D0221729

DECISION MAKING IN EDUCATIONAL LEADERSHIP

The increased focus on raising standards in education requires leaders to engage in complex decision making about teacher assessment, mandated accountability measures, and the collection and use of large amounts of data. Showcasing exemplary practices of school and district administrators, *Decision Making in Educational Leadership* covers issues concerning the role of emotion, ethical and legal ramifications, the use of data, and complexity in decision making. Chapter authors in this research-based volume explore what administrators and school leaders actually know about educational problems, how they draw upon and revise theories of action for responding to problems, and which theories are tenable in educational decision making. This important resource provides a broad and international perspective on effective models and methods of educational decision making and shares valuable knowledge about how theory can be translated into practice in a variety of school settings.

Stephanie Chitpin is Associate Professor of Leadership, Evaluation, and Curriculum at the Faculty of Education, University of Ottawa, Canada.

Colin W. Evers is Professor of Educational Leadership in the School of Education at the University of New South Wales, Australia.

DECISION MAKING IN EDUCATIONAL LEADERSHIP

Principles, Policies, and Practices

Edited by Stephanie Chitpin and
Colin W. Evers

Routledge
Taylor & Francis Group

NEW YORK AND LONDON

First published 2015
by Routledge
711 Third Avenue, New York, NY 10017

and by Routledge
2 Park Square, Milton Park, Abingdon, Oxon OX14 4RN

Routledge is an imprint of the Taylor & Francis Group, an informa business

© 2015 Taylor & Francis

The right of the Editors to be identified as the authors of the editorial material, and of the authors for their individual chapters, has been asserted in accordance with sections 77 and 78 of the Copyright, Designs and Patents Act 1988.

Library of Congress Cataloging-in-Publication Data

Decision making in educational leadership : principles, policies, and
    practices / edited by Stephanie Chitpin, Colin W. Evers.
        pages cm
    Includes bibliographical references and index.
    1. School management and organization—United States.   2. Decision
making—United States.   I. Chitpin, Stephanie.   II. Evers, C. W.
    LB2805.D354 2014
    371.2—dc23
    2014001676

ISBN: 978-0-415-84310-2 (hbk)
ISBN: 978-0-415-84311-9 (pbk)
ISBN: 978-0-203-75727-7 (ebk)

Typeset in ApexBembo
by Apex CoVantage, LLC

CONTENTS

ACKNOWLEDGMENTS

The editors wish to thank the following people and organizations for their support in assisting with the research reported here:

Dr. Stephanie Chitpin's research and planning of this work was facilitated by a period of sabbatical leave granted by University of Ottawa. In being able to spend time at the University of Ottawa for further writing and editorial work, Professor Colin Evers is grateful for a sabbatical leave granted by the University of New South Wales.

Work in progress by a number of authors was presented at annual meetings of the American Educational Research Association and also the Canadian Society for the Study of Education. We thank both these organizations for accepting proposals for the presentation of this work.

Further work in progress by several authors was reported at a meeting of the Canadian Principal Learning Network funded by the Knowledge Network for the Applied Education Research, the Ontario Ministry of Education, the University of Toronto and the University of Western Ontario. We are most grateful for this support.

Many of the ideas in this book have been presented to various graduate classes in educational leadership. We wish to thank the many students whose feedback helped shape these ideas. Further feedback and suggestions were provided by our many colleagues. Special thanks must go to Marielle Simon and Jeremy Chitpin for their ongoing wise counsel.

PREFACE

The aim of this book is to explore a range of aspects of educational decision making that are relevant to educational leaders in general and school leaders in particular. Because of the complexity of educational contexts, especially as a result of external initiatives that require a greater focus on raising standards of student achievement, that involve assessing the performance of teachers and require meeting a variety of mandated accountability measures that often demand the collection and use of large amounts of data, there is no established consensus as to how decision making should be conceptualized. Different issues may just require different strategies for coming to a decision. The approach we have adopted, therefore, is to invite the different contributors to this book to express their understandings of decision making relative to the decision contexts that most concern them. The book, in different chapters, covers both the descriptive aspect of decision making, drawing on detailed accounts of what administrators and school leaders actually know about educational problems, and how they make decisions for solving them, and the normative aspect of decision making, arguing how decisions ought to be made.

Issues covered for both descriptive and normative aspects include: how leaders draw upon and revise theories of action for responding to problems; which theories are tenable in educational decision making; which cognitive and contextual resources are important in such decision making; the use of data in decision making; the role of emotion and epistemology; the conceptual complexity of decision making; and ethical and legal issues.

This first chapter by Andy Hargreaves, Beth Morton, Henry Braun, and Alex M. Gurn begins with the Global Educational Reform Movement (GERM), described by Pasi Sahlberg, which aims to reduce the costs of teaching and simplify the work of teachers by using data-driven decision making. This chapter draws upon an analysis of 15 school districts that used GERM-influenced data-driven decision making to ameliorate their special education strategies and investigates the diversity of their data-informed discussions and solutions. Some schools chose to focus on improvements for target groups of students, yielding quick returns on threshold targets. Other schools used data more broadly to encourage a sense of collective responsibility among teachers for all students. Discussions and solutions worked well when teachers combined decisional capital in the form of accumulated experience for joint decision making. Hargreaves provides insights into successful navigation and leadership of data-driven decision making.

In the second chapter, Jingping Sun discusses the nature of student data and its use by principals and teachers to improve student achievement outcomes. Although the benefits of data-informed decision making are apparent, not all teachers share enthusiasm for the approach, and large variations can exist in the use of data by teachers inside a single school. By providing a framework that incorporates contextual factors such as the use of student data by principals and teachers, workplace factors, and student learning outcomes, this chapter explores the means by which school administrators and policy-makers can encourage teachers to adopt data-driven decision making in an enthusiastic and effective manner.

The third chapter by Stephanie Chitpin describes the professional learning of 12 principals in the context of the Canadian Principal Learning Network (CPLN), an online community of educational leaders. Equipped with the Objective Knowledge Growth Framework (OKGF), a framework for professional self-learning, principals were able to holistically describe the decision-making process when faced with complex and ambiguous problems and assess possible solutions from both a cognitive and emotional perspective. Together with discussion generated by the online forum medium, the OKGF provided a structure for principals to discover weaknesses in their tentative actions, as illustrated by two case studies.

The fourth chapter by Colin W. Evers argues against the use of static, linear decision making in education. Often, in order to achieve a goal, decision-makers collect information in order to determine which means to use. Once a procedure is selected and enacted, the process is finished. The process prior to decision making is thus highly information intensive. Unfortunately, social science knowledge is both fallible and context sensitive, thus weakening the effectiveness of static decision making. Stronger decision making therefore conceptualizes decisions and their consequences along an epistemologically progressive, continuous trajectory, whereby knowledge gained as a result of one decision informs future problems, decisions, and solutions. This chapter investigates decision making in the same cyclical Popperian context that informs Chitpin's Objective Knowledge Growth Framework and explores conditions required for this process to be epistemologically progressive and successful.

In Gabriele Lakomski's chapter, she assesses claims regarding the controversial concept of "emotional intelligence" (EI). EI is described as the ability to monitor the emotions of self and others and to use this knowledge to inform proper action. EI is traditionally thought to be an intelligence separate from cognition, and is thought to contribute to school leadership effectiveness. However, Lakomski argues that these two claims cannot be substantiated in light of current scientific knowledge showing that the neural pathways governing cognition and emotion are interconnected. It follows that the contribution of EI and cognition to effective school leadership cannot easily be disaggregated. Rather than assuming an emotion/cognition divide, Lakomski argues that a naturalistic theory of mind provides a superior framework for understanding human action. Effective educational leadership can thus be grounded in actual knowledge of how humans both think and feel, leading to a better understanding of human action and how to plan for it.

In the sixth chapter, Viviane Robinson and Rozanne Donald address the factors surrounding differing interpretations and enactments of policy within a school system. Although sense-making literature has contributed to our understanding of policy implementation by highlighting the nature of policy as an interpretation of an idea, rather than a static idea itself, it has provided little guidance as to how to predict and explain how particular policies may be interpreted and implemented by various agents. Robinson and Donald address these issues by providing a constraint inclusion model that explains how principals may make sense of policy ideas in order to solve problems and resolve conflicts. The model is then applied to the implementation of an innovative middle school curriculum designed to promote integrative inquiry learning. By applying constraint inclusion analyses, Robinson and Donald explain why the curriculum was adopted by schools and adapted at the individual teacher level. Ultimately, without understanding the ways in which individuals interpret policy, policies may be enacted in an uncoordinated manner, and may not contribute to school improvement. The specification of problems in terms of constraints (plus the demand that something be done) is the same as that employed by Chitpin and Evers in the way they define problems for their growth-of-knowledge analyses.

Peter P. Grimmett argues in his chapter that the effects of the micro politics of organizational life, particularly those relating to leadership and educational decision making, often conspire against efforts at school reform because they fail to take account of how the principles, policies, and practices on which reform is based become co-opted in specific organizational settings. His chapter examines this situation and argues that effective decision making and educational leadership in organizational settings necessitates symbolic and cultural forms of leadership, which use decision making and legal-rational power to infuse the work of teaching with value, meaning, passion, and purpose. Such forms of leadership relate closely with the development of an organizational culture that binds and bonds people together in productive ways. Decision making in such settings involves a strong commitment to understanding the role that myths, rituals, and ceremonies play in an organization, how they are used to envelope the mission and purpose at the heart of the school's culture, and how remystification is used to affirm and revision a desirable, normative professional culture. Hence, while experience in teaching and decision making will be valued and regarded as central to education, it will not be seen as sufficient; rather, experience will be purposefully examined to understand its complexities and nuances. Such understanding will be mediated through discourse in a manner in which decision-makers attend to how they frame its events and conditions. Leaders will thus study the specifics of context to focus on how meanings and a sense of agency are culturally constructed through language in social settings. In this way, they can avoid the trap of monolithic understanding to focus on how our beliefs and values influence the decisions we make, all of which need to be grounded in principle and embedded in policy.

In Chapter 8, Karen Starr focuses on principals as the primary agents of change at an individual school level. Governments hold principals accountable for enacting positive change, thus placing much pressure on principals to demonstrate measurable improvement and to avoid failure. However, managing change is often a daunting task. Research has shown that individuals are often resistant to major change and, as a result, school reforms are cursory or short-lived. This chapter focuses on the micro politics of resistance to major change, through reflections on principals' perceptions and experiences about leading and managing reform, and closes with suggestions for future research and leadership practice.

Dean Fink highlights the need for trust throughout the educational system in order for an educational leader to be successful. Although not often appreciated by rational, linear decision-making models, many forms of trust are necessary for successful decision and action in a school system, such as trust in the observations, judgments, and actions of oneself, another, or the system as a whole. Fink argues that trust is the defining ingredient that separates successful education from unsuccessful education across nations. Nevertheless, the necessity of trust must be balanced by reasonable strategies to verify the effectiveness of individuals and policy in order to avoid "naïve trust." The late American president Ronald Reagan coined the phrase "trust *but* verify." The modern educator, charged with making crucial decisions, must adapt the phrase to "trust *and* verify."

The chapter by Patrick M. Jenlink examines ethics in the context of decision making and educational leadership. Educational leaders are confronted daily with multiple complex, dynamic problems, which may be described as a *problématique*, a form of structural model that represents relationships among members of a set of problems. The educational leader must therefore discern not only the cognitive demands of the problem, but the contextual demands as well. As a result, examining the power-relations and interests of members becomes critically important before the question addressed by the problématique can be solved. Assessing the complex nature of educational problems and the various aspects surrounding them requires an understanding of the implicit and explicit nature of decision making and, as such, any decisions made by the educational leader assume a high level of ethical responsibility.

Justice Marvin A. Zuker discusses the concept of equitable education for all students. Although systems of education law differ from jurisdiction to jurisdiction, there is much to learn from a detailed case study of a particular jurisdiction, in this instance the Canadian province of Ontario. In past years, a number of provincial laws have been passed in Ontario to address the issue of youth who are left behind under the umbrella of the Safe Schools and Equity and Inclusive Education Strategy. This strategy, which includes the *Education Act* and the *Accepting Schools Act,* seeks to accommodate students who have been traditionally marginalized by the education system, such as lesbian, gay, bisexual, and transgender (LGBT) youth. Zuker argues that the accommodation of diverse groups of students creates a complex operational environment for principals and requires a multifaceted approach to address the needs of various students. In the case of students with learning disabilities or mental health issues, individual education plans may be established with a personalized curriculum when the student cannot benefit from the general curriculum, with the ultimate goal of allowing the student to integrate with the community upon graduation. Although all students should be accommodated, mental health issues combined with violent characteristics may pose a challenge for the principal. This chapter discusses challenges and resources accessible to principals, such as Section 265(m) of the *Education Act,* which allows the individual to be accommodated while maintaining a safe, effective school environment for all.

Howard Stevenson, in the concluding chapter of the book, raises the important and very large issue of how educational problems and decisions are framed. The currently prevalent perspective of neoliberalism has, as its focus, a market orientation, with issues framed in terms of cost-benefits, efficiency, performance indicators, appraisal mechanisms, and the like. This is a different language to that of educational values, worthwhile knowledge, student development, teacher professionalism, and social values such as equity, inclusion, and social justice. A neoliberal restructuring of public education, which emerged from the global economic crisis of the 1970s, is becoming increasingly aggressive. It seeks to become the new global orthodoxy. Stevenson argues that this is not a value-neutral technical adjustment of policy, but a fundamental repositioning of school systems, in which market values are privileged. His chapter analyses developments in global education policy and identifies how these changes are increasingly shaping the context in which school leaders do their work, and he argues that school leaders must join with others, and develop "dispositions of resistance" if they are to successfully challenge the trajectory of neoliberal restructuring and reassert the primacy of educational values over market values.

It is our hope that the range of perspectives offered in this book by its various authors will speak to the educational contexts where they may be most appropriately applied, and offer useful insights that will enrich decision making wherever it is applied.

—Stephanie Chitpin and Colin W. Evers

PART I

Data-Driven Decision Making

1

THE CHANGING DYNAMICS OF EDUCATIONAL JUDGMENT AND DECISION MAKING IN A DATA-DRIVEN WORLD

Andy Hargreaves, Beth Morton, Henry Braun, and Alex M. Gurn

Introduction

Among the many changes that affect us all in the first decades of the 21st century is the presence and impact of digital data. We use data to count our steps and our calories. Data track and target our online shopping preferences and customer purchasing habits. Data measure performance in business, sport, and health services, comparing individuals, units, and organizations against each other in areas as diverse as reputation indicators, infection levels, and injury rates. Facial recognition software can help us pick out a potential terrorist in a crowd, and data systems have also been used to trawl billions of phone calls and keyboard strokes among ordinary people across the world "just in case" they may have some use in the future. The use of data in the modern age can be superficial or sinister, helpful or harmful, a way to focus on core purposes or a device to distract people's attention from them.

In *Big Data,* Mayer-Schönberger and Cukier (2013) describe many of the ways that data enter into and also enhance our lives. Big Data, they say, are about "the ability of society to harness information in novel ways to produce useful insights or goods and services of significant value" (p. 2). They point to how the growing capacity to analyze vast volumes of data has made it possible to predict the spread of flu pandemics, to pinpoint the buildings most likely to be overcrowded fire hazards, and to use complex algorithms to provide just-in-time feedback in response to people's progress in their online learning.

But after their enthusiastic advocacy for Big Data, the authors then advise against turning to data for the answer to all our problems. They stress that there is a "special need to carve out a place for the human: to reserve space for intuition, common sense and serendipity." "What is greatest about human beings," they say, "is what is precisely what the algorithms and silicon chips don't reveal" (Mayer-Schönberger & Cukier, 2013, p. 196). This is equally true of those areas of life where problems are pervasive, inequities abound, and human suffering is rampant. Data can help in addressing these issues, but in the end, some of our most challenging educational and social problems will not mainly be solved by more or better data, just as they will not be solved by more technology or by any other silver bullet. More and better data can help us make more efficient educational decisions and judgments, but they will not, of themselves, help us make wiser or more humane ones.

In recent years, with our colleagues, we have been studying high performance, beyond normal expectations, in almost 20 cases in business, sport, and education. One of the explanations for the examples of high performance we have studied and witnessed has been not whether the organizations concerned use data as part of their quest to improve, but how they use those data. Let's turn to three examples of such data use and see what we can learn from them. The first two examples come from our multisite study of high performance in a study originally funded by the National College for School Leadership and the Specialist Schools and Academies Trust in the United Kingdom, and extended through a small number of additional cases once the funded period of the study had ended. In these cases, we collected data in intensive team visits of three days to interview leaders and managers of all kinds in the organizations about the reasons for high performance we had collected and that they provided in published and website information on organizational performance (Hargreaves & Harris, 2011). In the third example, we conducted a study of ten school districts and their approaches to whole school changes that benefit students with special educational needs in the strongly publicized, high-performing province of Ontario in Canada, according to international test results (Hargreaves & Braun, 2012).

Data and Judgment in Sport

In the spring of 2011, we sat in the basement of The Vancouver Coliseum, home to the well-known junior hockey team, the Vancouver Giants, whom Malcolm Gladwell had turned into a household name when he featured them in the opening chapter of his bestseller, *Outliers*. Since their establishment in 2001–2002, the Giants have become one of Canada's most successful junior hockey teams— winning the national championship Memorial Cup within six years and claiming the provincial title five seasons in a row.

Down beside the club's locker rooms, we talked to the team's 19-year-old captain, James Henry. James' face bore the brutal marks of his dedication to his sport. A scar on his left cheek, the swollen bridge on his nose, and gaps where his teeth should have been were clear signs of his commitment.

When James started to describe the Giants' year-upon-year success, he talked about the vision of the owners, the passion of his coach, and most of all, the importance of the team. It's a cliché to say that teams matter in sports. But at the Vancouver Giants, you can measure it. One of the most important things about a hockey player at this level is how much he is prepared to sacrifice for the team. In hockey, the biggest sacrifice is not just a moral one: It is also painfully physical.

"What's the identity of the Giants?" we asked. "We're brash," said General Manager Scott Bonner. "We like to be brash, really work hard, big and strong. We're the Vancouver Giants. We want to be the team that bangs and hits a lot, plays with no fear." James agreed. "Just relentless pressure, never really take your foot off the gas. We want to be known as a real hard team to play against." Everyone at the Giants agreed that they may not be the most skillful team or even the fastest and, by winning year after year, they could not stack their team with top-draft picks from the upcoming players either. The Giants were just tougher than anyone else. They worked harder. And they outlasted their opponents, game after game. They scored more goals in the third and final period than any other team. At the Vancouver Giants, brashness isn't just an idle boast. It's a statistical fact.

There are other metrics that drive the point home. One of the most bruising ones is known as "blocked shots." Blocked shot ratios are a strong predictor of high performance individually and collectively in hockey. A blocked shot occurs when a player puts his body in the way of a 100 mph puck to prevent an opponent getting a shot on goal. The Giants do well on blocked shots. So did James. His scars displayed the visible signs of how many times he had taken one for the team in this way.

So what happens when a player's own blocked shot ratio goes down? Well, it's more than a matter of simply being dropped from the team. The coach takes the player aside, goes through various video-plays with him, and reviews where he might have placed himself between puck and goal instead of standing aside. It's a learning experience. On the one hand, the data ensure total transparency. At the same time, high-quality coaching creates the critical and challenging conversations that convert digital data into individual and collective responsibility for evidence-informed improvement.

Michael Lewis's bestselling book, *Moneyball,* brought to popular attention how the use of performance statistics to select and deploy players boosted the underfunded Oakland Athletics baseball team to World Series standard, where they faced and often defeated teams with triple their payroll. Big Data got them big results. But data-driven improvement efforts in sport have not always had such a positive connotation as they have at the Vancouver Giants or Oakland A's.

One of the first exponents of data-driven improvement in sport was Valeri Lobanovsky—manager of the Dynamo Kiev soccer team in the former Soviet Union from the mid 1970s to the early 1990s. Lobanovsky decided to apply the principles of scientific Marxism to soccer management. Standing by the pitch, he made notations of different moves made by individual players and connected these to team performance outcomes. When Lobanovsky purchased a large computer, his goal was to combine science and technology to create the perfect soccer team.

Franklin Foer (2004) describes how Lobanovsky applied numerical values to every successful and unsuccessful action in the game. The data were put through the computer to produce calculations of "intensivity, activity, error rate" (p. 159), and so on. Lobanovsky was seeking a perfect data-driven system that his players could adopt automatically. He even organized practice matches where players were blindfolded. According to Foer (2004), Lobanovsky's system

> rewards a very specific style of play: physical and frenetic. Players work tirelessly to compile points. They play defense more aggressively than offense, because that's where points can be racked up. In stifling individual initiative, Lobanovsky's system mimicked the Soviet regime under which it was conceived. Nothing in Lobanovsky's point valuation measures creativity or daring. A vertical pass receives the same grade as a horizontal pass; a spectacular fake means nothing.
>
> (p. 160)

In sport, including the baseball world made famous by *Moneyball,* it is now understood that, while data are important, it is the use of data in combination with professional judgment and experience that is critical to success. Being driven by the numbers alone is little better than mechanistic Marxism.

Data and Judgment in Business

Data are a big deal in business as well as in sport, and not just in the obvious domains of profits and losses either. One example we have looked at in detail comes from the Internet retail sector. In 2009, Shoebuy.com was one of the Internet's top ten most-visited apparel and accessory shopping sites and one of the top ten "stickiest" websites in the Internet shopping sector (Evans, 2009). When shoppers reach the website, they tend to stay and keep coming back. Repeat buying grew from 17.5% of revenues in 2000, to over 36% of revenues in 2004, and more than 60% in 2009. Conservative estimates put the firm's available merchandising inventory at over $3.5 billion and annual sales figures at around $180 million (Kirsner, 2009). In 2011, Shoebuy realized, on average, about a 25% profit margin per customer (Keenan, 2011).

Shoebuy also has very high rates of staff retention. For example, in 2009, approximately 80% of its management team were the people who had originally been hired for those roles. Even in the midst of the global financial collapse in 2009, while Shoebuy's major competitor, Zappos, was forced to cut at least 8% of its staff (Smith, 2008), Shoebuy continued to hire employees. Company executives believe that if you expect high standards of every staff member and demonstrate loyalty to them, this fidelity of leadership enhances the work quality and the commitment of staff who feel supported and challenged as professionals (Keenan, 2011).

One factor that makes all this possible is Shoebuy's Web-based infrastructure and data-driven processes. Scott Savitz, one of Shoebuy's cofounders, loves numbers and how they can be used to inform and improve business practices. At Shoebuy, they permit complex analyses of users' interactions with the website and enable real-time responses to these engagements to be made. Shoebuy's product inventory is analyzed using an array of criteria including click-through, sell-through, margin, rate of return, repeat sales, customer surveys, and website feedback. Shoebuy's systems also analyze other information, such as how people move through the website and when they navigate away from it. The company uses A/B multivariate testing to reliably compare the usability of different Web designs. Real-time data lead to improved design—such as increasing the range and number of views that are offered in a bag or a purse. As a result, customers stay longer and longer on the site—giving Shoebuy its high rate of "stickiness."

However, while Shoebuy continually seeks ways to know customers better through triangulated sets of data, it doesn't rely on digital data alone. Savitz and others would also call customers personally when there was a problem. Shoebuy visibly lists its phone number on all Web pages and encourages customer feedback via Facebook, Twitter, and other digital media. The company has never outsourced its customer service functions. When Shoebuy receives an email inquiry from a customer, that customer will get a human, not computer-generated, response within 30 minutes. Customer calls are answered in less than 75 seconds (Keenan, 2011). Putting the customer first in business strategies is a top priority at Shoebuy. Technical data supported customer relationships, rather than replacing them.

Within the company itself, intelligent use of performance data guides people's decisions and actions and motivates a sense of ownership of their work. Savitz explained, "What we try to do is enable everybody to understand what their objectives are in each of their own individual areas of business." While Shoebuy leaders were explicit about staff expectations and benchmarks for successful performance, they also provided tools for staff to use themselves so they could exercise professional discretion and make their own judgments on the frontline.

With this evidence-informed approach, staff members regularly identify for themselves when something is not working or needs tweaking—"coming to us, saying I'm having troubles here." Savitz believed that "a lot of companies make the mistake of saying they don't want people individually to be that empowered." Yet, at Shoebuy, employees are encouraged to take risks because real-time monitoring permits swift interventions to correct errors and avert catastrophes. This enhances innovation and continuous improvement, increases employee satisfaction, and is one of the key reasons for Shoebuy's strong, award-winning record of staff retention (Internet Retailer, 2009).

This combination of good data with good judgment and its payoffs for employee satisfaction as well as customer experience is not always apparent in business, though. For instance, in a supermarket chain that Chris DeRose and Noel Tichy assisted, the company had used scanning metrics to set targets where checkout staff had to increase the numbers of shoppers they processed per hour. The threat posed by constant measurement on this single metric led staff to refuse help to older customers or to make eye contact with shoppers in case this involved time-consuming personal interactions. Target-driven monitoring undermined the human relationships with customers on which the supermarket ultimately depended. This, say DeRose and Tichy, is just one example of how businesses can overuse metrics to standardize performance in ways that undermine the judgments of front-line workers. In high-performing business, data are used to support high-quality judgment, not to replace that judgment.

Good Data With Good Judgment

So what have we learned from good and bad uses of data in business and sport? Data, it seems, lead to successful and sustainable high performance when they are

- *meaningful* and valid to the people who use them. The data measure what people in the organization truly value, and they make sense in terms of those values as well as in relation to the core purposes and processes of the organization.
- *balanced and fair* rather than single-minded in their focus and use. The data capture the range of what is important in the organization rather than judging and ranking people and their performance by one or two single and simple metrics.
- *integrated* with professional judgment, instead of overriding it. Data actually enhance people's ability and readiness to make good discretionary judgments at the point where their decisions have the most impact in relation to their own work. They do not undermine that judgment by using the numbers to place people's performance under threat.
- embedded in valued *relationships;* not imposed from on high or afar. Data-based decisions do not replace meaningful relationships with customers or among employees. They supplement and strengthen those relationships.
- *timely* in how they can be accessed in order to provide just-in-time corrections to and refinements in performance, innovation, impact, and design. They don't come to light so long after the fact that it is too late to make changes to performance of individuals or the community.
- *a shared responsibility* in cultures of collective commitment to shared goals and targets for improvement, not an imposition of hierarchical authority in high-threat cultures of sanction and fear.

In high-performing organizations and systems, people aren't blindly driven by data, or plunged into panic by the threat of imposed, short-term performance targets. Metrics are meaningful, data continually inform refinements in design and performance, targets are owned, and data strengthen employee judgments rather than undermining them. So are these the characteristics we are seeing in the increasing uses of data in public education?

Data and Judgment in Education

In education, terms like "evidence informed," "data driven," or their permutations are used to characterize decision-making processes, at various levels of the system, in which educators systematically collect and analyze "various types of data, including input, process, outcome and satisfaction data, to guide a range of decisions" (Marsh, Pane, & Hamilton, 2006, p. 1). The rationale is that use of data will help educators to select more effective strategies and make better decisions about resource allocations and, ultimately, "improve the success of students and schools" (Marsh, Pane, & Hamilton, 2006, p. 1).

Between 2009 and 2012, with a large team of researchers, we were asked to investigate the implementation of the special education reform strategy throughout the province of Ontario, Canada. In addition to quantitative data on achievement results at district and provincial levels, we also gathered data from a series of high-level policy interviews, and from intensive case study visits to ten varied school districts—almost a seventh of the districts in the province. Much of Ontario's special education reform strategy was focused on whole school changes that are essential for some (identified) children and good for all other children as well. This whole school focus incorporated a wide range of strategies in differentiated instruction, use of technology, and gathering and interpretation of data to track student progress, target those who may be falling behind, prompt and guide teachers to make just-in-time interventions, and also enable targets to be set for improvement at school, district, and province-wide levels. The organization and summarization of school-level data facilitated the construction of "statistical neighborhoods" that allowed schools to compare themselves and their students' test score performance with schools serving similar types of students. These strategies also formed part of the province's well-known literacy and numeracy reform strategy that has become associated with its success as a high performer in the world, according to international policy and consultancy organizations such as the Organisation for Economic Co-operation and Development (OECD, 2011), McKinsey (Mourshed, Chijioke, & Barber, 2010), and the National Center on Education and the Economy (Tucker, 2011).

Data-driven decision making is not a new phenomenon in education, and in Ontario, it has been at the core of many major school improvement strategies (Campbell & Fulford, 2009). The province has spent considerable time and resources developing a central data system—Ontario School Information System or ONSIS—to inform educational research and policy questions at all levels of the system. This growth in educational assessment and data-driven decision making has occurred in part because test-based accountability requires the tracking of student progress toward the attainment of system performance goals, based on the province-wide assessments in reading, writing, and mathematics for Grades 3, 6, 9, and 10, administered under the auspices of the Educational Quality and Account-ability Office (EQAO).

As part of its strategies for educating all students effectively, the province pro-posed that teachers use more precise assessment strategies to identify and track each student's patterns of learning, develop learning profiles for those students, and adjust their use of instructional strategies, making them more differentiated and customized for every student's needs. Considerable attention was therefore devoted to how to administer accurate and inclusive assessments within a continu-ous learning-teaching process that was organized into periodic cycles of imple-mentation and review (see Hall, 2002; Tomlinson, 2001).

How did the use of data and professional judgment in this data-driven, or evidence-informed, educational environment compare with the areas of best prac-tice we have documented in business and sport?

High Stakes Tests

First, while the ten boards that we studied used, between them, a wide range of evidence to inform decisions regarding instruction and intervention—including formal and informal teacher observations, classroom assessments, student work, previous results on EQAO assessments, and proxies for the EQAO outcomes for current students—test score data were by far the most frequently cited sources of evidence that were used to identify and address student needs.

The most commonly discussed and also most controversial areas of data use that emerged in our surveys and site visits were those pertaining to the EQAO assessments. In some cases, EQAO scores were examined in the aggregate to ret-rospectively identify and address achievement gaps. The EQAOs are summative, after-the-fact assessments where items and individual performances are guarded with scrupulous confidentiality in order to address accountability concerns. The assessments are administered in only a few grades at the end of the school year, so their utility in identifying specific student needs in a timely manner, especially in relation to students who have not yet been tested, is limited.

In open-ended survey responses, some teachers did note that EQAO's prior year results could give them a broad idea of where to focus or to identify key areas of learning that may have been missed. Principals and school district administrators were the most common supporters of EQAO as the results provided them with leverage to initiate change and improvement. "EQAO provides a starting point for teachers—to review what the strengths and weaknesses are from the previous year's results. Teachers then plan the (teaching-learning) cycles according to the needs of their students" (Hargreaves & Braun, 2012, p. 80). As one survey respondent put it:

> The Board-level focus on EQAO results actually helps me compare my identified students to all students that have written the EQAO. We try to

move our level 2 students to level 3, 3 to 4, etc. Teachers try to identify the gaps and to close it. It is no different for our identified students.

(p. 80)

Special education resource teachers were also inclined to favor the use of EQAO data as they felt the results demonstrated to fellow classroom teachers that students with learning disabilities were capable of achieving the proficiency level within the regular classroom program.

Classroom teachers were the most critical of the EQAO process—not because they didn't like to be assessed or be held accountable, but because they felt that they were being asked to divert their efforts toward students just below the borderline of proficiency and, consequently, toward those whose improvement would count more than that of other students. Ontario had set a high profile "Drive for 75" target (i.e., that 75% of students in every school in each tested grade and subject should meet or exceed the proficiency level). Although punitive consequences did not ensue for falling beneath this target, the pressures to move as many schools as possible to this standard were still often considerable. Teachers reported that these emphases were often conveyed to them by the administration in ways that created inner conflicts for teachers who wanted to improve the achievement of all students, not just those on the cusp of the proficiency cut score.

Teachers in one district, for example, reported that they were under constant pressure from the administration and the ministry to move students to the 3.0 threshold of measured proficiency and to concentrate especially on those students scoring in the 2.7–2.9 range on pre-EQAO assessments. Educators said that system leaders had told them "to push (these students) over to the next level" (Hargreaves & Braun, 2012, p. 81). One interviewee recalled being advised that "for those groups of children (near Level 3 proficiency), we need to do something different, a different skills set to work with those kids, more differentiating for that group." While educators recognized as a general principle that they must be "more precise in their teaching," these borderline students took priority over all of their other students—including those whose academic performance was lowest and arguably in need of the greatest attention (p. 81).

A chart hanging in the principal's office at one school represented this policy-driven hyper focus on those students at the 2.7–2.9 and 3.7–3.9 ranges, whose advancement was critical for a school to meet its established targets in the Drive to 75 on the EQAO. On the chart, the number of students who fell into these categories was circled in order to stimulate focused interventions that could possibly move more students to a 3.0 or 4.0.

In preferentially intervening with students near the borderline of measured proficiency, these teachers' efforts were drawn *away* from other students whose achievement needs may have been just as great or greater. "That's been a thrust in low performing boards. You need to look at results. You need to look at 2.7 to 2.9 and figure out how to get them over the 3.0 hump. There was no consideration for all the school has done to get kids into level 1" (Hargreaves & Braun, 2012, p. 81). Bumping these learners to the next level would raise the overall test results of a school and further its goal of meeting the system requirement to move higher percentages of students over the threshold of measured proficiency. Similar processes were reported in our survey results throughout the province. "We are clearly told to increase scores," said one educator. "This is best achieved at our school by working with the mid level group" (p. 81).

We had no evidence that there was a deliberate systemic push to have teachers concentrate most of their attention on the "bubble students" near the level of official proficiency (Booher-Jennings, 2005). But as John Seddon (2008) points out in his critique of target-driven policies in public sector work in the United Kingdom, once "the 'targets bureaucracy' takes over the management of the work; the focus becomes meeting the targets rather than improving the way the work works" (p. 119). The system then organizes itself to produce the required result by creating a set of "perverse incentives" to manufacture the numerical outcome (Bird et al., 2005; Seddon, 2008).

In short, although there is no evidence of policy intentions to have educators concentrate their efforts on those groups of students who will yield the quickest returns in results, the perverse incentives created in high-pressure environments still come into play, and teachers report feeling that their attention is drawn away from the students who, in equity terms, may need the most help of all. In this sense, imposed targets on singular metrics exact some of the same consequences in education, even in lower-threat environments, as they do in the crude use of performance data in soccer or checkout rate targets in supermarkets.

At the same time, the high-stakes testing process in Ontario is far less punitive in its consequences than is the case in most other systems that have used such tests—including England and the United States. Its intention has been to focus efforts and attention on measurable improvement at every level of the system in a serious and sustained way. The existence of the data provide system administrators and school principals with leverage to give their staff a clear reality check about their impact and to concentrate energy on improving standards and also increasing equity. Nonetheless, the nature of the data is a source of strong criticism among teachers who believe the evidence arrives too late, at the end of the year, to benefit the students from whom it has been collected. It is neither customized nor just in time.

Data Range

Because of these limitations of EQAO data, all the boards we studied also employed various types of diagnostic, interim, and formative assessments that provided information on students' current needs. Some of these, such as the Ontario Writing Assessments, aligned well with the portions of the EQAO. These assessments typically provided teachers with data that were closer to real-time issues of teaching and learning, and they were more precisely descriptive of gaps in students' understanding at the level of skills or subskills in a way that made it possible to make changes in instruction that were specific and immediate. In many cases, teachers were also encouraged to combine assessment data with evidence of student work, their own observations, and knowledge of their students' past performance.

Frequent diagnostic assessments can aid teachers in monitoring students' academic needs and progress, whereas periodic interim assessments can inform their teaching and instruction (Goertz, 2011), as well as track students' progress toward meeting performance standards. In this respect, many boards employed multiple measures of students' performance to build comprehensive profiles of students' academic strengths and areas of need. Multiple measures also enabled educators to customize the timeliness of the assessment or the level at which the curriculum standards were measured. In survey data collected from teachers in nine of the districts, teachers generally agreed that, since the onset of the special education strategy, the progress of students with special needs was being monitored through a variety of assessment and evaluation methods.

> The staff works as a team and seems to share responsibility for the growth of all students within their division. We use (diagnostic assessments in reading) DRA tests in my division (primary) to specifically target needs of specific students and we use the DRA to help our students set personal reading goals that are measurable and thus, more tangible for them. There is more of a sense of shared responsibility between teachers and their students, in my opinion.
>
> (Hargreaves & Braun, 2012, p. 70)

Strong, evidence-informed school systems don't just collect data, but they collect the *right* data to "inform the work of teachers and administrators" (Datnow, Park, & Wohlstetter, 2007, p. 6). Four of the ten boards we researched were using strategies to collect the right kind of data in relation to the needs of their identified at-risk populations. One board focused on literacy in the early grades, particularly among those students identified as being at risk of weak academic growth because of limited English literacy/fluency. Because obtaining valid and reliable assessment results for students with low levels of literacy can be challenging, teachers therefore began by setting entry-level targets for various components of early literacy. Diagnostic assessments were designed to provide teachers with information on students' status on domains such as key preliteracy skills. One of the board's teachers summarized how different types of data were collected for different purposes. "If you're really clear about what we're collecting that data for, and if it's system data, then we use it for a different purpose than interacting with a child on an everyday basis."

A second board focused its efforts more on early and middle grades, where students who were identified as showing limited growth were the targets of intervention efforts. The board used diagnostic assessments in reading (DRA) to identify students' needs and to differentiate instruction accordingly and augmented these with other instruments such as the WBTT (Web Base Teaching Tool) and Carmel Crevola's Screening of Print Concepts.

A third board used multiple instruments as part of the process of individualizing instruction. It instituted a cyclical process of assessment and instruction that began with administering the assessment in literacy. Coupled with evidence from classroom observations, teachers employed the resulting data to identify student needs and develop individual and class learning profiles. Teachers then used these profiles to make just-in-time instructional interventions. These cycles of assessment and instruction were repeated every eight to nine weeks and often involved the cooperation of classroom and special education teachers.

Some of the Ontario boards, therefore, deployed a range of data other than EQAO assessments in order to track and monitor student progress and guide interventions. As with best practice in business and sport, these boards stressed having a balanced scorecard of data and of measures that were regarded as valid and accurate and that were usable in real time by teachers making judgments about instruction and intervention that would help their students.

Data Walls

Many of the boards in Ontario developed data walls that enabled them to visualize the progress students were making toward the provincial benchmarks. The purpose of the walls was to track the literacy progress of each student. These data walls listed the various reading levels (emergent, early readers, transitional readers, and extending readers) and represented individual students and their current levels of achievement and progress by letters and numbers according to diagnostic assessments undertaken in October, February, and May. A red-yellow-green coloring system highlighted the progress of each student. Red represented students falling below provincial benchmarks; yellow indicated those at risk of falling below; and green showed students who had met the benchmarks. As students progressed, their marker changed color along the spectrum.

Teachers consulted these data walls weekly in order to track their students' progress. Students who were below the provincial benchmarks, as well as those just under the benchmarks, were flagged, and tailored interventions were then devised to raise proficiency. Teachers were trained to differentiate instruction in order to help these students. Teachers also referenced the data walls when establishing "Specific Measurable Attainable Realistic Timely" (SMART) goals that challenged students to move to the next level by giving them achievable short-term goals.

Like website tracking data in Internet retail and video data in sports performance, this technology for tracking progress increased the likelihood that students' problems would be picked up in real time, that interventions would be timely, that improvement goals would not be too vague, and that everyone would take responsibility for all students. In the best case scenarios, and in the views of administrative staff especially, the assessments raised expectations for all students, enabled teachers to set more specific goals for each student, prompted teachers to listen to each other's ideas more, created a common language for them to talk about their students' achievement, and developed a sense of collective responsibility for all students' success. In the words of one Board respondent, "We speak the same language when we discuss the aforementioned assessments; we know what the other is referring to, and can therefore more readily arrive at a consensus on approach to grading, critical thinking, etc."

> The Board's focus on data has increased my awareness of student achievement in the whole school. We have included French and English teachers in discussion about data and it has increased the capacity of all teachers working with special needs students. It has helped us set specific, measurable and attainable goals for our special needs students and all students.
>
> (Hargreaves & Braun, 2012, p. 80)

Data Cultures

As the previous section makes clear, effective judgments based on numerical and other kinds of data depend not only on the nature of the data, but also on the character and caliber of the professional conversations that occur in relation to the data. Survey results indicated that following the special education initiative, teachers mainly believed that their schools were making better use of assessment data to guide their instruction. Teachers in one board shifted their practice from an unsystematic method of assessing students' needs and adapting instruction, to a more thoughtful approach:

> (Previously), a child in grade 6 who was identified with special needs might simply have been given grade 3 academic work. This kind of practice was based neither on systematic knowledge of what students could perform nor on high expectations for students with learning disabilities. "Now we're definitely using our assessments as tools to see exactly where the child is at."
>
> (Hargreaves & Braun, 2012, p. 73)

The quality of these conversations depended on there being both a strong professional culture of collective responsibility for all students' success and supportive conditions where teachers could discuss and develop this sense of collective responsibility in relation to their own teaching strategies, as well with respect to the progress of students that teachers held in common. With additional support in place, staff in one board said that teachers began to see the value of data in relation to their professional judgments:

> The data really pushed them towards a paradigm shift, when they could see that students they thought were doing very well, in fact weren't; or students

who did not do very well and with some additional attention through interventions, they saw quick gains over a short period of time.

(Hargreaves & Braun, 2012, p. 74)

In a number of cases, though, data warehouses were more likely to be utilized by the board's evaluation team and by central office administrators than by educators at the classroom level. In one board, for example, teachers reported that entering diagnostic assessment data on students was time consuming and missed the high-touch simplicity of the physical binders containing students' profiles with which they were provided at the start of each year. "To look up a student's score quickly, [I] now have to turn on a computer, find the program, and enter passwords. Before, I could simply open a binder near my desk" (Hargreaves & Braun, 2012, p. 74), one of them said. This case serves as a reminder that digital data are not the only data or always the best data, but that many kinds of data, in many formats, can and should contribute to strong cultures of professional judgment and responsibility focused on improving student learning.

In at least half the boards we studied, data teams were one of the main mechanisms for analyzing student data and discussing instructional strategies to address student needs. About 70% of teachers who were surveyed said that since the start of the special education reform initiative, they were more likely to examine student work together. In each surveyed board, respondents reported that they were more likely to discuss data and student achievement results with their colleagues.

In one board, for example, the board leadership provided teachers with dedicated meeting time to analyze data, and to draw on their fellow teachers' expertise in data analysis and instructional techniques. In another board, a common language in the use of a set of assessments prompted deeper conversations among teachers and greater fluency in data use. Teachers drew on multiple measures of complementary evidence through common assessments or rubrics that provided them with a language with which they could discuss and compare their students' needs. Moreover, teachers were able to collectively set student achievement targets, jointly develop an understanding of their students' performance, and use the insights that were gained to inform pedagogical decisions.

I think five years ago we kept groups and they stayed the same all year long. We had our little reading group and this and that. I see groups changing all the time in all classrooms. The instruction is very focused now due to the DRA and other assessments. I'm very focused when I come into the classroom focused on certain students and certain topics.

(Hargreaves & Braun, 2012, p. 76)

Boards such as these seemed to have preexisting professional cultures of high trust and strong collaboration (Datnow, 2011). They were not so much data driven as evidence informed in the way they exercised collective professional judgments.

Their cultures valued many kinds of data, exercised judgments that included educators' expertise and their experience of professional and classroom relationships, and used the data to deepen understandings of students, not to replace or override those understandings.

Data Difficulties

Strong data cultures have great potential for enhancing and deepening individual and collective professional judgment, but a number of difficulties also arose in our research cases that were more than technical in nature and that paralleled the distinctions between good and bad practice in noneducation sectors. The first was the challenge of striking the right balance between assessment on the one hand and the instruction that was being assessed on the other, so that disproportionate time was not invested in assessing learning compared to undertaking the teaching and learning that was being assessed. Although teachers' survey responses indicated general agreement that assessment data were being better used to inform instruction, on average, teachers either agreed with or were neutral about the statement that there was too much reliance on data and not enough attention to professional judgment. Teachers and other educators in several boards said that assessment data were useful for informing instruction, but that the amount of testing of all kinds was excessive. They felt that they "miss out on too much valuable teaching time to do these assessments" and this left "very little time to cover curriculum." Finding ways to integrate assessment and curriculum more carefully—to convert assessment *of* learning into assessment *for* and even *as* learning—enabled teachers in two boards to incorporate assessment more into their everyday lessons over time, thereby making the time they spent on assessment more valuable. But remembering that data and assessment should support teachers' teaching—not distract them from it—remained a crucial concern.

Many of the board-mandated assessments, some teachers said, only told teachers what they already knew and took them away from teaching. Ironically, while a greater array of measurements and diagnostic assessments might avoid the pitfalls associated with employing one standardized instrument such as EQAO, a vast array of assessments could prove overwhelming and distracting instead.

> The diagnostic assessments, although very beneficial in tracking students' success and need for assistance, have taken over as the main focus. Our Board has now mandated the use of these assessments with set timelines for administration of these tests. Now, rather than using them when we feel it would be most useful, we have to interrupt the flow of learning to complete the tests, mark and input the data. The students' abilities often change within a short period, making the data invalid.
>
> (Hargreaves & Braun, 2012, p. 78)

Some teachers were more than merely skeptical about the assessment process. They were downright suspicious. Teachers in one board felt that the movement toward assessment and data use was a top-down mandate. They described a compliance-driven environment where everyone has to "collect their data. They have to have data walls." Indeed, some teachers felt that the focus on data signaled that "the watchdog at the Board is checking" (p. 78). Since the board was able to identify which teachers failed to input data into the system, the fears were not necessarily unfounded.

Other teachers were concerned that test data were being used not just to track the students but also to monitor the teachers in a type of professional surveillance. One teacher's open-ended survey response expressed it like this:

> I feel that too much emphasis has been placed on the EQAO results throughout the district and that too much of our professional development is used to address the EQAO results. I feel that my professionalism is questioned because some teachers are not doing what is asked and instead of those teachers being addressed there is a wide blanket thrown over all of us.
>
> (Hargreaves & Braun, 2012, p. 78)

Summary

This section has examined the nature of evidence-informed and data-driven cultures of improvement and intervention within Ontario. Three factors appeared to facilitate the development and maintenance of strong data cultures that supported and enhanced teachers' judgments rather than presenting a distraction from them:

- *Strong professional cultures of collective responsibility* that included classroom teachers, special education teachers, and other professionals and that were not hierarchical in their nature or conduct
- *Assignment of priority to just-in-time data* that were judged to be valid and accurate and that helped teachers to help the students from whom the data were collected
- *Collection of multiple measures* and other indicators of student achievement that focused on the progress of all students rather than mainly those with proximity to the threshold and that were combined with and did not overwhelm other sources of professional judgment and decision making.

Conclusion

Big Data need not be bad data. Accurate and relevant data can strengthen and support better judgment. It is not the existence or absence of digital data that will determine the effectiveness of professional judgment. After all, Finland, which was one of the highest performing educational systems in the world in the first decade of the 21st century, has relied very little on systematic uses of achievement and performance data to track the progress of the system or its students.

What matters most in a data-driven world in any and every sector is the actual and perceived quality and quantity of data that are employed; the coherent connection of the data to core judgments and purposes; and the caliber of the professional cultures in which digital, numerical, and other kinds of data contribute to the quality of professional interactions and judgment and the actions that result from that judgment.

In education, as in business and sport, the sorts of data use that lead to high performance and sustainable improvement are ones where we measure what we value instead of valuing only what we can easily measure. They are practices in which numerical performance targets and other uses of data are not mainly subjected to hierarchical top-down surveillance and authority but developed and applied in cultures of collective responsibility. They are practices where prudent and balanced scorecards of data are used rather than singular high-stakes metrics, or infinite numbers of indicators that distract people from their core tasks. And they are practices where the purpose of the data is to improve relationships throughout the organization and all it serves, not to replace or subvert those relationships. Like Margaret Mead, in the end, we should remember that the point is not to distract ourselves with dashboards or sequester ourselves in our offices with spreadsheets but to "personally measure success in terms of the contributions an individual makes to his or her fellow human beings" (Metraux, 1979, p. 249).

References

Bird, S. M., David, C., Farewell, V. T., Harvey, G., Tim, H., & Peter, C. (2005). Performance indicators: Good, bad, and ugly. *Journal of the Royal Statistical Society: Series A (Statistics in Society), 168*(1), 1–27.

Booher-Jennings, J. (2005). Below the bubble: "Educational triage" and the Texas Accountability System. *American Educational Research Journal, 42*(2), 231–268.

Campbell, C., & Fulford, D. (2009, April 15). *From knowledge generation to knowledge integration: Analysis of how a government uses research.* Paper presented at 2009 AERA Annual Meeting. Retrieved from www.edu.gov.on.ca/eng/research/AERA2009_KIPaper.pdf

Datnow, A. (2011). Collaboration and contrived collegiality: Revisiting Hargreaves in the age of accountability. *Journal of Educational Change, 12*(2), 147–158.

Datnow, A., Park, V., & Wohlstetter, P. (2007). *Achieving with data.* Los Angeles: University of Southern California, Center on Educational Governance.

Evans, K. (2009, June 26). Shoebuy.com steps up its traffic—eBay, however, isn't so lucky. *Internet Retailer.* Retrieved from www.internetretailer.com/2009/06/26/shoebuy-com-steps-up-its-traffic-ebay-however-isn-t-so-lu

Foer, F. (2004). *How soccer explains the world: An unlikely theory of globalization.* New York, NY: HarperCollins.

Goertz, M. (2011, September 22). *Multiple measures, multiple uses.* Paper presented at the 2011 Reidy Interactive Lecture Series, Boston, MA.

Hall, T. (2002). *Differentiated instruction.* Wakefield, MA: National Center on Accessing the General Curriculum (NCAC).

Hargreaves, A., & Braun, H. (2012). *Leading for all: A research report of the development, design, implementation and impact of Ontario's "Essential for Some, Good for All" initiative.* Ontario, Canada: Council of Ontario Directors of Education.

Hargreaves, A., & Harris, A. (2011). *Performance beyond expectations.* Nottingham, UK: The National College for Teaching and Leadership (NCTL).

Internet Retailer. (2009). *Top 500 guide: Profiles and statistics of America's 500 largest retail websites, ranked by annual sales.* Chicago, IL: Vertical Web Media.

Keenan, J. (2011). Retail online integration: 8 steps to Shoebuy.com's success. Retrieved from www.retailonlineintegration.com/article/8-steps-shoebuycoms-success/1

Kirsner, S. (2009, May 24). Tiptoeing to online success. *The Boston Globe.* Retrieved from www.boston.com/business/technology/articles/2009/05/24/tiptoeing_to_online_success/

Marsh, J. A., Pane, J. F., & Hamilton, L. S. (2006). *Making sense of data-driven decision making in education evidence from recent RAND research.* Santa Monica, CA: RAND.

Mayer-Schönberger, V., & Cukier, K. (2013). *Big data: A revolution that will transform how we live, work, and think.* New York, NY: Eamon Dolan/Houghton Mifflin Harcourt.

Metraux, R. B. (Ed.) (1979). *Margaret Mead: Some personal views.* New York, NY: Walker.

Mourshed, M., Chijioke, C., & Barber, M. (2010). *How the world's most improved school systems keep getting better.* London: McKinsey & Company. Retrieved from www.mckinsey.com/client_service/social_sector/latest_thinking/worlds_most_improved_schools/

Organisation for Economic Co-operation and Development (OECD). (2011). *Strong performers and successful reformers in education: Lessons from PISA for the United States.* Paris: Author.

Seddon, J. (2008). *Systems thinking in the public sector: The failure of the reform regime . . . and a manifesto for a better way.* Axminster, UK: Triarchy Press.

Smith, H. (2008, November 8). Zappos cuts work force by 8 percent. *Las Vegas Review-Journal.* Retrieved from www.lvrj.com/business/34137634.html

Tomlinson, C. A. (2001). *How to differentiate instruction in mixed-ability classrooms.* Alexandria, VA: ASCD.

Tucker, M. S. (2011). *Standing on the shoulders of giants: An American agenda for education reform.* Washington, DC: National Center on Education and the Economy.

2

PRINCIPALS' EVIDENCE-BASED DECISION MAKING: ITS NATURE AND IMPACTS

Jingping Sun

Introduction

Despite the increasingly acknowledged importance of data use in schools (Gallagher, Means, Padilla, & SRI, 2008; Leithwood, Aitken, & Jantzi, 2006; Sharratt & Fullan, 2012) and the 2001 federal No Child Left Behind Act that requires administrators to collect assessment data, disaggregate those data, and develop solutions to meet the needs of students, the conceptualization and vision of such data use are not clear; empirical research on its status and impact is thin and sporadic. Research on its impact on student learning is even rarer, but it has recently begun to emerge. An extensive search for studies on this important topic did not yield any reviews. This study aims to examine the nature, impacts, supports for, and barriers to principals and teachers' use of evidence to inform their decision making. Specifically, it asks the following:

- What data informs principals' and teachers' decision making to improve student learning?
- How do they use such data? For which purposes?
- What are the impacts of such data uses, especially on student learning?
- What are the challenges to and supports for such data uses?

Sources of Evidence, Search Criteria, and Data Characteristics

A preliminary scan of research conducted in the past 10 years using the online Scholars Portal with such key words as *student data, principal, teacher,* and *student learning* resulted in 49 studies (articles, reports, and books screened from an initial 200 studies) that met the inclusion criteria for this review (i.e., empirical studies investigating either principal or teacher use of student data). Six major peer-reviewed journals in educational administration were exhausted. Additional evidence was traced and added through references, as we digested these initial 64 studies. Finally, 73 studies were located and included in this review. These studies were carried out in elementary, middle, or high schools, or in mixed samples of schools. Approximately more than 1,000 K–12 schools, 1,300 principals, 7,500 teachers, and thousands of students with various social, economic, academic, and ethnic backgrounds were involved.

The Data Principals Use: Its Nature and Purpose

All studies reported the importance of principals looking at a variety of data to gain insight into student learning. Compared with teachers, who tended to focus on data specific to their grade level, classroom, and individual students, principals focused more on district-wide, school-wide, and grade-level data (e.g., Schildkamp & Kuiper, 2010). Seven types of data were identified that principals use to improve student learning. They are as follows in descending order of their frequency of use:

- State-wide standardized test scores or local benchmark assessments
- Attendance, and discipline or behavioral, data
- Teacher-generated authentic formative assessments and observation data
- Student demographic data, or input data
- Data or information about best practices for instruction
- Feedback/satisfaction data from teachers
- Parent and community perception data

Standardized test score data and data collected from local benchmark assessments (summative) were the types of data most often used by principals (e.g., Williams, 2011). The summative assessments are more formal and are used to measure students' mastery of the standards in a given pacing guide. Principals used summative assessment results to guide their decisions more often because of its core value of *standardization,* its time efficiency, its availability as a package of desegregated data, the lack of need to invent anything, the time for result presentation, and the fact that it presents a "snapshot in time," which is not possible with formative assessments. Student attendance and discipline data ranked next, which was used together with student achievement to find reasons for students' behaviors and student achievements, and was used separately to inform decisions on school-wide programs such as a model of positive behavior support (e.g., Shen et al., 2010).

Teacher-generated authentic formative assessments and observation data was the one type of data that principals used to a considerable extent and that was considered by them to be the most effective data as well (Williams, 2011). Examples of formative assessments are entrance/exit slips, quizzes, or homework assignments, reading fluency patterns of struggling readers, grades earned in core subjects, and overall motivation in the learning process. These data were usually generated by classroom teachers for their own students or by specific companies that were selected to work with schools to diagnose student states of learning outcomes or their skills.

Student demographic data, or *input data* as it was termed in a few studies, were often used when desegregating data analysis, when getting to know the contexts of schools and classes, and when making records of information such as race, addresses, phone numbers, etc. (e.g., SASI in Deike, 2009). Identifying data or information about best practices for instruction was also evidenced in a few studies. Principals can gather this kind of data through, for example, classroom observations by the instructional facilitators (e.g., Deike, 2009). These observations can be focused on rigor and student engagement and can be graphed and discussed during professional development monthly meetings. Best practices for instruction ranked very highly in terms of its value to principals but were used less often (Henry, 2011). This is perhaps partly due to the availability of such data, as the majority of principals did not "consider" it to be "data" and did not deliberately "collect" these data. However, experienced principals often have such knowledge accumulated in their heads. There is a need for such assessments to be identified and developed systematically so as to be available to educators, and it is recommended that principals use effective data proactively rather than available data passively.

Feedback data from teachers or teacher satisfaction data generally ranked lower than the above-mentioned data sources, though a couple of studies found valuing and collecting input from teachers to be one key successful leadership practice (Sanzo, Sherman, & Clayton, 2011). Principals may seek teachers' opinions by providing opportunities for teachers to give input on school-wide data-driven decision making through going to the principal's office, through team leaders, team minutes, and much less used opportunities such as grade-level meetings, monthly department meetings, questioning techniques, and special meetings (Godreau Cimma, 2011). Parent and community perception were mentioned by a few principals as an important tool used to measure the success of the school, although this was admittedly more difficult to measure. The frequency with which principals usually looked at data was reported as centering upon one month or more (e.g., Miller, 2007).

Principals often used the above sources of data for the following purposes:

- Improving learning and instruction
- Shared vision achievement and/or goal setting for school improvement
- Fostering collaboration around data use
- Staff development and evaluation
- Communication to students and parents
- Guiding resource allocation
- Managing public relationships
- Conducting longitudinal studies

How Principals Effectively Use Data

This section presents effective leadership practices principals enacted in using data that helped achieve the above-mentioned purposes identified in this review. These four sets of practices are more commonly reported than the others.

Evidence-Based Instructional Improvement

The main purpose for which principals use data as reported by all studies is to improve learning and teaching. This purpose was reported significantly more frequently than other purposes such as goal setting (Brooks, 2012). In order to achieve this, principals relied on data to do three things: to know what is going on with each student, in classes and in the school; to develop solutions; and to evaluate and monitor. Effective leadership practices in this regard include:

Leadership Practices for Knowing What Is "Going On"

- Analyzing multiple sources of longitudinal data and unpacking data in multiple ways
- Identifying trends, patterns, and gaps in students' knowledge and skills per state and curriculum standards
- Grouping
- Identifying the strengths, weaknesses, and needs of each individual student
- Identifying struggling students/placement
- Identifying needs in the curriculum
- Aligning assessment data with standards, standardized tests, and curriculum

Principals were reported to have used longitudinal data and examined performance by subgroup, by subject, by classroom, by grade, and by department. Looking at longitudinal data as well as multiple data in various ways helped them find trends, gaps, and patterns (e.g., Crum, Sherman, & Myran, 2009). They more often used summative assessment to identify trends and patterns over a period of time and compare between classes, grades, departments, and schools in comparison to their demographics. They used formative assessments to gauge whether or not their instructional leadership was having the desired impact on the teaching and learning that was going on at their sites in the short term and to know what the teachers at the site level *hoped* that their students learned vs. what the students *should* learn, as indicated by the summative measures (Henry, 2011). Both principals and teachers felt strongly that aligning the curriculum to the standards and having a variety of ways to measure progress toward those standards was a key factor in moving schools forward.

Leadership Practices for Developing Solutions

- Looking for meaningful guidance regarding how teaching practices can and should be altered, and creating instructional interventions
- Identifying and promoting teaching practices that work
- Customizing and/or developing instructional program, interventions, or remediation for each student and/or groups of students

Principals making decisions directly related to instruction and curriculum is an area that has high impact on student achievement (Shen et al., 2010). A typical example of using direct data for improving instruction, reported by the studies included in this review, was principals visiting classrooms and using these instructional observation data to identify best instructional practices, to assist teachers in developing appropriate instructional strategies to meet the needs of a diverse student population, to drive the professional development, and to promote best instructional practices (e.g., Crum et al., 2009; Deike, 2009). Principals used data analysis results to map curriculum for the next year and to adjust instruction (e.g., Shen et al., 2010), to meet accountability demands from school inspectorates, to redesign remediation program (e.g., Crum et al., 2009), and to schedule and plan professional development (PD) hours (e.g., Shen et al., 2010). Principals were reported to use formative assessment data and parent input, and their own observations for instructional management, such as grouping students and balancing classes. They also used indirect data, such as monthly reports from departments, to develop school learning plans (Sanzo et al., 2011).

Leadership Practices for Evaluating and Monitoring

Constant, regular evaluation and monitoring of the learning steps of each child, effectiveness of instructional strategies or programs was reported as key leadership practices (e.g., Simpson, 2011). Student achievement data helped determine concepts that students are missing and revealed gaps in the instructional program that might be causing gaps in student learning.

Formative assessment results, along with class work and course assessments, can be reviewed to provide appropriate intervention. Principals have monitored instructional strategies and have understood that data-driven decision making works successfully for the school overall through student academic growth data, attending meetings, and teacher feedback (e.g., Godreau Cimma, 2011).

Setting Coordinated, Tiered, Long-Term, and Short-Term Goals

The majority of the studies reported that principals used the data to communicate a vision or to change strategies for improvement with their staff and set school priorities. A theme about what really worked when principals and teachers used data is that the principal and the teachers focused on the common goal that all students would increase their academic achievement; once that goal was in place, they collaboratively created a process whereby teachers would meet on a monthly basis and sit down together to analyze student assessment data to ensure progress toward that goal. During those meetings, teachers came together at grade and/or department levels to look at common assessment data and student work data in relation to their students' achievement levels. They learned where each student was at and made changes as needed to whole group or small group instruction, or worked with students individually (Fischer, 2011; Miller, 2007).

Some also held a tiered goal related to preparing for students' college readiness, in which the students were (a) accepted to an institution of higher learning, (b) prepared for the rigorous academic challenges at that level, and (c) provided with the academic and psychological stamina necessary to prevail through all four years of college and to graduate with a degree (Rayor, 2010).

Several studies reported that it was effective for principals to develop and visually present to teachers various data analysis results in spreadsheets and diagrams, because just physically seeing a dot representing each and every student in the school made it real so that teachers were no longer talking in general terms about students not passing, and they could see the needs of each individual student, and where both small and large groups of students needed help with a skill (e.g., Fischer, 2011).

Determining Staff Development Needs and Developing Teacher' Instructional Capacities

Several studies (e.g., Dalton, 2009; Henry, 2011; Sanzo et al.2011; Schildkamp & Kuiper, 2010) reported that school leaders used several kinds of data (e.g., self-evaluation data, classrooms observation, and student test or assessment data) to determine PD needs for faculty, oriented toward school learning plans, to shape teachers' PD activities, and to evaluate teaching performance. School leaders shared data as a regular occurrence and used formative data as feedback given to the teachers. This sharing process allowed teachers to see and celebrate their successes along their way toward the final goals. Such data-driven instruction-focused professional development was reported by a few studies to be a successful school principal practice. It was of note that the PD for teachers should be differentiated to be effective (Deike, 2009; Simpson, 2011). Principals' modelling the use of the data presented to staff was reported as very helpful in making it easier for teachers to identify students' weak areas and to see a group of students who were struggling in the same strand of reading or math. Such processes helped prompt teachers to begin discussions about how they could supplement current instruction to ensure additional opportunities for students to go back and revisit concepts not mastered, and to begin to think about ways in which they could better support learning (e.g., Fischer, 2011).

Data-Advised Parent Involvement (DAPI)

Although principals' use of data for involving parents in teaching students col-laboratively was reported much less frequently than their use of data for other purposes (Brooks, 2012), evidence about principals' endeavors in this area is emerging and has proven this activity to be successful (e.g., Simpson, 2011). Student progress data shared with parents showed them whether the teaching strategies used at home were appropriate. In some schools, the principal spent considerable time providing parents with professional development to enhance their skills in using effective standards-driven strategies when working with their children. Parents expressed satisfaction with data-based communication with the school and teachers and were more cooperative and effective in help-ing their children learn at home when they received this information (Simpson, 2011). Much less frequently reported were principals' use of data for public rela-tions purposes. This was especially true in England where there was a particular emphasis placed by school leaders on the wide variety of school-level perfor-mance indicators reported in national tables and the media's school "league tables."

Impacts of Principal Use of Data

The majority of the principals in the majority of the studies commented on the value of data-informed decision making for instructional purposes and expressed that they used data to move their schools forward (e.g., Duke & Landahl, 2011; Henry, 2011). This observation is based on qualitative evidence, as most of the studies we reviewed are case studies or qualitative in nature. Quantitative evi-dence that statistically demonstrates the statistical relationship between princi-pals' use of data to inform decision making and student achievement is rare and inconsistent. The evidence included in this review suggests that the impact of principals' and teachers' use of data on student learning is indirect. It has a direct impact on fostering teachers' evidence-based instruction and more tailored and precise instruction, transforming school culture into a data-informed organism, the identification of evidence-supported/best teaching practices, and teachers sharing knowledge and instructional strategies, which are the keys to improving student achievement on a large scale. That being said, principals were reported to have direct and significant effects on the reading achievement gains on a state reading test by having one-to-one discussions with nonproficient students, focused on the review of their individual achievement reports, areas of relative strength, relative needs, and setting goals for the students on a state reading test (Silva, White, & Yoshida, 2011). Future research is needed to model statistically and conceptually in order to attest to the immediate impacts of principals' data-informed decision making and to identify from them the important contributors to student learning.

Factors Moderating Principal Data Use

- Data type
- Contextual factors
  - Performance status of school
  - School level
  - District size
- Principals' characteristics
  - Principal years of administrative experience
  - Principal years of experience at the current school
  - Education
  - Gender
  - Age

Three categories of factors were identified that significantly moderated principals' use of data. They were the nature of the data itself, contextual factors (i.e., school performing status), and principals' characteristics (e.g., their gender and age). Summative assessment was more often used by principals, as described in the above texts (e.g., Henry, 2011). The differences in principals' use of data to inform their decisions between high- and low-performing schools were reported to be significantly small to nonsignificant.

No consensus has been achieved regarding the moderating effects of school's performance status on principals' use of data. Williams (2011) reported that more principals in lower-performing schools used data more often than principals in higher-performing schools. In contrast, Hill (2010) and Martinez (2010) reported that principals and teachers in schools making the Adequate Yearly Progress (AYP) had higher mean scores for indicators of data use. Teigen's (2009) study reported, however, that the performance of schools (low vs. high) did not moderate the extent of principals' use of data. These contradictory results could be understood as showing that, when schools are in the process of making efforts to turn around/ meet the AYP requirements, school personnel tend to use data to a larger extent while, when the turnaround is not a pressure or emphasis, teachers and principals tend to be content with their current success and do not dig more; however, their school success could have resulted from greater use of data and higher competency in using data as well.

There was a significant contrast in principals' use of data between the elementary and the secondary schools. Most of the schools where the principals had created structures that supported professional development to promote data use were at the elementary level (Deike, 2009). The larger the school district, the more likely the principal was to use disaggregated data (Miller, 2007).

A few studies examined how principal characteristics moderated their use of data. As a principal's years of administrative experience increases, so may his or her perceptions that teachers are making data-driven decisions (Teigen, 2009).

Principals with three or fewer years in their current setting felt more strongly than those principals with more experience at their current school that a data-driven culture existed within their buildings (Teigen, 2009). The longer principals stayed in the current building, the more likely principals were to engage others in the school improvement process using data (Miller, 2007). Principals with nine or more years' experience in the same school believed satisfaction data is more effective in improving standardized mathematics scores than principals with only one to four years' experience in the same school (Williams, 2011). Female principals believed process-type data to be more effective than male principals in increasing student achievement (Williams, 2011). Female principals tended to use input data in high-performing than in low-performing schools. More female principals than males in the upper group used student language proficiency data to increase student achievement (Williams, 2011). Those 55+ years old in the lower-performing schools had a significantly higher mean for effectiveness ratings of input data in increasing mathematics scores than those 40–54 years old in lower-performing schools (Williams, 2011). The average use of satisfaction data was significantly lower in the 40–54 year olds than in those who were 55+ years old (Williams, 2011). Principals with a higher level of education were more likely to use data to monitor school improvement goals (Miller, 2007).

Supports for and Barriers to Principals' Use Data

Principals' ability to use assessment data, having support (e.g., reading coaches), technology support, availability of data, and collaborative culture in schools were rated as the top factors, in descending order, that supported principals' use of data. A few studies also reported that central office support was helpful in terms of providing requested data, training on data use, presentations of data results, and analysis in schools, though a lack of vision and alignment regarding data use from the central office and the lack of a system in place to offer professional development to all schools (e.g., Deike, 2009) tended to hamper these efforts. Someone (coaches or district persons) coming and presenting the results of a thorough analysis of data (Deike, 2009) is also very persuasive for school personnel to use data immediately.

Lack of time was reported as the number one barrier to principals' use of data, followed by the lack of technology systems, availability of data, a collaborative, knowledge-sharing culture, inconsistency in or lack of a district-wide support network, teacher' ability to use data, information about students being scattered among several different data sources—none of which talked to each other—and the difficulty of having to go to numerous sources to gather data for a particular student, a grade, or the entire school (e.g., Deike, 2009; Fischer, 2011). One system of data is needed for every school in which everything talks to everything else and all the information is provided. Data need to arrive at the schools in a user-friendly format that can be interpreted with ease (e.g., Deike, 2009).

Preparation for Principals' Data Use

Principals' attitudes toward data, their competencies with using data, and their professional development opportunities correlated highly with their actual use of data (Martinez, 2010). The principals' own studies ranked as the number one most useful source among the various sources of their preparation to use data to increase student academic achievement (Teigan, 2011). Ranked next were district training, mentoring from a colleague, and their doctoral program, with the latter three sources being useful to a much less significant degree than the principals' own studies. Administration credentialing programs provided the least helpful experience in preparation to use assessment data (Deike, 2009; Martinez, 2010; Teigan, 2011).

The Data Teachers Use: Its Nature and Purpose

Compared with principals, teachers looked at more formative assessment data in addition to summative data throughout the year (e.g., Courneene, 2009; Gates, 2008; Henry, 2011; Rayor, 2010). Summative scores give teachers a big picture and/or baseline knowledge of how the whole class or groups of students have been doing over a period of time. Short, informal, formative assessments give teachers a "pulse check" of where everybody is each day so as to adjust and plan teaching on a day-to-day basis. In particular, grade-level created common formative assessments that are aligned with curriculum and instruction were considered to be the most useful because teachers understand formative assessment better (Henry, 2011). Summative test results need to be combined with formative assessments so that teachers will have a good understanding of both "trends" and "group" information and individual information about each child in order to inform their daily, short-term, and long-term instructional plans.

Teachers use student data primarily to make instructional decisions, overlapping a lot with principals' use of data in making instructional improvement with their decisions focused more on classroom teaching. Teachers' overall use of data was reported to be limited more to assessment of student attainment and progress, and to planning for remediation rather than to tailor instruction and inform curriculum design. Teachers were skeptical about utilizing student attainment and progress data to inform assessments of their own teaching.

How Teachers Effectively Use Data

In general there is an inconsistent use of data among teachers (e.g., Barry, 2006). Effective practices in teachers' use of data that we identified, however, included analyzing data in groups periodically and sharing assessment data-supported practices; looking at individual students' reports to see where each student was and then addressing those problems in their work; talking to teachers from the previous year and the next year; looking at data to identify changes over a period of time; analyzing academic data to pinpoint the academic needs of the child and to ease students' behavioral and social issues; and reviewing test results with students. In addition, teacher leaders felt strongly that sharing data with parents is critical, helping to keep their conversations with parents focused on the learning needs of the child, helping parents to learn how they can help their child succeed, and thus creating buy-in into the school's learning philosophy.

Impacts of Teachers' Use of Data

The following are a few prominent impacts identified as themes in terms of the impacts of teachers' use of data: teachers' internalizing school or department goals by looking at the data; setting specific goals for their students and working subsequently toward the goals; motivating students when sharing data with students; and developing and providing more precise instruction to meet the needs of each student once they got to know each student's status. This goal-setting, sharing, alignment, and reinforcement achieved through multiple, ongoing data-informed decision making processes helped improve student achievement (e.g., Rayor, 2010; Simpson, 2011). Again, this claim is qualitative and tentative as a majority of the studies examining teachers' use of student data employed a case study method. Future research is needed to tease out these impacts, calculate their magnitudes, and test how these outcomes are associated with student learning outcomes.

Supports for and Barriers to Teacher Use of Data

Most teachers believe in using data for instructional purposes, but not all possess the knowledge and skills needed to do so. Six things were identified that promote teachers' use of data: principals' data-driven leadership, collaborative culture, providing time, availability of data, teachers' data-using skills, having one longitudinal user-friendly system in place for the storage of multiple data, analysis function, results reporting, assessment tool generation and evaluation functions, relevance and credibility of data to their teaching situation, and being well informed about their students and what can be done with various data (e.g., Barry, 2006; Fischer, 2011; Hill, 2010; Simpson, 2011; Wayman, Spring, Lemke, & Lehr, 2012). Teachers are much more motivated and committed to engage themselves in data use if principals model data use, help teachers to find the meaning and purpose of using data, conduct one-to-one conversations, set access goals for all users, communicate clear expectations for that data use, and provide multiple principal-led or data expert-led PD sessions, training led by professional communities, local association or agencies, or online training with flexible times throughout the year.

A collaborative PD culture where teachers share knowledge and problems associated with data, collaboratively develop common assessments and solutions, and share effective instructional strategies is also essential. In such a culture, the administrators trusted that the teachers were capable of doing their best work, and the teachers, in turn, needed to trust that the administration was supporting their work with children in their pursuit of academic achievement (Fischer, 2011). This trusting relationship, if nurtured, helps in establishing a high degree of buy-in for using data (Simpson, 2011). Principals can foster such collaboration by providing structure and tools around which to work, being involved in collaboration processes (e.g., Cruz, 2010; Wayman et al., 2012), providing time, setting expectations for collaboration, arranging coaches to help teachers make changes in their teaching (Barry, 2006), and building leadership teams and professional teams at every grade level (Sanzo et al., 2011).

Similarly to principals, teachers felt that the key to really moving school staff to engage in using data was having one longitudinal user-friendly system in place for the storage of multiple data, analysis functions, results reporting, assessment tool generation, and evaluation functions (e.g., Simpson, 2011). In addition, they indicated the importance of data relevance and being well informed about their students and what can be done with various data. Similar to their principals, teachers' formal training in learning is not helpful with their data analysis and Data-Informed Decision Making (DIDM).

Meanwhile, the factors that hinder teacher's use of data should be avoided. These include insufficiency of time and collaboration, lack of timely data and sensitive data tools, their relevance and usefulness, the cost of data systems, competition among teachers, unfriendly or threatening ways of displaying students' performance data, a lack of formal structure dedicated to teachers' data use, nondata-wise culture, lack of district formal and consistent support, and complacency with success (e.g., Cho, 2011; Deike, 2009; Fischer, 2011; Simpson, 2011).

Conclusion

Data-driven decision making is a process of principals and teachers taking data seriously and using multiple sources of student data to systematically inform their decisions to lead school change and provide data-informed instruction to improve student learning. Such data use is the most effective or, actually, the only way to make large-scale breakthroughs (i.e., substantial, continued gain in improving student learning and reaching every child in all schools) (Fullan, Hill, & Crévola, 2006; Kowalski, Lasley, & Mahoney, 2008) and is the number one key feature of a successful leadership (Crum et al., 2009). This review shows that the majority of schools are moving in this direction, that is, being knowledgeable about data use, using data for the purpose of improving teaching and learning, with some level of difficulty beyond accountability purposes. Limited but emerging evidence shows that, in a minority of the schools, principals have begun using student data to examine teachers' practices and determine teachers' professional development.

This review identified that principals use data to make decisions largely focused in two areas: using data to set school goals, and to prompt, help, and develop teachers to use data to adjust instruction. Many more efforts are needed on the part of principals to promote the use of formative assessments on a daily basis and the sharing of best evidence-proven instructional practices or strategies.

The study of the phenomena of analysis and practical uses of principals' and teachers' use of student data, as showed by the evidence in this review, is at an early stage (e.g., describing, conceptualizing, developing measures) but is moving from the infancy stage, as Wayman and Stringfield (2006) commented seven years ago. The majority of the studies explored in this chapter examined the fundamental questions related to this topic, such as what data principals and teachers use, for what purposes, and the barriers to and shapers of such data, but are "descriptive" in nature, trying to portray what is going on in ordinary schools (sampled schools in more than half of the studies) or what principals and teachers do in high-performing schools (less than half of the studies contextualized such schools). With this descriptive knowledge accumulated, systematic, large scale, and longitudinal studies with more sophisticated conceptualizing and statistical modeling can be used to examine the complex web in which principals promote data use among teachers and the conditions fostering such use, which in turn improves learning. The framework provided in this study serves as a start to frame thinking about this complex web.

Principal preparation programs, which were identified as the least helpful programs in developing principals' capacities in DIDM, should be seriously revisited. Principal preparation programs should be focused much more on skill development than on knowledge acquisition.

To promote the use of data, either on the part of teachers or principals, it is key to develop teachers' skills in doing so. This could be done either by principals, or on-the-job training or teacher preparation programs. Principals need to possess evidence-based decision-making skills themselves, but they also must possess the skills to develop teachers' capacities in this regard.

This review reveals that the "effective" principals analyzed data, graphed results, and presented visual data to teachers. Such endeavors are conceptualized as part of DIDM in current literature and principals have, unfortunately, been encouraged to continue this trend. However, this should not be the case. Decision making based on well-presented data should be the focus of principals' jobs as educational leaders. The former three activities should be done by the district, or school individuals, coaches, or data analysts, or by new positions created to fill this responsibility. Principal certificate or preparation programs should focus on the development of such abilities in aspiring principals as "know-ability," "do-ability," and "sustainability" in DIDM in schools.

This review finds, currently, that principals mostly look only at student data when making decisions on improving teaching and learning. Other information about the school conditions and teacher-related factors that significantly contribute to student learning, such as academic press, teacher collective efficacy, teacher trust in others, academic optimism (the combination of the above three variables), teacher organizational citizenship behavior, and school disciplinary climate (e.g., DiPaola & Hoy, 2005; Goddard, Hoy, & Hoy, 2004; Hoy & Miskel, 2013; Ma & Crocker, 2007; McGuigan, 2005; Tschannen-Moran & Barr, 2004), and, more recently, safe schools and focused instruction (Sun & Leithwood, 2013), should be also reviewed. However, only a few studies included in this review sporadically mentioned principals' use of teacher satisfaction data and other school process data for the purpose of student learning. Data about the status of such critical paths generally is not available to principals, let alone its analysis and results. Systematic data about these conditions should be provided to principals for them to make decisions, at least periodically. Principal certificate or preparation programs should, at least, provide preparation of principals' DIDM abilities in these domains and again should be focused on the development of such abilities as "know-ability," "do-ability," and sustainability in schools, rather than pure or merely conceptual understanding. Also they should provide data tools if principals have to collect data themselves.

In a similar vein, teachers should be prepared either through teacher education programs or on-the-job training to use data to make instructional decisions. Again, their job should be focused much more on decision making. They should be the experts to consult when developing either summative or normative assessments, rather than having school leaders develop those assessments themselves.

Figure 2.1 summarizes what was described in the above sections and visually presents the framework for understanding the nature of principal and teacher

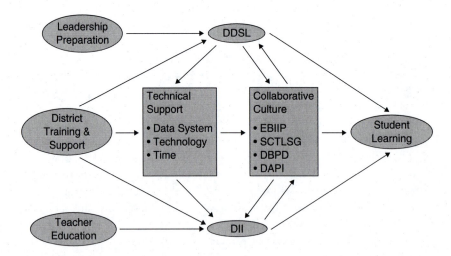

FIGURE 2.1 A Framework for Understanding the Nature and Impacts of Principals' and Teachers' Data Use to Improve Student Learning

use of student data and the multiple relationships between principals and teachers' use of student data, workplace factors, and student learning outcomes, developed through this review. It helps frame the thinking of school administrators and policy-makers who want to make evidence-based decisions to improve student learning and to improve teacher enthusiasm and effectiveness in student data use.

References

Barry, M. J. (2006). *A school's use of data for teaching and learning: A case study of data's impact on instruction in an urban school.* (Ed.D., University of Southern California). *ProQuest Dissertations and Theses.* (304967151).

Brooks, W. D., Jr. (2012). *South Carolina middle school principals' use of data-driven decision-making.* (Ph.D., University of South Carolina). *ProQuest Dissertations and Theses.* (1037995479).

Cho, V. (2011). *Educational data use and computer data systems: Policies, plans, and the enactment of practice.* (Ph.D., The University of Texas at Austin). *ProQuest Dissertations and Theses.* (900421672).

Courneene, J. L. (2009). *Middle school teacher use of data-driven decision-making to improve student learning.* (Ph.D., Marian University). *ProQuest Dissertations and Theses.* (305048702).

Crum, K. S., Sherman, W. H., & Myran, S. (2009). Best practices of successful elementary school leaders. *Journal of Educational Administration, 48*(1), 48–63. doi: http://dx.doi.org/10.1108/09578231011015412

Cruz, H. (2010). *Kids plus data equals student success! Investigating the use of a structured data portfolio on students' motivation and personal accountability.* (Ed.D., Arizona State University). *ProQuest Dissertations and Theses.* (304734584).

Dalton, M. (2009). *A school's use of data-driven decision-making to affect gifted students' learning.* (Ed.D., University of Southern California). *ProQuest Dissertations and Theses.* (304997923).

Deike, M. A. (2009). *The principal as an instructional leader within the context of effective data use.* (Ed.D., The University of Texas at Austin). *ProQuest Dissertations and Theses.* (305005467).

DiPaola, M. F., & Hoy, W. K. (2005). Organizational citizenship of faculty and achievement of high school students. *The High School Journal, 88*(3), 35–44.

Duke, D. L., & Landahl, M. (2011). "Raising tests scores was the easy part": A case study of the third year of school turnaround. *International Studies in Educational Administration (Commonwealth Council for Educational Administration & Management (CCEAM), 39*(3), 91–114. Retrieved from http://connection.ebscohost.com/c/articles/69959683/raising-tests-scores-was-easy-part-case-study-third-year-school-turnaround

Fischer, B. E. (2011). *Using data to increase student achievement: A case study of success in a sanctioned school.* (D.Ed., University of Minnesota). *ProQuest Dissertations and Theses.* (873812798).

Fullan, M., Hill, P., & Crévola, C. (2006). *Breakthrough.* Toronto, Canada: Ontario Principal's Council.

Gallagher, L., Means, B., Padilla, C., & SRI International (2008). *Teachers' use of student data systems to improve instruction: 2005 to 2007.* Report prepared for U.S. Department of Education Office of Planning, Evaluation and Policy Development Policy and Program Studies Service. Washington, DC. Retrieved from www.ed.gov/rschstat/eval/tech/teachers-data-use-2005–2007/teachers-data-use-2005–2007.pdf

Gates, A. A. (2008). *Wyoming teachers' knowledge and use of formative assessment.* (Ph.D., University of Wyoming). *ProQuest Dissertations and Theses.* (304452083).

Goddard, R., Hoy, W. K., & Hoy, A. W. (2004). Collective efficacy beliefs: Theoretical developments, empirical evidence, and future directions [Electronic version]. *Educational Researcher, 33*(3), 3–13.

Godreau Cimma, K. L. (2011). *A middle school principal's and teachers' perceptions of leadership practices in data-driven decision-making.* (Ed.D., University of Hartford). *ProQuest Dissertations and Theses.* (851186662).

Henry, S. S. (2011). *Principals' use of assessment data to drive student academic achievement.* (Ed.D., California State University, Fullerton). *ProQuest Dissertations and Theses.* (912193587).

Hill, K. L. (2010). *Predictive indicators of high performing schools: A study of evaluative inquiry and the effective use of achievement test data.* (Ph.D., University of Minnesota). *ProQuest Dissertations and Theses.* (610058860).

Hoy, W. K., & Miskel, C. G. (2013). *Educational administration: Theory, research, and practice* (9th ed.). New York, NY: McGraw-Hill.

Kowalski, T. J., Lasley, T. J., & Mahoney, J. W. (2008). *Data-driven decisions and school leadership: Best practices for school improvement.* Boston, MA: Pearson/Allyn and Bacon.

Leithwood, K., Aitken, R., & Jantzi, D. (2006). *Making school smarter: Leading with evidence.* Thousand Oaks, CA: Corwin.

Ma, X., & Crocker, R. (2007). Provincial effects on reading achievement. *The Alberta Journal of Educational Research, 53*(1), 87–109.

Martinez, G. (2010). *Investigating school principals' personal variables related to the use of data: Implications for professional development.* (Ed.D., New Mexico State University). *ProQuest Dissertations and Theses.* (734420206).

McGuigan, L. (2005). *The role of enabling bureaucracy and academic optimism in academic achievement growth.* Unpublished Dissertation, Ohio State University, Columbus.

Miller, J. K. (2007). *The use of data to inform decisions by elementary building principals.* (Ed.D., The University of Nebraska—Lincoln). *ProQuest Dissertations and Theses.* (304841876).

Rayor, L. F. (2010). *Multiple perceptions of teachers who use data.* (Ed.D., University of Southern California). *ProQuest Dissertations and Theses.* (375548771).

Sanzo, K. L., Sherman, W. H., & Clayton, J. (2011). Leadership practices of successful middle school principals. *Journal of Educational Administration, 49*(1), 31–45. Retrieved from www.emeraldinsight.com/journals.htm?articleid=1902018

Schildkamp, K., & Kuiper, W. (2010). Data-informed curriculum reform: Which data, what purposes, and promoting and hindering factors. *Teaching and Teacher Education, 26,* 482–496. doi: 10.1016/j.tate.2009.06.007

Sharratt, L., & Fullan, M. (2012). *Putting FACES on the data: What great leaders do.* Thousand Oaks, CA: Corwin.

Shen, J., Cooley, V. E., Reeves, P., Burt, W. L., Ryan, L., Rainey, M. J., & Yuan, W. (2010). Using data for decision-making: Perspectives from 16 principals in Michigan, USA. *International Review of Education, 56*(4), 435–456.

Silva, J. P., White, G. P., & Yoshida, R. K. (2011). The direct effects of principal-student discussions on eighth grade students' gains in reading achievement: An experimental study. *Educational Administration Quarterly, 47*(5), 772–793.

Simpson, G. H. (2011). *School leaders' use of data-driven decision-making for school improvement: A study of promising practices in two California charter schools.* (Ed.D., University of Southern California). *ProQuest Dissertations and Theses.* (901883434).

Sun, J.-P., & Leithwood, K. (2013). *The nature and impact of leadership practices aimed at developing the capacities of school staffs: A meta-analytical review of evidence.* Paper presented at the annual meeting of the AERA, San Francisco, USA.

Teigen, B. N. (2009). *A systematic examination of data-driven decision-making within a school division: The relationships among principal beliefs, school characteristics, and accreditation status.* (Ph.D., Virginia Commonwealth University). *ProQuest Dissertations and Theses.* (305175153).

Tschannen-Moran, M., & Barr, M. (2004). Fostering student learning: The relationship of collective teacher efficacy and student achievement. *Leadership and Policy in Schools, 3*(3), 189–209.

Wayman, J. C., Spring, S. D., Lemke, M. A., & Lehr, M. D. (2012, April 14). *Using data to inform practice: Effective principal leadership strategies.* Paper presented at the 2012 annual meeting of the American Educational Research Association, Vancouver, British Columbia, Canada.

Wayman, J. C., & Stringfield, S. (2006). Technology-supported involvement of entire faculties in examination of student data for instructional improvement. *American Journal of Education, 112*(4), 549–571.

Williams, J. (2011). *A comparison of secondary principals' use of data systems to increase student achievement in mathematics as measured by standardized assessments.* (D.Ed., Indiana University of Pennsylvania). *ProQuest Dissertations and Theses.* (867800169).

PART II

Emotional and Epistemological Decision-Making Structures

3

CAPTURING PRINCIPALS' DECISION-MAKING PROCESSES IN AN ONLINE PROFESSIONAL LEARNING COMMUNITY

Stephanie Chitpin

Introduction

The roles and responsibilities of principals have radically changed over the last decade, and the burdens placed upon the shoulders of these individuals are increasing (Darling-Hammond, LaPointe, Myerson, Orr, & Cohen, 2007). They are not only managers, heads of finance, efficient schedulers, and rigorous followers of bureaucratic regulations, but also curriculum leaders, reflective practitioners, and builders of collaborative cultures. They are also tasked with the responsibility to forge powerful visions for their schools and lead significant organizational change (Darling-Hammond et al., 2007; Fahey 2011, Farkas, Johnson, Duffett, Foleno, & Foley, 2001; Marzano, Waters, & McNulty, 2005; Wagner & Kegan, 2006; Waters & Cameron, 2007).

It is clear that, at the school level, principals play a pivotal leadership role and that these additional responsibilities have, no doubt, impacted upon their decision-making activities. How, and on what basis, they make decisions around important aspects of school improvement is also significant both to their development as curriculum and instructional leaders and to educational reform itself. Simply because principals are required to be curriculum and instructional leaders, their decisions around raising student achievement and the assessment of teachers becomes consequential. This work is challenged both by the isolated, unreflective context in which it often occurs and a lack of clarity around the exact nature of principals' work.

As a remedy to this issue, an understanding of how principals make decisions is predicated upon an awareness of the knowledge and theories from which principals draw in making those decisions. Robinson (1993) states that practitioner problems "are problems about what to do, and what counts as a solution is constrained both internally by their own beliefs and values, and externally by material conditions and institutional and cultural expectations" (p. 13). The knowledge used in decision making is complex and characterized by explicit and tacit structures (Baumard, 1999; Marquardt, 1996; Newton & Sackney, 2005). Similarly, principal theories include both theories-in-use and espoused theories (Argyris & Schön, 1978), and therefore, a sophisticated methodological framework, complete with a supporting matrix, capable of capturing the variety of knowledge and theories involved in principal decision making, is needed.

This study examines principals' decision making in an eastern-district school board in Ontario, Canada. The purpose for this study concerns the school district's adoption of site-based decision-making approaches. This decentralization of school improvement initiatives provides the opportunity to study localized examples of how principals make decisions. This district has faced challenges in the realm of principal decision making for school improvement, and this study has the potential to provide robust findings in terms of how principals make their decisions.

Furthermore, the school district has a mature and well-established policy context centered on accountability and school-level strategic planning. In Ontario, the *School Effectiveness Framework* mandates school improvement plans and the regular review and evaluation of these plans; this policy provides an ideal context for exploring principal decisions regarding school improvement. All decisions and accountabilities are borne by schools, with principals ultimately being held responsible and liable. Schools are expected to make improvements and to solve their own problems through wise and timely decision making.

Methodology

The focus of this research is principals' decision making. Twelve principals voluntarily participated in the study. Researchers coached participating principals in the use of the Objective Knowledge Growth Framework (OKGF) (Chitpin, 2010; Chitpin & Knowles, 2009) as a reflective tool to examine their decision-making processes and problem-solving strategies when faced with challenges and opportunities. The OKGF prompts participants to critically reflect on their beliefs and decision-making strategies, so that their solutions become bolder and sharper in empirical content. The OKGF is cost efficient and relatively easy to implement, as evidenced by a study funded by the Social Sciences and Humanities Research Council–Research and Development Initiatives (SSHRC-RDI) with preservice teachers focused on solving assessment related problems (Chitpin, 2010; Chitpin et al., 2012; Chitpin & Knowles, 2009). Participants are essentially asked to document their decision-making process, using a template (see Figure 3.1) as they try to solve situational problems.

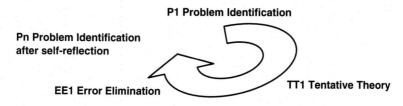

FIGURE 3.1 The Objective Knowledge Growth Framework

The OKGF: A Framework for Decision Making

The most important influence on the development of the Canadian Principals Learning Network (CPLN) has been Chitpin's Objective Knowledge Growth Framework (OKGF) (Chitpin & Knowles, 2009; Chitpin 2010). The OKGF builds upon Popper's (1979; 2002) critical rationalism, which emphasizes that the dynamic growth of knowledge is stimulated by problems of practice, inconsistencies, and intellectual conflicts. Crucial to this process is the users' willingness to critically reflect upon and revise a hitherto accepted body of beliefs. This method encourages users to discover weak points in theories and to question their arguments. In the current context, we focus on the theory's process of systematic and explicit reflection, rather than whether knowledge can be said to be objectively true.

Figure 3.1 depicts the cyclical process of identifying an initial problem, proposing, first, a tentative theory to address or solve the problem, then testing tentative theories against experience or the criticisms of others to arrive at a new problem identification process arising from error elimination. The schema then becomes iterative.

The comprehensive yet simple OKGF has repeatedly been shown to support professional learning (Chitpin, 2010, 2011; Chitpin & Knowles, 2009; Chitpin & Simon, 2012; Chitpin, Simon, & Galipeau, 2008; Simon, Chitpin, & Yahya, 2010). For example, when the teachers in the study by Simon et al. (2010) were interviewed in depth, and their teaching artifacts were analyzed in detail, the OKGF schema emerged as a useful tool for assisting their professional learning, regardless of their professional training, background, or prior experience. This schema has helped people to explicitly examine (1) how they make decisions; (2) how they devise tentative theories and consider their accuracy; (3) how others influence the decision process and what that means; and (4) how and why they eliminate certain options in favor of others. The OKGF is sensitive to experience, contexts, and exigencies (Simon et al, 2010).

Perhaps the best known attempt at incorporating all three—experience, contexts, and exigencies—is the model of the reflective practitioner developed by Schön (1983), which focused on broad procedures for specifying conditions under which *reflecting on* and *in* practice could flourish. However Schön's work did not provide a structure to guide self-reflection or prompt learners to report on their process when making key decisions. The OKGF, on the other hand, systematically tracks the progression of decision making (challenges and opportunities) employed by the participants. Thus each strategy employed becomes bolder and sharper in empirical content.

Finally, the OKGF is cost efficient and relatively easy to implement—as demonstrated in a pilot study in an Eastern Ontario Board (Chitpin & Knowles, 2009) as well as in a study with preservice teachers on assessment issues funded by the Social Sciences and Humanities Research Council (SSHRC) (Chitpin, 2010). Participants are essentially asked to document their decision making (using a template) as they try to solve organizational problems. When the OKGF is adopted within a natural school setting as a reflective tool, it offers several advantages: Participants are provided with a structured form to record their decision-making processes and their explanations on actions taken when faced with opportunities or challenges. They also have the freedom of choosing the number of cycles they want to complete.

The CPLN and the OKGF

To contribute to the existing knowledge on principals' decision-making skills, a strategic knowledge mobilization matrix, called Canadian Principals Learning Network (CPLN), was created in the spring of 2011. Through online activities, it collaboratively links an international group of practicing principals and university-based researchers with related expertise in order to explore the potential of an online professional learning community (PLC) using the OKGF, a reflective model of self-directed professional learning based on the critical rationalism of Karl Popper (a detailed description of the framework will follow).

First, this paper, through the use of the CPLN website, attempts to describe the context within which the professional learning of these principals has occurred. Second, it seeks to answer two research questions: (1) How do principals make decisions when faced with complex and ambiguous problems? (2) To what extent does the use of the OKGF provide a more holistic and comprehensive description of participants' decision-making process when faced with complex problems? Third, a description of the context of the study in the area of principals' decision making is provided, followed by a discussion differentiating between decision making and problem solving. Fourth, a description of the OKGF and how it provided a structure for participants to discover weak points in theories and to question their arguments is illustrated, using two dilemmas faced by school principals in their contexts. Finally, arguments are made for a matrix, such as the CPLN, for principals to use the OKGF to try out theories/solutions/ideas and to reflect more deeply about their decision-making skills within their curricular and instructional leadership practice.

Context: The CPLN Matrix

In November of 2010, the Ministry of Education in Ontario, Canada's largest province, announced the creation of the Knowledge Network for Applied Education Research (hereafter referred to as KNAER or the Knowledge Network).

KNAER provided the funding for the development of the CPLN, a website to support school principals in the area of decision making. Taken from a business model, the CPLN is broader than the concept of communities of practice in that, in addition to the shared learning and interests of its members, it encourages the development of new relationships with peers, academic researchers, and policy-makers involved in the professional development of school principals. It is a step toward the recognition and development of the conceptualization of knowledge production (Gibbons et al., 1994) where researchers and participants (school districts, principals, etc.) are associates in the generation and utilization of knowledge through applied partnerships (Bickel & Hattrup, 1995; Bradley, 2002; Brew, 2003; Department for Education and Employment, 2000; Gravani, 2008).

Characteristic of such knowledge is that it is interdisciplinary, rather than focused on a "knowledge for knowledge's sake" basis, and it is responsive to a wide range of social, political, and economic priorities outside the university itself (Gibbons et al., 1994). A further major trait is that knowledge is generated by groups of researchers and users who lose their hierarchical identity within their teams. In short, they become partners in knowledge creation, validation, adoption, dissemination, and diffusion.

This project is committed to bringing together practitioners and researchers in new forms of online PLCs because, as Wenger (1998) points out, "Elements of discourse travel across boundaries and combine to form broader discourses as people co-ordinate their enterprises, convince each other, reconcile their perspectives and form alliances" (p. 128). It proposes to yield robust descriptions of what principals actually know about educational problems, how they draw upon and revise theories of action for responding to problems, which theories are tenable in school improvement decisions, and which cognitive and contextual resources are important in principals' decision making. As such, the CPLN promises to promote online professional learning and to enhance school principals' decision-making skills by sharing valuable knowledge about how principals in a variety of locations and settings translated formal and informal theory into practice. The knowledge produced within this context would support the principals moving from a tentative knowledge base to one that is more objective, grounded, and sustainable.

In the summer of 2011, the principal author and researcher in this project met with the collaborator from an Eastern Catholic District School to solicit the participation of 15 high school principals from his school district. Since the principals from his school district had already been meeting for a whole day once a month, participating in yearly fall and spring retreats with their board's administrative officials, and regularly meeting as a PLC for professional development, they welcomed the opportunity to participate, celebrate, and share their success in an online forum with other school boards across Canada and internationally. However, they also believed that something else was needed for them to continue to be effective in their leadership roles that included additional responsibilities that impacted on their decision making in relation to teaching, learning, and school improvement in general. While they argued that mentoring had been vital with respect to the technical aspects of the position, they also required a place they could go to when needs arise to discuss challenges and to obtain feedback from their colleagues with respect to their knowledge and skills in the area of decision making. Thus, in order to meet this need, the CPLN was developed.

Decision Making and Problem Solving

Principals make countless number of decisions daily. Two primary challenges they face are separating consequential from inconsequential decisions and engaging in decision analysis for the more consequential issues (Kowalski, Lasley, & Mahoney, 2008). According to scholars in the area of decision making, there are two major categories of decisions: programmed decisions and nonprogrammed decisions (Davis & Davis, 2003). Programmed decisions are those that are simple, routine, highly structured, repetitive, familiar, low level, and quantitative in nature. It is argued that analytical approaches are most suited in making programmed decisions. Because nonprogrammed decisions are novel, unfamiliar, ambiguous, complex, nonsystematic, and qualitative in nature, analytical approaches are often of little use in resolving such problems in order to make suitable decisions (Davis & Davis, 2003).

Conversely, problem solvers tend to rely on heuristics or intuition or a combination of both (Cuban, 2001; Razik & Swanson, 2001). While, in theory, simple problems require programmed decisions whereas complex problems require nonprogrammed decisions, in reality, however, problems and decisions tend to exist on a continuum from very simple to highly complex with a mixture of simple and complex characteristics. The following example, Sam's problem of ice fishing (discussed at length in the analysis section) was taken from a posting on the CPLN and serves as an illustration of a nonprogrammed decision.

Sam needed to make a decision regarding the request of a teacher and a parent about taking students for ice fishing. Having just a couple of years of experience as a principal, Sam had never made such a decision. Based on her experience and assessment of the request, she was inclined not to grant the teacher and the parent permission to take the Grade 4–7 students ice fishing for a school trip. She also recognized that such a decision could produce negative consequences for her and the school. Her concerns were exacerbated by the fact that school district policy on this matter was vague and colored by an awareness that no principal in the district had ever granted such permission in past years. Uncertainty, risk, and potential consequences made this decision highly nonprogrammed. In this case, Sam was required to assess and evaluate the situation and provide insights when framing the problem (Simon, 1986) because there was no well-known, agreed-upon choice.

By way of contrast, an example of a programmed decision occurs when a principal must decide to order additional school supplies. In the past she has made this decision numerous times after the school secretary informed her that teachers were asking when they will receive more supplies and, in each instance, she has followed the existing school policy by ordering the same quantity from the same vendor. As illustrated, the decision she must make is highly programmed.

The terms *problem solving* and *decision making* are often used interchangeably and erroneously. According to Davis and Davis (2003) problem solving is "broader and encapsulates all of the tensions, turbulence, goals, strategies, agendas, preferences, demands, complexities, and potential outcomes of a problematic event." (p. 37). On the other hand, decision making is the specific process that an individual or a group engages in to solve a problem. One can look at problem solving as the frame and canvas of an artist, whereas decision making can be viewed as the paint and brush of the artist. Leadership requires decision making, which is what principals do every day (Davis & Davis, 2003). Decision making, the paint and brush of the artist, is a subset of problem solving, the frame and canvas of an artist.

However, with simple or routine problems, decision making and problem solving can be synonymous events. For example, there is a job posting for Grade 10 math and science. The deadline for applying is July 1. At the close of the competition, there are six applications. Four of the six applications are incomplete, with missing references, even though the individuals are highly qualified and have had many years of teaching experiences in a variety of settings. The principal is faced with the problem of determining how to deal with the four qualified applicants who have missed the deadline for submitting all application materials. The decision of the principal is to be fair and consistent with the process and, thus, she needs to exclude all applicants whose applications are incomplete. Her problem is solved.

Thus, the value of the decision is often determined by its effect on solving a problem. According to Welch (2002), a decision has three components: (1) a goal, (for example, how do I get the child to stop crying); (2) options for attaining the goal (different tentative theories or solutions employed to solve the problem); and (3) the selection of the preferred option (making decisions as to which of these tentative solutions to try out).

Problem solving, on the other hand, is a five-stage process. These stages are: (1) understanding; (2) formulating; (3) applying; (4) reflecting; and (5) improving. At the *understanding* stage, the problem-solver is required to understand what he or she is trying to do. There are two steps in this stage: framing the problem and analyzing the problem, which corresponds to the identification of the problem through using the OKGF. Even though, educators might have similar levels of education and personal experience, they often understand or identify their problems differently. This is due to personal cognitive processing of personal knowledge, values, and experiences.

There are also two elements at the formulating stage. At this stage, the problem-solver is required to *identify possible solutions* and *select a preferred solution* to solve the problem, which is what OKGF calls the *tentative solution or theory* (TT1). Due to time and information constraints, principals usually identify one of the most plausible solutions to solve the problem.

At the *applying stage,* the preferred solution is applied to solve the identified problem. The effectiveness of the solution depends on a variety of factors such as the quality of application, and the context in which it is applied. It is important to separate the potential solution from its application.

At the *reflecting stage,* it is highly recommended that the problem-solver assess the applied solution in an objective manner. Both formative and summative assessments ought to be used to assess the effectiveness of the applied solution. The summative assessment will determine the extent to which the solution actually resolved the problem and the formative assessment ice will determine what could be done to improve the solution if the problem has not been solved.

At the *improving stage,* the final stage of the process involves making a decision among three possibilities which are (1) the problem is resolved and no further action is necessary; (2) the preferred solution is adjusted and the application stage is repeated; or (3) the solution is found to be ineffective and the problem cycle is repeated by returning to the understanding stage (Kowalski, Lasley, & Mahoney, 2009). The last three stages of the five-stage process of problem solving are similar to the *error elimination process of the OKGF* in the sense that the problem-solver may apply the tentative theory to solve the problem and eliminates any errors contained in the tentative theory/solution so as to either keep the theory because it works, modify it to make it more epistemically progressive, discard it, and replace it with a bolder, stronger theory, or refine the problem.

Analysis: A Structure for Principals to Improve Decisions

We begin our analyses with two narratives that serve as parables to illustrate dilemmas faced by school principals in their daily contexts. The stories illustrate the point that real-world administrative decisions do not always conform to theories about or expectations for analytical planning and rational thinking. While the application of rational/analytical approaches to certain organizational problems or issues can lead to effective decisions, dilemmas faced by principals are often messy, complex, ill-defined, and not easily solved through algorithmic reason or the application of rules (Miranda, 2000), as evidenced by the two stories, the first of which has been described and the second story is to follow, provided by Sam, a second year teaching principal in a small suburban elementary school. These two scenarios may sound familiar to many school administrators. In fact, anyone who has occupied a leadership position may be able to identify with Sam's decision dilemmas. There is nothing new in these two situations as principals deal with similar issues every day. Sam's situation represents only a small example of the difficult decisions faced by principals in their daily work.

In the previous situation, Sam had arrived at school one early morning in late January where she was met at her office door by a teacher and a parent who asked her to allow them to take the Grades 4–7 class ice fishing one day in February. In this second scenario, one day, partway through the school year, Sam entered her second-grade classroom to find a pupil, named John, in her class who had been a very happy and content child, but who had been diagnosed two years ago with mixed receptive and auditory communication disorders. John cried over everything since his parents, a successful business couple, had gone on a business trip about three weeks ago to Toronto.

John was an only child and, since his parents had gone on the business trip, started to cry and complain about soreness all over his body. His mother had brought him to see a pediatrician at the Children's Hospital to ensure that John was not ill. When John continued to complain about all these aliments, his mother took him to see his family doctor for a second opinion. This doctor confirmed that John was in good health, but John continued to have problems focusing on the task at hand. For example, during guided reading, he noticed that he had a pen mark on his arm. He could not focus on his reading until the pen mark was washed off. He claimed that the pen mark was hurting him. The behavior that John was exhibiting was new for his teachers and parents. Although the parents were supportive of the school, they did not agree with the school that John's new behavior came about as a result of their business trip. So, where did that leave Sam in terms of solving the dilemma that she was faced with?

Faced with the problem of having a student in her class crying all the time over everything and, given the emotional intensity of the situation confronting her, Sam had little use for the classical model of programmed decision making, which is particularly effective for dealing with routine, simple, quantitative, and unambiguous situations (Davis & Davis, 2003). In this case, a naturalistic decision-making approach is based on the premise that there is no single right way of making a decision when faced with such complex problems (Bower, 1998). Arguably, Sam's problem was a complex one that required her to apply qualitative judgment. The OKGF template filled out by Sam revealed how she developed and used new strategies as she progressed through her decision-making process.

Sam knew she had a problem when she noticed that John cried and said that he felt "soreness all over his body" (P1, Initial Problem). From Sam's initial perspective, this is a simple problem with a clear solution; that is, suggest to John's parents that they seek medical attention from both Children Hospital and his family doctor (TT1, Tentative Theory). After speaking with the child's parents, things changed somewhat. In other words, feedback from John parents indicated that John was well and there were no medical issues (EE1, Error Elimination). What appeared to be a routine problem took on an entirely new dimension as documented in her OKGF template. The issue, which appeared to be a medical one at the outset, did not seem to be the best solution or response. Faced with this situation, getting a clear and accurate definition of the real problem, crying over the "soreness all over his body" was not only difficult but crucial to the successful resolution of the problem of "how to get the child to stop crying" (P2).

The way Sam identified her revised problem (P2) not only influenced potential solutions but also shaped her perception of the problem and that of her peers when she decided to post her problem on the CPLN website to seek advice from her colleagues. She, along with her colleagues, could view the problem as being a threat for the well-being of the child, as well as an opportunity for her to try out new strategies shared by her peers or her own solution based on her past experiences. When problems are perceived as threats, the tendency for the problem-solver is to look for solutions that avoid conflict or harm. On the other hand, when problems are viewed as opportunities, the focus shifts from avoidance to addressing the issues (Davis & Davis, 2003). Evidence from Sam's OKGF template reveals that she did not see the problem as a threat to the health of the child when she ignored some of his crying in the classroom (TT2). Sam became less reactive and more proactive, less constrained and more creative (Pashiardis, 1994; Simon, 1986). When she ignored his crying, she found that he would go and play with other students (EE2).

When ignored, John decided to play with other students, and Sam moved back and forth between perceiving the problem as an opportunity to perceiving it as a threat, as evidenced by her problem identification (P3); that of, "How do I ensure that the child does not have a medical problem?" She did not use a predefined pathway in solving her problem. According to Cuban (2001) and Wagner and Kegan (2006), most complex problems involve a recursive and episodic process whereby the problem–solver moves forward, backward, and laterally through the problem-solving steps. This is precisely what Sam did when she said that she would "continue to suggest that the parents speak with their family doctor" (TT3).

It is evident from Sam's OKGF template that she was reframing the problem as the process unfolded. Weick (1995) describes the process as: "Goals evolve and change during action, which means that both the existing and the desired state are fluid. Gaps open and close, widen and narrow" (p. 88). It is important to note that problem solving is often intuitive in nature and is accompanied in ways that defy explanation or description (Wagner & Kegan, 2006). Feedback from speaking with John's parents revealed that John did not have a health issue and that no further testing was recommended by his family doctor. However, the family doctor suggested that John might be suffering from anxiety (EE3). Her decision-making strategies or solutions were supported by her peers, as evidenced by Brad, a newly promoted high school principal, who said, "My guess is that you are on the right track with ignoring some of this behaviour, as he may be gaining new behaviours by the extensive attention he is getting." Sam was making a marginal adjustment in the pursuit of finding a resolution to the problem of John's crying all the time.

This incremental model of decision making, under the umbrella of naturalistic decision theory, enabled Sam to nibble at the problem until she found the "best fit" solution (Davis & Davis, 2003). She wanted to explore to see if, indeed, John had an anxiety issue. She framed her next problem as, "What do I do with a child who has anxiety?" (P4) and posted it on the network (CPLN) site to solicit responses from her peers. One of her colleagues suggested that she refer the parents to the Phoenix Centre, (The Phoenix Centre for Children and Families is a children's mental health treatment center run by a volunteer board of directors and funded by the provincial government) (www.phoenixpembroke.com) where John could either join a group class or enter a private session to deal with his anxiety issue. His family could also get assistance in acquiring strategies to deal with John's anxiety (TT4). While the family was waiting to hear back from the Phoenix Centre, Sam continued to ignore John's crying behavior in class and she noticed that John eventually had stopped complaining about his pains and the crying stopped (EE4). Cuban (2001) describes this type of problem as a "wicked problem." This wicked problem is a dilemma that can only be managed, not resolved.

In the first scenario, Sam had to respond to both her teacher's and the parent's request to take the Grades 4–7 class ice fishing, even though she was reluctant to give them permission because of the anticipated risks. She again decided to seek the counsel of her colleagues by posting her problem on the CPLN website. She asked, "What decision should I make regarding the request of a teacher and parent about taking Grades 4–7 for ice fishing in February?" (P1). When prompted by her colleagues as to what response is appropriate to both teacher and the parent, she wrote, "My tentative solution is to find out how thick the ice is before making a final decision. I am not too worried about the temperature, but rather the thickness of the ice" (EE1). Feedback from one of her peers, Theresa, indicated that letting the Grades 4–7 class go ice fishing would not be an issue as she had recently allowed the students in her school to do so. Although, there are no two communities or schools alike, and no two principals exactly alike, nevertheless, it is possible to develop an understanding of the factors that commonly influence the choices principals make in relation to their responsibilities (Kowalski, Lasley, & Mahoney, 2008). Sam refined her problem to "What do I need to do to ensure that I have taken students and staff's safety into consideration?" (P2).

It appears that the school district has an open climate environment since Sam felt comfortable sharing her problem with her peers. Hoy and Miskel (2008) describe an open climate environment as one where there exists "cooperation and respect within the faculty and between the faculty and principals" (p. 187) and by a desire to exchange information with the external environment (Hanson, 2003). One of her peers, an elementary principal, suggested that she ask the parents and students to go ice fishing on Family Day, instead (TT2). As Sam conveyed this suggestion to her teachers and parents, she was reminded that students would prefer to go ice fishing with their peers instead of with their families (EE1).

There are two common problems that plague administrative work. They are uncertainty and inadequate coping strategies for dealing with uncertainty (Thompson, 1967). In this case, it is possible that Sam could not predict the future outcome accurately when she asked how she could ensure the students' and staff safety. According to Milliken (1987), uncertainty has three environmental dimensions. They are (1) future conditions, (2) effects of future conditions, and (3) responses to future conditions. Sam is concerned with the safety of her staff and students. Using Sam's scenario, the following examples of uncertainties could exist with respect to each environmental dimension. With respect to the *future conditions level,* Sam would not know the safety of her staff and students would be ensured if she accepted the advice of the teachers and parents regarding ice fishing. As for the *effects of future conditions,* Sam would not know what effects her decision would have on her staff and students. Finally, with the *response level,* if she allowed the students and staff to go for ice-fishing, she would not know what effect this trip might have on future school trips.

It is evident from Sam's OKGF template that she had a low tolerance for uncertainty and she kept on coming back to the problem of "what to do to ensure student and staff safety" (P3). Instead of basing her decision solely on what she personally favored, she opted to check the safety regulations on ice fishing, recommended by a high school principal, Paul (TT3), which would likely eliminate some of the risks and uncertainties associated with this sport. Despite having checked the regulations and safety issues around ice fishing, Sam was still not convinced that she had found the answer she was looking for in the ice fishing regulations (EE3). She went back to her problem of "How do I ensure the students' and staff safety?" (P4). When it was noted that Sam was still struggling with finding a solution to her problem of ice fishing, a researcher and expert in the field of curriculum then posted a solution for her to consider (TT4). The researcher wrote:

> I want to reinforce what Paul has said. Any activity, whether in the classroom or outdoors, like ice fishing, has to be connected to the curriculum. That is, we always have to link activities back to the learning outcomes we and the students are trying to achieve. And students can learn a great deal from such trips. Our job as teachers is to ensure student safety and provide opportunities for them to make connections. We do that by thinking about them first (Researcher).

The feedback provided by the researcher prompted her to refine her problem from one of ensuring the safety of her staff and students to that of aligning the learning outcomes and activities (P5). In reviewing the Grades 4–7 curriculum, she proposed the solution of playing a hockey game in an arena instead of ice fishing (TT5). She consulted the parents and teachers and implemented her decision. Feedback from the staff and parents indicated that they were happy with the decision she made, as it fulfilled both the curriculum and safety requirements.

Discussion

Schools are human service organizations; problems faced by principals are often complex. In other words, the problems are rarely simple and often possess no clear solution. In schools, when students act out in class, it is often difficult to pinpoint a particular reason as the prime culprit. The different variables that interact to influence student behavior (peer pressure, home situation, student temperature, teacher beliefs, and teaching style) are simply too many to track and consider. Moreover principals are pressured to act quickly and decisively with little time for reflection or deliberation (Cuban, 2001; Krabuanrat & Phelps, 1998), which, in turn, renders rational systems of control and decision making less useful.

Like Sam, for most principals, a typical day consists of a variety of fragmented and paradoxical activities, as well as requests for assistance, and innumerable disjointed conversations. Their work is often interrupted by trivial issues and concerns, which result in rapid mood shifts. The constant flow of issues to deal with means that principals must attend to numerous tasks simultaneously, and few of these ever capture the principal's full attention. Deal and Peterson (1994), as well as Fullan (1997), have described principals as "victims of the moment" (Fullan, 1997, p. 37) because of the intensity, immediacy, and physical proximity of the problems they face. They are also often dragged into the "crisis of the moment" (ibid., p. 37) as evidenced by Sam's decision-making process when faced with her crying student.

When principals have a place to post their questions and can feel comfortable in so doing, they can bring up sensitive or complex dilemmas for discussion. In the case of the CPLN, it has been fruitful for the participating principals, because many of the principals have faced or experienced similar problems and have the experience to offer helpful answers. Even when the principal did not have a positive outcome, it could help the requesting principal because he or she could benefit vicariously from the experiences of the explaining principal. Furthermore, it is an informal place, which allows give-and-take in a positive manner for discussion. Sensitive issues are freely discussed because colleagues do not rate or judge each other. Thus, principals can be at ease to ask advice and seek feedback from those who share and understand the decision-making nature of problematic situations.

Conclusion

Understanding how principals in schools make decisions has been a popular topic of interest for researchers. This is due to the fact that, over the last three decades, the importance of principals' decision making has been elevated markedly by school reform initiatives. Principals are expected to be both reliable managers and effective leaders. There is no doubt that, as schools become more complex, so do the decisions faced by the principals. The present study reveals that, as these decisions become more complex, the ability to solve them through rational means alone becomes increasingly difficult. Intuition has the potential to assist principals in making good decisions under complex and stressful conditions.

Problems in human service organizations such as public schools come in different forms and contexts. These problems rarely exist in neatly packaged bundles, as evidenced by the two stories of Sam. How do principals enhance their decision-making skills about leading, and how do they make sense of the complex and changing sets of demands that they face? This study suggests that principals can learn from reflective professional communities by building a professional community for themselves. The CPLN is one answer as to how this might be done.

This particular group of principals had collaboratively examined problems of practice they encountered and learned together to resolve the issues at hand. The engagement of these principals begs the question of what is different about what happens with the CPLN? The analysis of the problems faced by the participants suggests that the use of the OKGF allows participants to learn from one another in a collegial and nonjudgmental environment. They shared and reflected on their peer's practices and challenged each other as they used the OKGF. Furthermore, the principals not only learned about online professional communities through the CPLN, but their learning also affected their decision-making processes. The CPLN was a place for principals to use the OKGF to try out theories/solutions/ideas and to reflect more deeply about their decision-making skills in their leadership practice. Much as the OKGF provided a place for Sam to pose questions, to try out her tentative solutions, and to listen and reflect upon the advice of her peers, the CPLN provided a unique place for them to be reflective and to learn about their decision-making practices.

This study suggests that how principals make decisions and how the OKGF provides them with a comprehensive description of their decision-making process, when faced with complex and ambiguous problems, might have three characteristics. First, there needs to be an ongoing structure. In this study, the principals have posted their questions or dilemmas online for the past year and continue to do so. The role of the principal has become so complex that it seems unlikely that these administrators can be effective without continuously rethinking and reinventing their craft (Mitgang & Maeroff, 2008). This can only be achieved over time. Second, the study suggests that any learning structure, such as CPLN, needs to have a mechanism for maintaining rigor as the principals learn. In this case, the use of the OKGF supported the participants' learning and encouraged them to try out their theories and to seek feedback from their peers in order to eliminate errors contained in the theory that, essentially, is helping them to go deeper into the dilemmas they face so as to find stronger and bolder theories to solve their problems. Third, principals were solving actual dilemmas faced in their practice. It was not a learning exercise, but an authentic problem faced by principals.

References

Argyris, C., & Schön, D. (1978). *Organizational learning: A theory of action perspective.* Reading, MA: Addison-Wesley.

Baumard, P. (1999). *Tacit knowledge in organizations.* Thousand Oaks, CA: Sage.

Bickel, W. E., & Hattrup, R. A. (1995). Teachers and researchers in collaboration: Reflections on the process. *American Educational Research Journal, 32*(1), 35–62.

Bower, B. (1998). Seeing through expert eyes. *Science News, 154*(3), 44–46.

Bradley, G. (2002). A really useful link between teaching and research. *Teaching in Higher Education, 7*(4), 443–455.

Brew, A. (2003). Teaching and research: New relationships and their implications for higher education. *Research & Development, 22*(1), 3–18.

Chitpin, S. (2010). A critical approach for building teacher knowledge. *The International Journal of Education, 2*(1), 1–14.

Chitpin, S. (2011, November). Should Popper's view of rationality be used for promoting teacher knowledge? *Educational Philosophy and Theory, 45*(8), 833–844. doi: 10.1111/j.1469-5812.2011.00803.x

Chitpin, S., & Knowles, J. G. (2009). A principal's view on the use of the Objective Knowledge Growth Framework (OKGF) as a reflection tool. In. M. P. Caltone, *Handbook of Lifelong Learning Developments* (Chapter 12, pp. 1–15), New York, NY: Nova Science Publishers.

Chitpin, S., McMurtry, A., & Starr, K., Evers, C., & Grimmett, P. (2012, April). Knowledge mobilization on decision-making for school improvement: A peer-to-peer network for school principals, *The American Educational Research Association,* Vancouver, pp. 12–17.

Chitpin, S., & Simon, M. (2012). OKGF: An alternative tool for gathering introspective data on problem-solving processes. *Teacher Education & Practice, 25*(2), 302–319.

Chitpin, S., Simon, M., & Galipeau, J. (2008). Pre-service teachers' use of the Objective Knowledge Growth Framework for reflection during practicum. *Teaching and Teacher Education, 24*(8), 2049–2058.

Cuban, L. (2001). *How can I fix it? Finding solutions and managing dilemmas: An educator's road map.* New York, NY: Teachers College Press.

Darling-Hammond, L., LaPointe, M., Meyerson, D., Orr, M. T., & Cohen, A. (2007). *Preparing school leaders for a changing world: Lessons from exemplary leadership development programs.* Stanford, CA: Stanford University, Stanford Educational Leadership Institute.

Davis, S. H., & Davis, P. B. (2003). *The intuitive dimensions of administrative decision-making.* Lanham, MD: Scarecrow Press.

Deal, T. E., & Peterson, K. D. (1994). *The leadership paradox: Balancing logic and artistry in schools.* San Francisco, CA: Jossey-Bass.

Department for Education and Employment. (2000). *Best practice research scholarships.* London, UK: DfEE News.

Fahey, K. M. (2011). Still learning about leading: A leadership critical friends group. *Journal of Research on Leadership Education, 6*(11), 1–35.

Farkas, S., Johnson, J., Duffett, A., Foleno, T., & Foley, P. (2001). *Trying to stay ahead of the game.* New York, NY: Public Agenda.

Fullan, M. (1997). *What's worth fighting for in the principalship?* New York, NY: Teachers College Press.

Gibbons, M., Limoges, C., Nowotny, H., Schwartzman, S., Scott, P., & Trow, M. (1994). *The new production of knowledge.* London, UK: Sage.

Gravani, M. N. (2008). Academics and practitioners: Partners in generating knowledge or citizens of two different worlds? *Teaching and Teacher Education, 24*(1), 649–659.

Hanson, E. M. (2003). *Educational administration and organizational behavior* (5th ed.). Boston, MA: Allyn and Bacon.

Hoy, W., & Miskel, C. (2008). *Educational administration: Theory, research, and practice* (8th ed.). New York, NY: McGraw-Hill.

Kowalski, T. J., Lasley III, T. J., & Mahoney, J. W. (2008). *Data driven decisions and school leadership.* Boston, MA: Pearson Education.

Krabuanrat, K., & Phelps, R. (1998). Heuristics and rationality in strategic decision-making: An exploratory study. *Journal of Business Research, 41,* 83–93.

Marquardt, M. J. (1996). *Building the learning organization: A systems approach to quantum improvement and global success.* New York, NY: McGraw-Hill.

Marzano, R., Waters, T., & McNulty, T. (2005). *School leadership that works: From research to results.* Alexandria, VA: ASCD.

Milliken, F. J. (1987). Three types of uncertainty about the environment: State, effect, and response uncertainty. *Academy of Management Review,* (12), 133–143.

Miranda, T. (2000). Rationality and critical education. In *The Encylopaedia of Educational Philosophy and Theory.* Retrieved from http://eepat.net/doku.php?id=rationality_and_critical_education

Mitgang, L., & Maeroff, G. (2008). *Becoming a leader: Preparing school principals for today's schools.* New York, NY: The Wallace Foundation.

Newton, P. M., & Sackney, L. (2005). Group knowledge and group knowledge processes in school board decision-making. *Canadian Journal of Education, 28*(3), 434–457.

Pashiardis, P. (1994, May 15–27). *Problem and dilemma identification and formulation as the most critical element of the decision-making process: Behavioral biases and characteristics.* Paper presented at the international Intervisitation Programme in Educational Administration, Toronto, Canada.

Popper, K. (1979). *Objective knowledge.* Oxford, UK: Oxford University Press.

Popper, K. (2002). *Conjectures and refutations.* Oxford, UK: Oxford University Press.

Razik, T. A., & Swanson, A. D. (2001). *Fundamental concepts of educational leadership.* Upper Saddle River, NJ: Merrill Prentice Hall.

Robinson, V. M. (1993). *Problem-based methodology: Research for the improvement of practice.* New York, NY: Pergamon Press.

Schön, D. (1983). *The reflective practitioner: How professionals think in action.* New York, NY: Basic Books.

Simon, H. A. (1986). Decision-making and problem-solving. In *Research Briefings 1986: Report of the research briefing panel on decision-making and problem-solving* (pp. 1–24). Washington, DC: National Academy Press.

Simon, M., Chitpin, S., & Yahya, R. (2010). Pre-service teachers' thinking about student assessment issue. *The International Journal of Education, 2*(2), 1–22.

Thompson, J. D. (1967). *Organizations in action: Social science bases of administrative theory.* New York, NY: McGraw-Hill.

Wagner, T., & Kegan, R. (2006). *Change leadership: A practical guide to transforming our schools.* San Francisco, CA: Jossey Bass.

Waters, T., & Cameron, G. (2007). *The balanced leadership framework: Connecting vision with action.* Denver, CO: Mid-continent Research for Education and Learning.

Weick, K. E. (1995). *Sensemaking in organizations.* Thousand Oaks, CA: Sage.

Welch, D. A. (2002). *Decisions, decisions: The art of effective decision-making.* Amherst, NY: Prometheus Books.

Wenger, E. (1998). *Communities of practice: Learning, meaning, and identity.* Cambridge, UK: Cambridge University Press.

4

DECISION MAKING AS PROBLEM-SOLVING TRAJECTORIES

Colin W. Evers

Introduction

The central argument of this chapter takes the following form. First, it is noted that a wide variety of accounts of decision making involve primarily a one step process. Bring as much knowledge to bear, as possible, on the decision task, trying to ensure that the result will be the best decision that can be made. That is, the process places a heavy premium on the "front-end-loading" of knowledge in order to get a good result. A class of decision models that I call "rationalistic" especially embody this approach. Second, it is noted that this knowledge, for a variety of reasons, is fallible in the sense that it could be wrong, or could contain errors. Well-known arguments employed by Simon (1991) in his defense of bounded rationality figure here, with some additional theoretical ones included. The upshot is that one step approaches to decision making can lead to bad decisions. Suggestions from an alternative naturalistic tradition (Zsambok & Klein, 1997) are explored, since decision making in natural settings is the norm for educational leaders and the tradition has a focus on professional learning of expertise. The alternative proposed here, but within the broad naturalistic tradition, is to incorporate knowledge derived from the results of making decisions into the improvement of decisions. On this proposal, decision making comes to resemble a trajectory of decisions, with the trajectory including the consequences of earlier decisions and an opportunity to incorporate knowledge of these consequences into subsequent decision making.

Rationalism in Decision Making

To frame discussion, it is useful to draw two sets of distinctions. One concerns the difference between rationalism and naturalism in decision making; the other, the difference between normative and descriptive accounts of decision making. Perhaps the best known nontechnical account of rational decision making is that provided by Herbert Simon in his classic *Administrative Behavior* (1945/1976). Simon lays down three requirements for "objective rationality." The first is "complete knowledge and anticipation of the consequences that will follow on each choice." The second requirement was to be able to anticipate how we might value the future outcomes of each choice. The third requirement was that all alternatives be considered (Simon, 1945/1976, p. 81).

Although Simon went on to criticize each of these conditions, they live on in more elaborate models still discussed in the literature. For example, Hoy and Tarter (1995, p. 16) discuss a model that employs a probability event chain. Suppose you want to decide on a plan for, say, improving student learning outcomes in your school. This is something that admits of multiple possible courses of action. Let's label three of these as A, B, and C. The model then considers the possible consequences of each alternative. Let's suppose there are three possible consequences of each plan and label them as follows. For plan A, these would be C1A, C2A, and C3A. And analogously for plans B and C. The next step in the probability event chain is to assign probabilities for each consequence: P(C1A), as the probability for consequence C1A occurring, P(C2A) for the probability of C2A occurring, and so on. Given the resulting full tree diagram, how are decisions made? They say that the "consequences of each alternative are considered using the criteria for a satisfactory solution" (Hoy & Tarter, 1995, p. 17). The best set of alternatives is the one chosen. But what counts as "best?" So far, this model just considered the probability of consequences occurring. But it's entirely possible that the most probable way of solving the problem is the one that is least attractive. Suppose, for example, that the most probable way of boosting student learning outcomes involves putting students under levels of pressure that would be considered ethically unacceptable by students, teachers, families, and the community in general. Clearly, the model needs to include Simon's second requirement concerning how we value consequences. The usual way of doing this is to attach a numerical estimate of preference, which is a proxy for value, for each consequence. The best solution, that is the most rational, is the one whose sum of the products of preferences and probabilities is the greatest. Technically, value or preference is called "utility," and the product of utility and probability is known as "expected utility."

Here's a very simple example, often called a "toy universe," of how this sort of approach works. (For an elaboration, see Evers & Lakomski, 2000, pp. 89–94.) You want to solve the problem of bad weather in travelling from home to work, with your main alternatives being whether to carry an umbrella or not. How do you decide? Let's suppose the probability of rain is 50% (or 0.5). If you bring the umbrella and it rains then you will attach a high value (say +6.0) to this consequence, and if it doesn't rain and you have the consequence of unnecessarily carrying the umbrella, you value that consequence negatively (say −2.0). You then consider the consequences of not carrying the umbrella. If it rains, you attach a high negative value (say, −8.0), and if it doesn't rain, you attach a positive value (say +2.0). Using this model, how do we rationally decide what to do?

The standard way is to construct a decision matrix and use it to calculate the expected utility of each alternative course of action. Using the above data, your decision matrix will look like this:

Decision Matrix

	Rain	No Rain
Bring umbrella	+6.0, 0.5	−2.0, 0.5
Leave umbrella	−8.0, 0.5	+2.0, 0.5

The expected utility of each alternative is then calculated thus:

Bringing: 6.00.5 + −2.00.5 = 2.0

Leaving: −8.00.5 + 2.00.5 = −3.0

Since bringing an umbrella on that particular day (the day of a forecast 50% probability of rain) has the highest expected utility, that is the rational decision to make.

There is a huge literature on the question of whether rationality should be defined as maximizing expected utility (for a sample, see Heap, Hollis, Lyons, Sudgen, & Weale, 1992). One complication is the presence of altruism (Simon, 1993). I don't propose to go into the details of this debate except to note two issues. The first is that whatever definition of rational decision making we accept, it opens up the possibility of distinguishing between that view as a normative view, namely as an account of how people ought to make decisions, and descriptive views of how people actually make decisions. This issue has been well studied, especially in contexts where rationality is easily defined, such as probability theory or logic (Kahneman, 2011). The second, which is worth discussing at length, is the issue of whether it's empirically possible to implement the kind of view of rational decision making that is captured by even the simple toy universe of the umbrella example.

Here are some difficulties with the front-end-loading required of knowledge for this model. The first is that attaching probabilities to consequences can be quite difficult. The reliability of weather forecasts varies from location to location. Second, the concept of rain needs a bit of unpacking. Rain in a place like Hong Kong can come in the form of a deluge, whereas in Melbourne it may more often look like drizzle. It is, of course, possible to adopt a more fine-grained set of categories for distinctions along the rain/nonrain continuum, but this will put pressure on the accuracy of assigning probabilities. Assigning value to carrying an umbrella in the rain oversimplifies context. The umbrella is not much good if rain is accompanied by strong wind, and its utility will vary along the continuum between deluge and drizzle. Flexibility of work arrangements will figure here. You may have the option of staying home until a deluge passes, and likewise for staying at work, an option you may be less likely to exercise for drizzle. At this point, only poverty of imagination makes utility maximization decision making in this toy universe seem remotely plausible. That it should be thought to scale up to a real organizational context such as deciding in a school how to improve student learning outcomes is wishful thinking. Hoy and Tarter (1995, p. 17) are more sanguine: "Although such a formal procedure may not always be used, remember that every alternative has a number of probable consequences." Following Simon (1945/1976, p. 81), I would just add that we almost never know every alternative, that probabilities are hard to know, and that how we attach values to future consequences may be different to our current valuations of consequences. (A good example of this last point is buyer's remorse.)

The above arguments illustrate practical difficulties in acquiring and using the knowledge required to make good decisions under conditions where such knowledge needs to be had in advance of the decision. However, there are two more theoretical arguments that have been advanced to show the limits of social prediction or knowing consequences. Imagine a prediction as a deduction one might make about the future state of a social system on the ideal assumption that you had complete knowledge of its present state and all relevant deterministic laws that governed its evolution through time. Popper (1950) used an argument that made use of Godel's incompleteness theorem to show that there will always be some true claim about the future that cannot be derived from all this present ideal knowledge. (The relevant Godel result is that any system of axioms strong enough to give elementary arithmetic will contain at least one true theorem that cannot be proved in that system. And if the system is strengthened to permit a proof, then there will exist at least another true theorem that cannot be proved.) The conclusion Popper (1957) drew was that social engineering needs to be small scale and piecemeal so that we can learn from the consequences of an intervention. Large scale change sets in train too many causes and effects from which one must then learn. Better to have fewer things in motion.

A second theoretical argument about the limits of knowing consequences concerns the problem of complexity, at least under certain special conditions. Consider, first, the case of weather forecasting. Data, from day_1, represented here by X_1, are fed into a set of equations, f, to yield the forecast for day_2, thus: $X_2 = f(X_1)$. To get the forecast for day_3, the process is, roughly speaking, repeated: $X_3 = f(X_2) = ff(X_1)$. The problem is that since all measurements of data contain small errors, this iterative process causes these errors to accumulate exponentially. Forecasts much beyond eight days have no predictive value whatsoever (See Silver, 2011, pp. 118–122). Now any modelling of aspects of a social system, say economic aspects, that employs this kind of iterative methodology, will suffer the same kind of problem, known as the "butterfly effect" thus setting a limit to decision making based on predictions of consequences further along the causal chain. For leaders working in school settings, this kind of problem is mostly avoided by the simple process of monitoring the effects of modest, relatively piecemeal decisions that are the stuff of school life. There's little scope for iteration to occur, although even decisions with small effects can create the conditions for later decisions by changing the causal structure of conditions for consequences. I'll have more to say about this later.

Simon's response to limits to our knowledge, our cognition, and our social science is to argue not for optimal decision making, but for satisfactory decision making, we should "satisfice" not optimize (Simon, 1991). This position is sufficiently well known not to require further comment here, except for me to signal a basic agreement where up-front knowledge for decision making as a one step process cannot be avoided. There is, however, an important ambiguity in the nature of knowledge required for decision making, with the rationalist tradition assuming some kind of symbolic representations. Against this assumption, some ideas from a naturalistic tradition need to be taken into account.

Naturalism in Decision Making

Consider the following example. On the 15th of January, 2009, US Airways flight 1549 left LaGuardia Airport, New York City, to fly to Charlotte, North Carolina. With First Officer Jeff Skiles flying the plane, it struck a flock of Canada Geese at about 3000 feet, disabling both engines. At that point, the senior pilot, Captain Sullenberger, announced "my aircraft" and took control of the plane. The first important decision after that was to try to restart the engines. The checklist for doing so ran to about three pages, clearly based on the assumption that a critical engine failure would not occur at such low altitude. After about half a minute, and with the plane losing altitude, it was further decided that the engines couldn't be restarted. (Canada Geese are much larger than the kind of birds for which aircraft jet engines were designed to survive a strike.) One consequence of the decision to restart the engines, and it not being successful, was that it functioned as a constraint on the next decision: where to land the plane. After some brief discussion with air traffic control, Captain Sullenberger decided that no airport could be reached. The only decision possible, therefore, was to land the plane in the Hudson River. This was a feat of astonishing difficulty, requiring the pilot to glide the plane into a descent onto the river within a narrow range of speeds and at an upward angle of 11 degrees. This was accomplished successfully, and all 155 passengers and crew were able to leave the ditched aircraft safely. The time between the bird strike and the successful landing was about four minutes.

The kind of expertise required for this sort of decision making is not easily codified into symbolic representations of propositions, representations that can be assigned values and probabilities. That's only part of the story. Much of what went on falls more readily into what Aristotle called "phronesis," or practical wisdom. Captain Sullenberger had extensive experience flying gliders, as well as many years as both a military pilot and a pilot of commercial airliners. The practical wisdom that accumulates from this amount and variety of experience, though difficult to codify into decision-theoretic models, is certainly formidable and, in this case, probably unique. For example, when the data from flight 1549 were entered into a flight simulator, no one was able to produce a flight trajectory that would have resulted in a successful landing. What is also missing from the simulations is the sheer emotional stress that attended the real thing. Indeed, it is now widely recognized that emotion, instead of being the antithesis of reason, is essential for good reasoning (Lakomski & Evers, 2010).

The importance of understanding decision making in natural settings has been recognized by a number of researchers. (See, for example, Zsambok & Klein, 1997, for an overview.) Of particular importance is how such decision-making expertise is acquired. According to Klein (1997), expertise can be acquired in natural settings by engaging in a number of distinctive practices. The first is that when learning in natural settings, one should actually do those things that the experts did when they were acquiring their expertise. That is, learning is by doing, or going through the motions as it were. But it's more than that. Learning to fly an aircraft certainly involves acquiring a "feel" for the positions and movements of the various controls. Klein (1997, p. 348) adds, however, that, in engaging in practice, one also have in mind the goals of the practice and how it might be evaluated. He's drawing attention to the importance of attending to feedback, in much the same way as someone learning to serve in a game of tennis allows their acquisition of the relevant combination of motor skills to be shaped by where the ball goes when it is hit.

A second suggestion of Klein's (1997, p. 348) is to sample alternative courses of action so as to build up a sense of what might work best in a given situation. Again, what counts as "best" is driven by goals and criteria for success; another example of learning by doing and attending to normatively understood feedback.

A third suggestion, well known to experts in many fields, is to accumulate a large repertoire of possible strategies or courses of action. Captain Sullenberger had among the items in his mental database of courses of action, something that very few other airline pilots had: the knowledge to successfully glide a commercial airliner.

As a fourth suggestion, Klein lays great emphasis on not just attending to feedback, but creating the circumstances that promote it, and with additional attention to its accuracy. In many natural settings, the feedback that is being promoted is nonlinguistic, or even nonsymbolic.

Fifth, and this is an attempt to integrate the nonsymbolic with the symbolic, engage in reflection. Many years ago, Schön (1983) made popular the notion of professionals engaging in reflection as part of their professional learning. The most extensively used technique was keeping a diary as an aide and memoir of reflection. In the next section, I'll be proposing an alternative model of reflection that can guide critical self-learning in a more structured way than the keeping of diaries.

The final suggestion is one that is being increasingly adopted by senior levels of management, namely accepting the practice of coaching. This can be interpreted quite broadly, but the key idea is that a coach provides both a source of feedback and an interpretation of a learner's actions that are external to the learner. A coach offers another point of view. Access to alternative viewpoints helps to reduce the possibility of confirmation bias, the habit of interpreting information or feedback as supporting the learner's viewpoint even when it doesn't.

Decision Making, Problem Solving, and Critical Self-Learning

In this section, I elaborate a view of decision making that accepts the fact of bounded rationality, remains skeptical of the applicability of formal rationalistic models of decision making, but attempts to describe and defend as normatively useful a model that is applicable in natural, realistic decision contexts. Bounded rationality is reconstructed epistemically as fallibilism, and it makes use of the ideas of the philosopher of science, Karl Popper, for promoting the growth of our fallible knowledge. The model is normatively useful because it uses feedback in a way that makes for self-correcting learning. The proposed mechanism for self-correction comes from Popper's notion that knowledge grows, not through confirmation of our theories but through the process of trying to falsify those theories. Finally, by the use of one fairly clear and practical example, namely one that describes an actual decision problem and its processes, I try to show that it is realistic in natural decision contexts that educational leaders, in particular, face.

In attempting to understand how scientific knowledge grows, that is, what makes for the improvement of our theories or leads to the replacement of bad theories by good ones, Popper (1959) came to the view that theories could flourish for hundreds of years enjoying any number of confirming instances and still later be found to be wrong. He concluded that the real test for a scientific theory is not how well it is confirmed but how well it passes the most stringent tests aimed at refuting, or disconfirming, it. Scientific knowledge grows by a process of conjecture and refutation. Our currently held best theories are conjectures, fallible and provisionally accepted. Or knowledge grows when we manage to falsify these conjectures and replace them with new conjectures that pass the falsifying tests. In his later work, Popper (1979) proposed a simple schema for describing this process:

$$P1 => TT1 => EE1 => P2$$

In this schema, P1 is some initial problem, TT1 is our first tentative theory for dealing with it, EE1 is the process of error elimination, or rigorous testing of our first tentative theory, and P2 is some new problem that might emerge as a result of error elimination. Actually, we might also manage to solve the problem on our first attempt, so ending the cycle of conjecture and refutation, or we might end up with exactly the same problem and so have to come up with a new tentative theory. Although easily described, this schema has a number of technical difficulties. Take, for example, the process of error elimination, or falsification. Scientific theories and their background of assumptions are quite complex, and it is not always obvious which claim, or set of claims, within this complex needs revision or replacement in the presence of falsifying evidence. A famous example in the history of science can be used to illustrate this point. By the early nineteenth century, enough was known about the solar system to give full confidence in the descriptive and explanatory power of Newtonian mechanics as an account of the motion of the planets, with one worrying exception. Observations of the motion of the planet Uranus did not quite match what Newtonian mechanics predicted. Was Newtonian mechanics therefore falsified? An alternative approach was to hold to the theory and suggest that its failure to match observation was due to some unknown other cause, in this case perhaps the influence of another planet beyond the orbit of Uranus. The theory was then used to predict where this other planet could be found, and these calculations were subsequently used by astronomers to locate the planet Neptune. So the theory was judged correct but a background assumption, namely that Uranus was the last planet in the solar system, needed to be revised. (The theory, which also failed to match data on the precession of the perihelion of Mercury's orbit, was finally replaced by General Relativity, which did match those data.) Another difficulty is that the notion of observation has its own complexities. For example, in science, most observations are mediated by apparatus, from Galileo's telescope to the giant particle detectors of the Large Hadron Collider. What is observed is therefore subject to assumptions about the value of the theory that informs the construction and operation of such apparatus. Indeed, what even counts as an observation may be determined in this way. The upshot is that we don't have a situation where observations can be used to falsify a theory. It's also a case of theory being used to falsify theory, for the observations are theory laden.

In social science, which is most often the kind of theory that informs decisions by educational leaders, this point is obvious. All data are interpreted data. Thus, what do the PISA 2012 rankings mean given that the top seven jurisdictions are, to varying degrees, Confucian heritage cultures with large shadow education systems? In making policy decisions informed by ideas about what can be learned from these jurisdictions, while it may make sense for countries like Australia, Canada, or the United States, to borrow methods of teaching, or leadership training, it makes no sense at all to borrow another country's culture. Policy-makers making decisions about improving their country's PISA performance need to interpret these data very carefully.

Despite these sorts of difficulties, it is possible to make progress with the use of feedback-driven learning in social contexts. The first attempt at applying the Popperian schema for promoting the growth of knowledge in educational contexts, can be found in Chitpin (2003). In her study, the initial aim was to discover the role of portfolios in teachers' professional development, with six elementary school language arts teachers who had kept portfolios for at least a year being the primary source of data. Since the initial interpretive framework had been a form of social constructivism, where one would expect a certain amount of variability to derive from a teacher's experience, social and cultural background, education and training, whether they themselves had children, and other such factors, the big surprise was the lack of variability. It turned out, on closer analysis, that the most important factor reducing variability was the structure of the problems teachers were trying to solve. Once that became clear, it made more sense to look at the growth of teachers' professional knowledge within an objective knowledge framework. The obvious framework to try (since I was consulted and had trained as a philosopher) was that proposed by Popper. (See Chitpin & Evers, 2005, 2012.)

To see how it works both descriptively and normatively in response to bounded rationality and the conditions of naturalistic settings, consider the following case of practical educational decision making. It's an old case dating from my time, 20 years ago, as a School Council President of a high school in the Australian city of Melbourne. The problem concerning which we needed to decide upon a solution was the high levels of student absenteeism, about 20%, on Fridays and then on the following Mondays. Students were giving themselves long weekends. Although there's no textbook answer—social science cannot deal well with the particularities of context variety—the consensus view, both in the research literature, and in our Council, was to involve the parents. Table 4.1 below sets out our experience of the decision-making procedure cast in the form of a succession of Popper Cycles that trace out a decision trajectory through time.

In elaborating this methodology, I want to comment in some detail on each of the steps in the process. The first issue concerns the nature of problems. This model assumes that a problem can be defined in terms of a set of constraints plus the demand (which is also a constraint) that something be done. If there's no requirement to do anything then a condition is not presenting as a problem. The pattern of absenteeism was clearly a problem for the school as it was disrupting teaching, notably the pacing of learning for classes. Teachers were wanting something to be done. Further, the problem had the great virtue of having a proxy for easy measurement. We couldn't easily measure the degree of learning disruption, but we could readily measure the amount of absenteeism. This proxy allowed us to track quite quickly whether we were making progress in solving the problem. Indeed, we mainly spoke of the problem as absenteeism rather than learning disruption, or used the two interchangeably. Unlike some other models of professional self-learning, or learning from feedback on one's practice, this model sees reflection not as something that enters the scene after an action, but as something that needs to be done right at the beginning, at the stage of problem formulation and definition. The most important feature of problem definition is for the definition to let you have criteria for knowing whether the problem is being solved. A useful problem definition will be both guided by theory and point the way to a first tentative theory. Note, however, that there are also limits to the value of easy measurement that need to be reflected upon at this stage. Educators would

TABLE 4.1 Decision Making to Solve Absenteeism

Popper Cycle 1	Popper Cycle 2	Popper Cycle 3	Popper Cycle 4
P1: Absenteeism among students peaks at 20% on Fridays and Mondays disrupting the pacing of classroom teaching.	P2: How can we communicate with parents of students who are absent on Fridays and Mondays?	P3: How can we arrange for letters to reach parents without being intercepted by students?	P4: How can the school communicate directly with parents of chronically absent students?
TT1: Mark the roll when school starts and then utilize all general staff to phone the home of all absent students.	TT2: Send a letter from the school to the address where students live, asking parents to contact the school to discuss the absenteeism problem in relation to their child.	TT3: Send letters to parents in unmarked envelopes.	TT4: Adopt a more piecemeal approach. Review all school functions where parents are able to attend, such as parent-teacher evenings, reporting meetings, etc. Attempt to adapt these so that there is more opportunity to raise the absentee problem for discussion.
EE1: There are very few parents at home to answer the calls. The strategy has very little impact on the level of absenteeism.	EE2: Very few parents make arrangements to discuss the problem, and data from roll calls still indicate high levels of absenteeism. This is puzzling so further analysis and investigation was undertaken. It appeared that students who were almost always home before parents were intercepting the letters easily identified by their official school envelopes.	EE3: There is some improvement in the number of parents responding to the letter and a modest improvement in the absenteeism problem. But given the number of letters sent, the modest response rate is still puzzling. More follow-up produced the following likely explanation. The school's population is highly multicultural with some 36 different community languages spoken in homes. And the letters were in English. Evidently, it was common for students to translate the letters.	EE4: Progress is gradual, but parents are slowly made aware. School council and staff begin to explore other strategies for dealing with the problem. For example, student welfare policy, adjusting the timetable to reduce some of the bad effects of student absenteeism on Fridays and Mondays.

see value in making decisions aimed at promoting and providing good education, conceived in a fairly broad way; but adopting a measurement proxy like standardized test scores can easily compromise the achievement of this goal. One trade-off might be to have multiple proxies that permit measurement. That way, the achievement of a broad goal is less likely to be compromised by a single, narrow measurement proxy.

Another matter to take into account in formulating a problem for subsequent decision making is to be aware of relevant other problems. Schools always have to deal simultaneously with multiple problems and leaders need to hedge against the possibility that a tentative theory designed to solve one problem will not exacerbate another problem. So, in working out the constraints on, say, the problem of improving student learning outcomes, one might note that the problem of improving staff morale is part of the wider decision landscape. In taking into account this wider problem context, there is now a premium on coherence. Problems and their solutions need to form a coherent whole. Given the realities of bounded rationality, one may only discover the incoherence of a set of decisions during their implementation. Again, procedural fallibilism counsels making adjustments through time as further evidence suggests.

The tentative theories in Table 4.1 have, in the main, only one hypothesis for a course of action. In Popper's usage of TT, a theory is a rather large structure of interconnected propositions. Despite appearances, the social science equivalent is also a large structure. The use of the model as exemplified in Table 4.1 merely fails to mention all the other assumptions, keeping them in the background and focusing on just the one hypothesis that is central to initiating a particular course of action. It may turn out that, in acting on this hypothesis, we discover that one or more claims informing our background assumptions are wrong. Then we will need to make adjustments along the trajectory, as is often the case. The choice of a tentative theory will be in part dictated by the nature of the problem and what is known about its defining constraints. Although the model's epistemic process of learning from feedback is self-correcting, the number of cycles can be shortened, to some extent, by trying to start with the best known theory for dealing with such problems. School leaders should therefore be prepared to do some research, such as reading the relevant literature, or consulting others with relevant experience on the matters to be decided. If solutions are being canvassed by a group, a variety of people with different opinions and experiences will widen the search option space so that more alternatives can be considered. The speed with which a problem is solved can make all the difference as to whether it is solved. For example, a school that is falling below some mandated enrolment threshold may be given only a certain amount of time to fix the problem before being closed down.

There are, nevertheless, some structural limitations to reducing the number of Popper Cycles in a decision-making problems/solutions trajectory. Here's an analogy that will illustrate this point. Suppose you are trying to do a jigsaw puzzle that requires you to locate pieces on a board. There's no point in starting with pieces that are likely to be toward the center because there are no constraints available to define the location problem. For those pieces, the constraints come into existence as other pieces are put in place. Initially, the most constraints are provided by corners, and then edges. Only after a fair number of pieces have been put in place can we know what would even count as a correct location for a center piece. Decisions about staff performance development and appraisal can be like this, requiring a prescribed sequence of steps to be followed.

The length of a sequence of Popper Cycles can also be shaped by pragmatic considerations. Take the case of a single sex school that is failing to meet its prescribed enrollment target. There is no question that converting to become a coeducational school would solve the problem. However, this may be a very expensive and complex option, compared with mounting an advertising and promotion campaign in the school's local district. Here we have a trade-off between the probability of success and the costs of achieving it. Cost, functioning as a constraint that contributes to defining the problem, therefore helps to select the first tentative theory. The extent to which cost is a soft constraint will emerge later as other cheaper methods of problem solving fail. A bit like the jigsaw puzzle example, you won't get to the problem of converting the school to coeducational until a prior sequence of problems/solutions failures has helped redefine the original constraint set. In this way, failure becomes a condition for success.

I want to make a last point about the nature of tentative theories and knowledge growth. It is customary to assume some kind of divide between theory and practice. In this model, that distinction is much diminished because the description of the tentative theory doubles as a description of what is done. The TT describes an implementation. Without an implementation you don't get knowledge growth. This means that, in schools (and many other organizations), knowledge growth needs to be both theorized and practiced, not as something that goes on in an individual's head, but as a social process involving patterns of epistemically progressive shared practices. Klein's suggestions, in which natural settings are also social and organizational settings, are meant to inform in these contexts.

Without feedback, we don't have knowledge growth. At best, a single Popper Cycle confirms that our current theory is suitable for solving the problem in the context in which it exists. While making the right decision, first go, is a virtue not to be discounted, even easily defined problems often require a number of decision iterations for a solution to emerge. It is under these conditions that error elimination proves vital, driving the trajectory in a progressive, self-correcting way. Moreover, the value of testing our theories through feedback is enhanced if the tests are more rigorous. The solution of some problems admits not of a bivalent judgment of success or failure, but of a graduated one. The Popperian framework urges that the goal be set high where this is an advantage. It's analogous to having high standards in teaching and learning as a way to promote better achievement.

The principal enemy of learning through feedback, of persuading us or a group to change viewpoint, is confirmation bias. Several strategies can be helpful here. The first is to rely on feedback that is as unambiguous as the appropriateness of evidence will permit. Data-driven decision making is therefore a key part of the Popper Cycle process. The question of what counts as evidence will be mostly settled at the prior stages of problem formulation and theory formulation. The trade-off to watch and calibrate that I mentioned earlier is that between ease and clarity of data and the compromising of a broader, more valuable, goal through the use of a narrower, less valuable, measurement proxy.

Since decision feedback data in schools are often interpreted by teams, group-think can be avoided, as in the case of choosing theories, by having a group of diverse opinions. This will enable a bigger variety of data interpretations to be critically tested before a consensus, or majority, view emerges. Again, there's an important trade-off to watch. Groups with strong leadership, in this epistemic sense, a person whose viewpoint has a strong influence on the viewpoint others in the group adopt, will be more efficient at making decisions, but are also more prone to confirmation bias. Errors, once in place, are very hard to eliminate. On the other hand, groups with weak leadership take longer to make decisions but are much less prone to confirmation bias. (See Evers, 2012, for an overview an analysis of the literature.)

The two trade-offs discussed above indicate that learning from experience is no simple algorithmic process. The process of Popper Cycle trajectories should itself inform the tuning and adjustment of the knowledge we use to initially set our trade-offs. This sounds circular, but it is better seen as promoting overall coherence among the various elements that go into the decision process.

There is a third significant trade-off that introduces further indeterminacy into learning from feedback. Earlier, I mentioned that the failure of prior tentative theories to solve problems may be a necessary condition for the development of a theory that is successful. The implicit assumption was that the successful theory would be different. This is, however, not always the case. Sometimes an approach, or course of action, is not working because it hasn't been tried enough times. Giving it another go versus cut and run is the issue here. Owing to the role of context in determining success or failure, there is no general heuristic available, and I doubt that one can be constructed. For one case, it may just be obvious after the first trial that the proposed solution could never work. For another, it may not be at all clear, or there were special factors that compromised the implementation. And pragmatic factors can figure prominently. The number of other goes can be constrained by budget or time, or even just the demand to try something new. Experience, especially a lot of it, helps with this issue.

In addition to driving theory improvement, error elimination also helps define the next problem. Notice in Table 4.1 that, while P1 is the problem of absenteeism, error elimination prompted P2 to be defined as the problem of communicating with parents. That remained the case for P3 and P4. However, the final error elimination, EE4, in the set of cycles, suggested more. It suggested that seeking a solution to absenteeism in terms almost exclusively of parent involvement was a mistake, and it raised the issue of exploring multiple strategies. The school did indeed begin to explore and then implement some of these, and significant progress was eventually made on the original problem.

Conclusion

The trade-offs and indeterminacies afflicting decision making in natural school settings are not meant to discount the value of the proposed Popperian model of decision making as problems/solutions trajectories. The afflictions are typical of the complexities of making decisions in any social context. Nevertheless, the methodology can be extremely useful, as the examples in our research have shown (Chitpin & Evers, 2005, 2012). An unformulated element that contributes significantly to its usefulness is the practical wisdom that educational leaders bring to decision tasks. In not admitting of a rule-based formulation, Aristotle's notion may not appear to be a very helpful addition. It does, however, enjoy the virtue of being true.

References

Chitpin, S. (2003). *The role of portfolios in teachers' professional growth and development: A knowledge building analysis.* Unpublished PhD thesis, University of Toronto.

Chitpin, S., & Evers, C. W. (2005). Teacher professional development as knowledge building: A Popperian analysis. *Teachers and Teaching: Theory and Practice, 11*(4), 419–433.

Chitpin, S., & Evers, C. W. (2012). Using Popper's philosophy of science to build pre-service teachers' knowledge. *International Journal of Education, 4*(4), 144–156.

Evers, C. W. (2012). Organisational contexts for lifelong learning: Individual and collective learning configurations. In D. N. Aspin, J. Chapman, K. Evans, & R. Bagnall (Eds.), *Second international handbook of lifelong learning* (pp. 61–76). Dordrecht, Germany: Springer.

Evers, C. W., & Lakomski, G. (2000). *Doing Educational Administration.* Oxford, UK: Elsevier.

Heap, S. H., Hollis, M., Lyons, B., Sudgen, R., & Weale, A. (1992). *The theory of choice: A critical guide.* Oxford, UK: Blackwell.

Hoy, W. K., & Tarter, J. (1995). *Administrators solving the problems of practice.* Needham Heights, MA: Allyn and Bacon.

Kahneman, D. (2011). *Thinking fast and slow.* New York, NY: Penguin Books.

Klein, G. A. (1997). Applying hybrid models of cognition. In C. E. Zsambok & G. A. Klein (Eds.), *Naturalistic decision making* (pp. 331–370). Mahwah, NJ: Lawrence Erlbaum.

Lakomski, G., & Evers, C. W. (2010). Passionate rationalism: The role of emotion in decision-making. *Journal of Educational Administration, 48*(4), 438–450.

Popper, K. R. (1950). Indeterminism in quantum physics and classical physics: Part II. *British Journal for the Philosophy of Science, 1*(3), 179–188.

Popper, K. R. (1957). *The poverty of historicism.* London, UK: Routledge and Kegan Paul.

Popper, K. R. (1959). *The logic of scientific discovery.* London, UK: Hutchinson.

Popper, K. R. (1979). *Objective knowledge.* Oxford, UK: Oxford University Press.

Schön, D. (1983). *The reflective practitioner.* New York, NY: Basic Books.

Silver, N. (2011). *The signal and the noise.* New York, NY: Penguin Press.

Simon, H. A. (1945/1976). *Administrative behavior* (3rd ed.). New York, NY: The Free Press.

Simon, H. A. (1991). Bounded rationality and organizational learning, *Organization Science, 2*(1), 125–134.

Simon, H. A. (1993). Altruism and economics. *The American Economic Review, 83*(2), 156–161.

Zsambok, C. E., & Klein, G. A. (Eds.). (1997). *Naturalistic decision making.* Mahwah, NJ: Lawrence Erlbaum.

5

EMOTIONS, EMOTIONAL INTELLIGENCE, AND LEADERSHIP: FROM FOLKPSYCHOLOGY TO NEUROSCIENCE

Gabriele Lakomski

Introduction

The concept of Emotional Intelligence (EI) has thoroughly captured the public imagination. It has become absorbed into the vernacular as a description that seems to say something authentic about an important aspect of being human, our emotions, and how to deal with them. To be thought of as "emotionally intelligent" somehow elevates a person, while appearing to be without it is practically considered a character flaw. When applied in organizational contexts, as, for example, in the case of leadership, Goleman enthusiastically declares that ". . . emotional intelligence is the sine qua non of leadership" (Goleman, 2004, p. 82; Goleman, Boyatzis, & McKee, 2002). Its possession is declared to trump an excellent analytical mind, the best training, and even the best ideas. Similar enthusiasm is also evident in education contexts in general where EI is advocated as being able to predict school success (Mayer & Cobb, 2000; Zeidner et al., 2010).

While few advocates of EI or leadership theorists are as effusive, what such emphasis indicates, so it is claimed, is nothing less than the "transmutation of emotions in organizations from negative and irrational to a positive attribute of successful leaders . . ." (Fambrough & Hart, 2008, p. 740; see also Ashkanasy & Tse, 2000; Dulewicz, Young, & Dulewicz, 2005). The focus on the emotional skills of the leader thus appears to herald a new age of leadership development, in marked contrast to the cognitive-rational approach in the H. A. Simon tradition of decision making and organization behavior that had split values and emotions from reason, subject to its positivist epistemology, and sought to reinterpret emotions within the rationalist framework instantiated in the symbol processing view (Evers & Lakomski, 2000). Although discussion of emotion and affect generally are not new to education and administration, the concept of Emotional Intelligence is put forward by its advocates as a new dimension for all social-emotional education, including more effective leadership.

Given the large and exponentially growing advocacy and critical literatures on EI and the extraordinary range of topics available to discuss—from assessing conceptual issues of the EI construct as opposed to "cognitive" intelligence, to whether EI itself is, or is not, an intelligence, to construct validity, the true meaning of EI, how its categories differ from those of personality characteristics and social skills generally, the various EI models with their differing emphases, terminological and definitional quagmires, issues of application, the multitude of changing measurement instruments and their validity, and other methodological problems such as self-reports—the interested scholar is spoilt for choice (Matthews, Zeidner, & Roberts, 2004, provide a comprehensive critical overview; also see Fineman, 2004 and Zeidner, Roberts, & Matthews, 2004).

Rather than addressing any one of the specific issues above, I want to examine the claim that EI is a scientifically valid concept. The focus of the discussion is the model of EI offered by Mayer and colleagues, as it is claimed to be the most coherent and scientifically defensible account (Mayer, 2000; Mayer, DiPaolo, & Salovey, 1990; Mayer & Salovey, 1993; Mayer, Caruso, & Salovey, 1999; Mayer, Salovey, & Caruso, 2000, 2004; Salovey & Grewal, 2005; Salovey & Mayer, 1990). In particular, I argue that EI (1) assumes the untenable, dualistic theory of mind that splits cognition from emotion; (2) is a theoretical construct that shows all the hallmarks of the hypothetico-deductive methodology of positivist science; and (3) trades on common-sense meanings of emotion, Folkemotion, a central feature of positivism's invalid theory of mind. EI relies on Folkemotion as a core concept, but as the core concept is invalid, so is EI as a consequence. It collapses as an empirical theory. What remains is a colloquial expression *without* explanatory force.

While folk psychological *descriptions* of mental phenomena will remain part and parcel of our everyday accounts for some time, scientific *explanations* are currently developed in both emotion science and affective neuroscience. The most promising account is to recast emotions in terms of dynamical systems theory that is biologically realistic, coheres with our currently best knowledge of brain function and architecture, and is able to account for emotions' variability, context-dependence, and time-boundedness. In addition, considering emotions as dynamical systems also makes it possible to explain both how emotions (and moods) can stay stable over time, and how they change. Although there is much controversy within and between emotion science and affective neuroscience, there are some initial implications we can draw for rethinking emotion in educational leadership, policy, and practice.

This chapter is organized into six sections. In the following I discuss the concept of Emotional Intelligence, as developed by Mayer and his colleagues, followed by considering an application of EI to leadership as one example. In the third section, I examine the philosophical-theoretical problems of EI as Folkpsychology and then introduce in the fourth section new research currently conducted in emotion science and affective neuroscience. Section five revisits EI on the basis of recent scientific results on the nature of emotion that show why EI is a false empirical theory, rather than a fledgling science. In the final section, I introduce some elements of a theory of emotional coherence as a species of a biologically realistic dynamical systems theory, based on the work of Thagard and colleagues. One important feature of this theory is that it helps explain (and model) emotion states and how they change, critical knowledge to have for educators and policy-makers alike.

Emotional Intelligence: The Scientific Model

The concept of EI is used by different writers in different ways and incorporates different features, depending on whose concept it is. Ruling out what serious minded EI writers describe as the "trade" texts, such as Goleman's (1995) and Goleman et al. (2002) popular formulations (e.g., Mayer et al., 2004), the focus in this section is on the claims made by Mayer and his colleagues for their four-branch model.

As Mayer and Salovey (1997, p. 4) explain, the concept of EI requires that both its component terms need to be explored. They accept the three part division of the mind as "basic to modern psychology" (p. 27, Note 3), which consists of *cognition* or thought, *affect* (including emotions), and *motivation* (or conation). Intelligence belongs to the cognitive sphere and is generally characterized by reasoning, judgment, and the ability to engage in abstract thought; emotions are part of the affective sphere "of mental functioning" and include the emotions themselves as well as moods, evaluations, and other feeling states. Motivation is thought to be secondary and is not discussed further. Of importance is that "Definitions of *emotional intelligence* should in some way connect emotions with *intelligence if the meanings of the two terms are to be preserved*" (p. 4; second italics added). This definition makes quite clear that Mayer and Salovey adhere to the traditional theory of mind and behavior, that of Folkpsychology (Ravenscroft, 2010).

The scientific nature of Mayer and Salovey's model is said to consist of the fact that it presents a unitary ability-model as opposed to mixed-model proposals in that it deliberately excludes the common personality characteristics found in mixed models that combine EI with other personality traits. (For more detail see Mayer's extensive EI website). In this way, Mayer et al. (2004) believe that their ability model is the most theoretically coherent. (A detailed overview of their ability model and how it differs from others is found in Mayer et al., 2000, pp. 396–398; see also Mayer, Roberts, & Barsade, 2008; Salovey & Grewal, 2005; further discussions, overviews, as well as critiques, are compiled in www.eiconsortium.org/index.html#.)

In one of their earliest presentations, Salovey and Mayer (1990, p. 186) place their EI concept within the emotion tradition that considers emotion as "an organizing response because it adaptively focuses cognitive activities and subsequent action" in line with modern theories of emotion:

> The full expression of emotions seems to be a primary human motive . . . and it may therefore be worthwhile to consider it from a functionalist

perspective . . . we view the organized response of emotion as adaptive and as something that can potentially lead to a transformation of personal and social interaction into enriching experience.

(Salovey & Mayer, 1990, p. 186).

They posit that EI is an intelligence, using Wechsler's broad definition: ". . . intelligence is the aggregate or global capacity of the individual to act purposefully, to think rationally, and to deal effectively with his environment" (cited in Salovey & Mayer, 1990, p. 186). The very broadness of the definition has the added advantage, in their view, of encompassing what people normally understand by "intelligence" (Salovey & Mayer 1990, p. 186). More specifically, Salovey and Mayer (1990, p. 189) define EI as a subset of *social intelligence* in that it "involves the ability to monitor one's own and others' feelings and emotions, to discriminate among them and to use this information to guide one's thinking and actions." (See Landy, 2005, for a critical discussion of the origins of social intelligence. He provides examples of how the concept was misused in the emotional intelligence literature.)

The EI concept was initially constructed on the background of scattered research largely descriptive in nature. Salovey and Mayer's hope was, via the examination of scale development, to reveal underlying constructs "and the means by which they operationalize portions of what we call emotional intelligence" (Salovey & Mayer, 1990, p. 190). The result of this research was expected to unearth "a set of conceptually related mental processes involving emotional information, that is, *reveal a unitary emotional intelligence*. The four-branch model is said to represent just that and consists of four abilities:

- to perceive emotions, especially through the nonverbal reception and expression of emotion, based on facial expressions (e.g., happiness, sadness, anger, and fear), or voice of others.
- to access and generate emotions so as to assist thought; the capacity of the emotions to enter into and guide the cognitive system and promote thinking.
- to understand emotions and emotional knowledge; as emotions convey information, it is important to understand emotional messages and the actions associated with them.
- to reflectively regulate emotions so as to promote emotional and intellectual growth. Emotions often can be managed (Mayer & Salovey, 1997, p. 5; see Figure 1.1, p. 11, for a tabular overview).

The primary research methodology associated with the model is known as the MSCEIT—the Mayer-Salovey-Caruso Emotional Intelligence Test—the latest in a line of instruments, following criticisms of earlier self-report scales (Salovey & Grewal, 2005) and reconfirmed as the "gold standard" in the field of EI (Ashkanasy, 2013, p. 311). Designed to measure each of the four branches, it consists of two tasks per branch (for details see Mayer et al., 2004, p. 200) and can be completed either by computer or on paper. (For critical commentary, see Locke, 2005.)

As these test items have been operationalized to generate more or less correct answers, show specific patterns of correlations reminiscent of those of known intelligences, and thus describe a "factorially unified domain," EI is said to meet the standards for traditional intelligence and should correlate with other intelligences, albeit only modestly. More importantly in the authors' view, "EI should develop with age," what it predicts, and what a person high in EI is like (Mayer, et al. 2004, p. 200).

In essence, the concept of Emotional Intelligence was initially formulated to unify and bring together disparate fields of research in order to examine how "people appraise and communicate emotion, and how they use that emotion in solving problems" (Salovey & Mayer, 1990, p. 190). It was to provide conceptual integration and thus make a substantive contribution to psychology. In the next section, I consider briefly one application of the four-branch model that has been influential in the leadership literature.

Applying Emotional Intelligence to Leadership: An Example

Although there is research on the impact of emotions on leadership by way of research on the charismatic leader and transformational leadership, George's (2000) influential argument proposes that the renewed focus on emotions and leadership is an important development as a response to the predominant cognitive orientation in leadership and organization studies. Moods and emotions play a much more central role than previously acknowledged, because, George claims, "leadership is an emotion–laden process . . ." (George, 2000, p. 1046). The following serves to give the flavor of the argument to establish the connection between moods and effective leadership, taken up by Daus and Ashkanasy (2005) and Dasborough and Ashkanasy (2003), in their work on leadership and EI. The spirited exchange between Antonakis, on one hand, and Ashkanasy and Dasborough (2009) on the other, provides an excellent critical source on EI for leadership.

The claim George makes is broad, and goes something like this. Just as emotions and feelings play an important part in human behavior generally, so it is likely that they are also influential in leadership, and more specifically, effective leadership. Subsequent research appears to support her claim. (See the Special Issue of *The Leadership Quarterly,* 2002, p. 13.) Emotional intelligence theory, in the form of the four-branch model, is able to provide answers to how (positive) mood connects with effective leadership. George acknowledges the difficulties in determining what makes for "effective leadership," and constructs her own list based on select elements of effective leadership models (George, 2000, p. 1039). Without going into detail about individual elements, a subjective selection, she agrees, the main results of applying EI theory (George, 2000, p. 1039 onward) boil down to (1) leaders who are in a positive mood are likely to develop and communicate organizational vision better while being able to monitor and adjust their own mood; (2) leaders are able to appraise the moods of their followers' feelings and make them aware of problems; (3) leaders can manage followers' feelings appropriately; (4) leaders high in EI are able to differentiate between followers' "real" as opposed to merely "professed" feelings and are able to detect "faked" from "real" excitement and enthusiasm and instill the real thing; (5) leaders high in EI are able to resolve conflicts constructively; (6) leaders create high quality interpersonal relationships and trust; (7) leaders high in EI are able to know the causes of their emotions; know what they are, and therefore use their positive (or deflect their negative) emotions in effective decision making; (8) such emotion knowledge enables leaders to consider the consequences of positive or negative emotions and consider alternatives; (9) a leader high in EI is also able to detect "relationships" (or patterns) between issues and is thus able to respond to multiple issues at once; (10) leaders bring about organizational change and instill and manage organizational culture. What needs to be done now, she asserts, is to test these claims empirically both in laboratories and field settings, and employ the measures of EI currently available, such as MSCEI.

There are many points to be made about George's argument, but a sample will have to suffice here. First, the argument is circular. High EI is presumed to be both the cause and result of leader effectiveness, leaving aside an examination of "effectiveness" itself. Second, there is no indication whether it is even possible *to learn* how to become an effective leader. Possessing and being aware of one's positive mood seems to be a given. Third, "positive mood" appears to be the same as being high in EI. There is no discussion or any criteria given of what is to count as being "high in EI." Fourth, mood is taken to be a static quality, without explanation. Fifth, the examples of organizational behaviors George provides all require cognitive appraisal as well as emotion; they are a mix of emotion and cognition, as is to be expected in all real-life decision-making contexts. Finally, at a time in the history of leadership studies where more collaborative or distributed models have been widely advocated, the model underlying George's proposal falls squarely into the traditional "leader as superhero" category and is an example of "methodological individualism" (Evers & Lakomski, 2013) where the individual leader's action controls and explains organizational activity, a false assumption.

It is difficult to see how such a general, over-inclusive conception could be tested empirically, as nothing is ruled out and everything (positive) is ruled in. (See Walter, Cole, & Humphrey, 2011, for discussion). I will return to some of these issues later. To understand more fully what the problems are with the model of EI proposed by Mayer and colleagues, and applied by George, a closer examination of its theoretical structure follows.

Theoretical Problems

Returning to Mayer et al.'s definition of EI, the characteristic theoretical-methodological structure of their model is the hypothetico-deductive approach of logical empiricism, an account of scientific theory and practice no longer accepted as valid (see Evers and Lakomski, 2000, especially p. 66, Figure 4.1, the Generic Leadership Model). Bowers and Seashore's (1973, p. 447) formulation, developed for traditional leadership studies, serves equally well in the present context. It contains the following features:

- Measures reflecting a theoretically meaningful conceptual structure of leadership (EI)
- An integrated set of systematically derived criteria
- A treatment of these data, which takes account of the multiplicity of relationships and investigates the adequacy of leadership (EI) characteristic in predicting effectiveness variables.

Recall that Mayer and colleagues portray their model of EI as scientific because it "arises in the context of associated scientific terms and their meanings . . . as a nomological network—a system of meanings with which most scientists are familiar and that have been established because of their utility" (Mayer et al., 2008, pp. 509–510). Practically, EI "concerns the ability to carry out accurate reasoning about emotions and the ability to use emotions and emotional knowledge to enhance thought" (p. 511).

This broad definition denotes the *General EI Construct* at the top of the (pyramidal) structure (see Figure 4.1, p. 66, Evers & Lakomski, 2000), further defined in terms of the four branches underneath it. These are further specified and *operationally defined* in terms of *observable behaviors* (instantiated in MSCEI test items); these behaviors/test items in turn are gathered by means of the MSCEI, and analyzed in terms of correlations, regularities, or patterns. This analysis then leads to *evidence* or *confirmation* of the study and is taken in support of the initial EI model, as stipulated at the top of the hierarchy.

The immediate problem is the broadness of the definition that allows many different observable behaviors to be defined and operationalized as indicators. These are, in principle, endless, only delimited by the researcher's ingenuity. So, endemic uncertainty about what does constitute EI is built into its generic construct. More importantly, even if unambiguous, operationalizable behaviors could be identified, the case for EI would not thus be strengthened as the notion of *operational definition* is in principle indefensible. This is so because the basic assumption of logical empiricism (positivism) is that the foundations of science are observations, or observation reports that need to be secure and beyond doubt. This principle also applies to nonobservable entities, such as EI, that had to be rendered "visible." The solution was to stipulate behaviors that are to count as evidence for (aspects of)

EI; that is, to provide *operational definitions* of them. This, however, is not a successful move as there is no principled epistemological distinction between observable and nonobservable entities. All observations are "theory laden;" that is, they rely on networks of prior knowledge, for both physical and nonphysical objects. For humans, there is no camera-like recording of observations. Indeed, vision is always "affective vision" because visual processing happens in a context shaped by extensive communication between amygdala (highly involved in emotion generation) and the visual cortex (Pessoa, 2012, p. 159).

The hypothetico-deductive methodology of EI does not establish that it, or any of its branches, really exists. The MSCEI may provide evidence (weak or strong) for some of the branch subconstructs, but all this means is that it provides evidence for items predetermined by the initial construct, which is taken as given. It does not provide independent evidence for the construct's validity, and all its subcategories are defined within its set of assumptions. Just because Emotional Intelligence has become a commonly used term does not mean that EI, therefore, is real. The issue at stake here is the tacit assumption that a linguistic representation means that the entity referred to exists in nature. It does not. To put this point in a more general way, the psychology of everyday understandings to which EI belongs is not that of science but of Folkpsychology. The latter employs descriptive, functionalist terms but does not offer *explanations* of causal relationships, which is an important objective of science. Let's consider the functionalist nature of Folkpsychology more closely.

Although there are arguments for why a functionalist theory does not need to offer causal explanations to be considered valid, as its main feature consists in it being a semantically coherent system, as intimated above in Mayer's characterization, and because logical relations are not reducible to causal relations, for advocates of Folkpsychology, any worry over causality simply drops away (see Lakomski, 2008). Given this functionalist theory, in principle, many exchangeable entities can be instantiated in many different physical systems, the main requirement being consistency of semantic systems. One such prominent example is Simon's (1987) proposal that the chess player's *intuition* can be instantiated in productions of if-then pairs and stored in computer memory (Evers & Lakomski, in press). So for EI, the function of a mental state-like mood, however defined, is in theory like the function of a computer or a jackhammer. Of course this strikes us immediately as absurd as we "know" that moods/feelings/emotions are nothing like jackhammers, for example, whose functions and properties are fairly well understood because of scientific principles underlying their manufacture and operation, etc. No such scientific knowledge, however, underpins folk moods. We just assume them because we have always known them; they are innate, part of the "Given" of human experience. But, insofar as EI alleges mental states linked to actual behaviors, such as "positive mood X causes leadership behaviors Y," it has content. The four-branch model makes empirical claims and is thus an empirical theory open to refutation or even elimination, as any empirical theory is.

It is at this point that the spuriousness of EI as an empirical theory becomes clear. Content is not exchangeable willy-nilly; it just so happens that humans are natural, not functional, kinds whose brains have evolved as they have. Computational and pattern recognition capacities allow the brain to represent the internal as well as external world. There is thus a fundamental mismatch between the sentential structure of EI on the one hand and the actual biological architecture of the brain on the other. As Ramsay (2012) observes regarding sentential structure, "Whereas the former involves discrete symbols and a combinatorial syntax, the latter involves action potentials, spiking frequencies and spreading activation" (p. 13).

Given that the account of EI contributes nothing to an explanation of mental phenomena, it is appropriate to turn instead to what affective neuroscience, as well as the new emotion science, tell us about "emotion," the key component of EI. To say that current research in this area is complicated, is a massive understatement, as will become clear in the following, beginning with a brief look at the history of the word emotion and the current state of determining "emotion" in the emerging emotion science and affective neuroscience.

Emotion in the New Emotion Science and Affective Neuroscience

The word emotion has had an interesting history and has not become applied to the systematic study of mental phenomena until the mid-19th century. The concept of emotion has been characterized by a fundamental tension, as emotions were believed to be determined by mental constituents on one hand, or by bodily ones on the other (see Dixon, 2012, for a brief history). This dichotomy persists in current research in psychology on emotion, as does ambiguity regarding its "proper" definition. In fact, following Izard's (2010) recent survey, there are 34 different definitions of emotion—one for each of the scientists he asked! Despite this general lack of agreement on the meaning of "emotion," Izard (2010) reports substantial agreement regarding the structures and functions of emotion ". . . in motivating and focusing individual endeavours, social interactions, and the development of adaptive and maladaptive behaviors" (p. 368; also Izard, 2009). This ambiguity is reflected in contemporary emotion science and affective neuroscience, albeit in different degrees and with different consequences.

Perhaps the simplest way to describe what both psychological science—that is, emotion science—and affective neuroscience are researching is the question of the nature and origins of "emotion," the term we use regardless of what science we work in. The answers, however, differ. Affective neuroscience is primarily interested in the causal, underlying, neural substrates of emotion and mood (Dalgleish, Dunn, & Mobbs, 2009), while the new emotion science is more concerned with the specification or classification of what emotions are. As De Gelder (2010, p. 1) notes, the first challenge for an emotion science is to determine exactly how many emotions there are, followed by issues such as whether

> all emotions [are] alike, what is there to measure, how do we measure emotions, what does interdisciplinarity mean, how important is interaction, what are the issues for modelling emotions, what is the part of context, do feelings matter, consciousness, and emotions.

Clearly, the scope of emotion science is vast.

Accounts to answer the emotion question empirically have taken two opposite approaches; the basic or discrete emotions account (e.g., Ekman, 1999; also, with modifications, Panksepp, 1998; Damasio, 1996, 1999; Izard, 2007; LeDoux, 1996, 2012) and the dimensional or *constructionist* approach (e.g., Gendron & Barrett, 2009). The main focus of the ongoing controversy is the question of what the basic units of emotion are "and whether these units are essentially dimensional or discrete" (Hamann, 2012, p. 458).

For basic emotion theorists, emotion categories (such as fear and anger) have evolved as part of our biological nature. They are not decomposable into constituent psychological elements (Hamann, 2012, p. 461). In contrast, dimensional theorists argue for combinations of underlying dimensions of discrete emotions, "such as emotional arousal (strength or intensity of emotion) and emotional valence (degree of pleasantness or unpleasantness), in combination with cognitive processes, such as appraisal and attribution of meaning" (Hamann, 2012, p. 458). In the latter account, the basic emotion of fear, for example, would result from a "combination of negative valence, high arousal, and other attributes that are not specific to the category of fear *per se*" (Hamann, 2012, p. 458). Whether the basic emotions approach or the dimensional account better explains emotional phenomena is still a matter of controversy. But, as all mental states, ultimately, are expected to be mapped onto their corresponding brain mechanisms, neuroimaging was thought to be able to provide evidence for one or the other. Recent results, however, do not support an either/or solution (Hamann, 2012).

Although various meta-analyses have provided some evidence of consistent neural correlates underpinning basic emotions, the major finding is that there is no specialization of brain regions responsible for one type of emotion (e.g., Anderson, 2010; Bressler & Menon, 2010). Rather, individual brain regions often contribute to multiple emotions, making it therefore more appropriate to conceive of emotions as represented in networks across the brain. In short, as Pessoa (2012) puts it, "the mapping between structure and function is both *pluripotent* (one-to-many) and *degenerate* (many-to-one)" (p. 158). The combination of the two indicates that there are no "necessary and sufficient" (Pessoa) brain regions. Networks are the prime unit of analysis, and it is the interaction between the networks that generates the processes that emerge dynamically through such interaction, and thus support behavior (Witherington & Crichton, 2007). Contrary to traditional conceptions, it is no longer appropriate that brain regions be viewed as either "cognitive" or "emotional"; brains are not "decomposable in terms of emotion and cognition" (Pessoa, 2012, p. 159). It follows from these results that emotion and cognition "are *functionally integrated systems,* namely, they more or less continuously impact each other's operations" (Pessoa, 2012, p. 159).

This argument, it should be noted, thus counts as much for explaining the (lack of) localization and specification of cognition as it does for emotion (Lakomski & Evers, 2010, 2012). So what implications can be drawn from this complex picture of the state of the art in the study of emotion for emotional intelligence and the business of emotions?

Emotional Intelligence Revisited

In considering that some of the implications of the preceding discussion are for educators, including leaders, an important distinction needs to be kept in mind: The causal account of emotion (in affective neuroscience), as outlined above, and second, the language of the emotions we continue to employ when talking about our own mental states, and those of others. Given the dynamical systems account of brain function briefly outlined above, the manifestation of an emotion, an emotion episode, can be understood as

> the form or second-order constraint that emerges from the self-organization of various processes (i.e. neural, autonomic, behavioral, etc.) and that entrains such processes into a meta-stable configuration or pattern. Reciprocal interactions among these various processes embody first-order constraints and contribute to the formation of an emotion as an overarching form. Events in the environment—traditional 'emotional stimuli'—also influence the emotion form, and can be seen as control parameters. . . . An emotional episode thus conceptualized can 'vary' in the sense that the processes constituting it can organize themselves in different ways . . .
>
> (Colombetti, 2009, p. 415; also, Lewis, 2005).

An interesting example in this context is the emergence of facial configurations, such as different types of smiles, from local synergies of various muscles (e.g., Camras, 2000; Camras & Witherington, 2005; Scherer & Ellgring, 2007). Furthermore, given dynamical self-organizing patterning of emotional behavior, there are no clear distinctions between emotional and nonemotional episodes, or even between emotional and cognitive phenomena (Colombetti, 2009, p. 420). Nor should one expect anything different, given that all mental phenomena emerge in a brain that is itself a self-organizing system.

Returning to the EI construct proposed by Mayer and colleagues, and on the basis of the recent empirical and theoretical work in affective neuroscience and emotion science, it is now easy to see that the construct begins from a radically false conception of the mind and, subsequently, of emotion (see Evers & Lakomski, 2000, pp.10–14, on the functionalist mind). EI's methodological approach (the MSCEI) only "captures" the model's linguistic representations of what is to count as emotionally intelligent behaviors (operationalization). Furthermore, test items are administered as pencil and paper tasks, or by computer, usually under laboratory conditions. This is an additional problem as test situations deny the variability and context-dependence of emotion episodes as they are experienced in everyday life and, thus, distort the results even further.

We do not have direct introspective access to the contents of our own minds (LeDoux, 1996; also Churchland, 1984), and our verbal reports on our mental processes can be systematically misleading (see Nisbett & Wilson's, 1978, now classical study). Indeed, we appear to suffer from "affective ignorance" (AI) (Haybron, 2007). Moods, as distinct from emotions, for example, are elusive, but can nevertheless affect us for a long time and, strange as this seems, there is evidence that we can systematically mistake what mood we are actually in; we may even be mistaken about the *valence* of current emotional experience; that is, be unable to tell pleasant from unpleasant experiences (see Haybron, 2007, p. 405, for examples; also Lambie & Marcel, 2002).

As psychologists, including EI theorists, often use scales to measure experience, affective ignorance is a serious problem known as *scale norming:* that is, people assess their own experience in different and widely diverging ways, subject to their previous experiences, with different outcomes at different points in time. This problem has been noted as applying to the four-branch model (Zeidner, Roberts, & Matthews, 2010, p. 218). As Haybron (2007, p. 403) notes,

> [It] generates . . . ignorance about the *relative* quality of our experience . . . it undermines interpersonal—and *intra*personal—comparisons insofar as we aren't sure whether two individuals, or two time-slices of the same individual, are rating their experience using similar scales. More importantly, scale norming suggests that we often fail to recognize how our experience rates in relation to the possibilities . . . we don't know what we're missing, and therefore don't know how good (or bad) what we've got is.

In light of these difficulties, we might note that, given that awareness and correct identification of mood in George's advocacy for effective high EI leaders plays such a central role, "mood" may not be the reliable indicator for predicting leader effectiveness, as assumed. We may be mistaken, perhaps even systematically, in our own assessments of the mood we are in. And if this applies to our own moods, it is equally likely to apply to gauging the moods of others.

In conclusion, the foregoing discussion served to indicate that the issue of consciousness and emotion experience are highly complex and remain the subject of ongoing scientific controversy. We do, however, have empirical and theoretical support for the view that emotion experience does not have a single form or content, and is varied and variable between emotions as well as individuals (See Lambie & Marcel, 2002, for a detailed discussion on consciousness and the varieties of emotion experience; also Winkielman & Berridge, 2004).

Where Do We Go From Here?

The biologically realistic dynamical systems view explains emotion experience as characterized by variability within emotions and persons, dependent on time-scales, and are highly sensitive to context. This perspective thus helps explain what we experience every day in terms of changing moods and emotions, changes that sometimes are only mild and subtle, and inconsequential in terms of action, but that can also be volatile and qualitatively different at other times, and sometimes lead to (self-)destructive behavior. The folk psychological view of emotion/s—characteristic of EI—is merely able to describe such experience but is unable to explain it. And importantly, as emotional intelligence was conceived of as a stable individual ability, how emotional states emerge, and how one state can be followed by a completely different one, remain unanswered.

Viewing emotion experience, or affect generally, as explicable by means of the dynamical systems perspective provides the theoretical, as well as computational tools, to explain (and model) how emotional change happens, in Thagard and Nerb's (2002) terms, how *emotional gestalts* emerge and how *emotional gestalt shifts* come about. The first specification is that emotional change is considered as a transition in a complex dynamical system whose specifications are those of extended neural networks that are able to perform parallel constraint satisfaction. *Emotional gestalts* are states that come about as the result of constraint satisfaction processing that includes both cognitive and affective constraints. Transitions in the system are called *emotional gestalt shifts*. Accounting thus for both stability and change in the system, Thagard and Nerb (2002, p. 275) employ an explanation schema from dynamical systems theory that fits the explanation of psychological phenomena:

- *Explanation Target:* Why do people have stable but unpredictable patterns of behavior?
- *Explanatory Pattern:* Human thought is describable by a set of variables.
- These variables are governed by a set of nonlinear equations.
- These equations establish a state space that has attractors.
- The system described by the equations is chaotic.
- The existence of the attractors explains stable patterns of behavior. Multiple attractors explain abrupt phase transitions.
- The chaotic nature of the system explains why behavior is unpredictable.

Variables would include descriptions of environmental, bodily, and mental factors; equations are nonlinear as the causal relationships between variables are driven by complex feedback relations between them; the system is chaotic in that one small perturbation in one variable can have large effects on the others and thus on the overall system. For example, sometimes it only needs one friendly word to change the complexion of an act or behavior, replacing your grumpy mood with a cheerful one. But it is also the case that moods can remain stable over a considerable period of time, and in dynamical system's terms such stability is explainable in terms of the system's "tendency to evolve into a small number of general states called attractors, and the shift from one mood to another can be described as the shift from one attractor to another" (Thagard & Nerb, 2002, p. 275). The duck-rabbit example from Gestalt psychology might help make this clear. The two images—duck and rabbit—can be considered as attractor states; focusing on parts of the drawings produces a gestalt switch that allows you to transition from one to the other (and also back again). So, analogously, an emotional state as a *gestalt* emerges from complex interacting environmental, bodily, and cognitive variables, and an emotional state change can be seen as a *gestalt* switch.

Based on his theory of thinking as parallel constraint satisfaction—many representations are involved simultaneously in our thinking that constrain or place limits on one another and that operate in parallel to maximize constraint satisfaction—Thagard (2000, 2006; Wagar & Thagard, 2003) has developed a series of artificial neural networks that implement the variables and equations listed above in an increasingly biologically realistic way. The most recent is GAGE (named in honor of Phineas Gage), a network that models spiking neurons, a feature of real brains. GAGE incorporates interactions between emotion and cognition that mimic how the biological brain operates (Thagard, 2006).

Broadly supportive of Damasio's somatic marker hypothesis (SM) that discusses the centrality of the VMPCF for covert effective decision making (Damasio, 1996, 1999, 2000, 2003; Lakomski & Evers, 2010, 2012), Wagar and Thagard (in Thagard, 2006, p. 92 onward) expand the SM mechanism by highlighting the role of the *nucleus accumbens* (NAcc) as an important gateway through which signals must pass to access brain areas responsible for higher-order reasoning (Thagard, 2006, p. 110). In effect, the *nucleus accumbens* limits throughput to those signals that are consistent with the current context, thereby reducing the number of alternative choices that can access higher-level cognitive processes. In addition, as GAGE is able to model the spiking behavior of real neurons, it thus "shows that temporal coordination between the VMPCF and the amygdala is a key component to eliciting emotional reactions to stimuli" (Thagard, 2006, p. 91). Thagard's earlier constraint satisfaction model has thus been expanded to account for more actual real brain mechanisms in emotional decision making, which makes GAGE a very powerful network indeed.

It is easy to see that this model of emotional coherence "fits" with appraisal views of emotion, such as Damasio's for example, insofar as somatic body states or markers may give rise to awareness of options, and then to conscious evaluations, *valences,* either positive or negative. The theory of emotional coherence, Thagard and Nerb (2002) suggest, provides the specific mechanisms that generate evaluations and elicit emotions, and it can thus serve as a realistic explanation of, for example, how cognitive therapy works (Thagard, 2000, p. 208 onward).

Conclusion

It is quite conceivable that the theory of emotional coherence, as a species of a biologically realistic dynamical systems theory, in its explanation of how emotional *gestalts* emerge and also how they change, could be of enormous benefit in education. As EI has shown itself to be inapplicable "to real world emotional challenges" (Zeidner et al., 2010, p. 219), an explanation (with potential computational modeling) of how moods and emotions can change, and stay the same, would be enormously helpful to teachers. Schools have to deal with increasing incidents of aggressive behavior, bullying, poor self-image of teenage girls and boys, and self-harming behaviors, just to name some problems. Getting a better, scientifically grounded understanding of the causes of mood and emotional state emergence and understanding how they can change should be a policy proscription for all educators, including school leaders (Mayer & Cobb, 2000).

References

Anderson, M. L. (2010). Neural reuse: A fundamental organizational principle of the brain. *Behavioral and Brain Sciences, 33,* 245–313.

Antonakis, J., Ashkanasy, N. M., & Dasborough, M. T. (2009). Does leadership need emotional intelligence? *The Leadership Quarterly, 20,* 247–261.

Ashkanasy, N. M. (2013). Neuroscience and leadership: Take care not to throw the baby out with the bathwater. *Journal of Management Inquiry, 22,* 311–313.

Ashkanasy, N. M. & Dasborough, M. T. (2009). Does leadership need emotional intelligence? *The Leadership Quarterly, 20,* 251–254; 257–259.

Ashkanasy, N. M., & Tse, B. (2000). Transformational leadership as management of emotion: A conceptual review. In N. Ashkanasy, C. E. J. Härtel, & W. J. Zerber (Eds.), *Emotions in the workplace: Research, theory, and practice* (pp. 221–235). Westport, CT: Quorum Books.

Bowers, D. G., & Seashore, S. E. (1973). Predicting organizational effectiveness with a four-factor theory of leadership. In W. E. Scott & L. L. Cummings (Eds.), *Readings in Organizational Behavior and Human Performance* (p. 447). Homewood, IL: Richard D. Irwin.

Bressler, S. L., & Menon, V. (2010). Large-scale brain networks in cognition: Emerging methods and principles. *Trends in Cognitive Sciences, 14,* 277–290.

Camras, L. A. (2000). Surprise! Facial expressions can be coordinative motor structures. In M. Lewis & I. Granic (Eds.), *Emotion, development and self-organization* (pp. 100–124). New York, NY: Cambridge University Press.

Camras, L. A., & Witherington, D. C. (2005). Dynamical systems approaches to emotional development. *Developmental Review, 25,* 328–350.

Churchland, P. M. (1984). *Matter and consciousness* [Rev. Ed.]. Cambridge, MA: MIT Press.

Colombetti, G. (2009). From affect programs to dynamical discrete emotions. *Philosophical Psychology, 22,* 407–425.

Dalgliesh, T., Dunn, B. D., & Mobbs, D. (2009). Affective neuroscience: Past, present, and future. *Emotion Review, 1,* 355–368.

Damasio, A. R. (1996). *Descartes' error.* London, UK: Macmillan.

Damasio, A. R. (1999). *The feeling of what happens.* New York, NY: Harcourt.

Damasio, A. R. (2000). A second chance for emotion. In R. D. Lane & L. Nadel (Eds.). *Cognitive neuroscience of emotion* (pp. 12–23). New York, NY: Oxford University Press.

Damasio, A. R. (2003). *Looking for Spinoza.* New York, NY: Harcourt.

Dasborough, M. T., & and Ashkanasy, N. M. (2003). Is emotional intelligence training for leaders justified? *Australian Journal of Psychology,* Supplement 2003, 120–121.

Daus, C. S., & Ashkanasy, N. M. (2005). The case for the ability-based model of emotional intelligence in organizational behavior. [Comment/Reply]. *Journal of Organizational Behavior, 26,* 453–466.

De Gelder, B. (2010). The grand challenge for frontiers in emotion science. *Frontiers in Psychology, 1,* 1–4.

Dixon, T. (2012). Emotion: The history of a keyword in crisis. *Emotion Review, 4,* 338–344.

Dulewicz, C., Young, M., & Dulewicz, V. (2005). The relevance of emotional intelligence for leadership performance. *Journal of General Management, 30,* 71–86.

Ekman, P. (1999). *Annotated update of Charles Darwin's "The expression of the emotions in man and animals."* New York, NY: HarperCollins.

Evers, C. W., & Lakomski, G. (2000). *Doing educational administration.* Oxford, UK: Pergamon.

Evers, C. W., & Lakomski, G. (2013). Methodological individualism, educational administration, and leadership: Philosophical reflections. *Journal of Educational Administration and History, 44,* 1–15.

Fambrough, M. J., & Hart, R. K. (2008). Emotions in leadership development: A critique of emotional intelligence. *Advances in Developing Human Resources, 10,* 740–758.

Fineman, S. (2004). Getting the measure of emotion—and the cautionary tale of emotional intelligence. *Human Relations, 57,* 719–740.

Gendron, M., & Barrett, L. F. (2009). Reconstructing the past: A century of ideas about emotion in psychology. *Emotion Review, 1,* 316–339.

George, J. M. (2000). Emotions and leadership: The role of emotional intelligence. *Human Relations, 53,* 1027–1055.

Goleman, D. (1995). *Emotional intelligence: Why it can matter more than IQ.* New York, NY: Bantam Books.

Goleman, D. (2004). What makes a leader? *Harvard Business Review, 82,* 82–91.

Goleman, D., Boyatzis, R. R., & McKee, A. (2002). *Primal leadership: Realizing the power of emotional intelligence.* Boston, MA: Harvard Business School.

Hamann, S. (2012). Mapping discrete and dimensional emotions onto the brain: Controversies and consensus. *Trends in Cognitive Sciences, 16,* 458–466.

Haybron, D. M. (2007). Do we know how happy we are? On some limits of affective introspection and recall, *NOUS, 41,* 394–428.

Izard, C. E. (2007). Emotion feelings stem from evolution and neurobiological development, not from conceptual acts, corrections for Barrett et al., *Perspectives on Psychological Science, 2,* 404–405.

Izard, C. E. (2009). Emotion theory and research: Highlights, unanswered questions, and emerging issues. *Annual Review of Psychology, 60,* 1–25.

Izard, C. E. (2010). The many meanings/aspects of emotion: Definitions, functions, activation, and regulation. *Emotion Review, 2,* 363–370.

Lakomski, G. (2008). Functionally adequate but causally idle: W(h)ither distributed leadership? *Journal of Educational Administration, 46,* 159–171.

Lakomski, G., & Evers, C. W. (2010). Passionate rationalism: The role of emotion in decision-making. *Journal of Educational Administration, 48,* 438–450.

Lakomski, G., & Evers, C. W. (2012). Emotion and rationality in educational problem-solving: From individuals to groups. *Korean Journal of Educational Administration, 30,* 653–677.

Lambie, J. A., & Marcel, A. J. (2002). Consciousness and the varieties of emotion experience: A theoretical framework. *Psychological Review, 109,* 219–259.

Landy, F. J. (2005). Some historical and scientific issues related to research on emotional intelligence. *Journal of Organizational Behavior, 26,* 411–424.

LeDoux, J. (1996). *The emotional brain.* New York, NY: Simon & Schuster.

LeDoux, J. (2012). A neuroscientist's perspective on debates about the nature of emotion. *Emotion Review, 4,* 375–377.

Lewis, M. D. (2005). Bridging emotion theory and neurobiology through dynamic systems modelling. *Behavioral and Brain Sciences, 28,* 169–245.

Locke, E. A. (2005). Why emotional intelligence is an invalid concept. *Journal of Organizational Behavior, 26,* 425–431.

Matthews, G., Zeidner, M., & Roberts, R. D. (2004). *Emotional intelligence: Science and myth.* Boston, MA: MIT Press.

Mayer, J. D. (2000). Emotion, intelligence, and emotional intelligence. In J. P. Forgas (Ed.), *Handbook of affect and social cognition* (pp. 410–431). Mahwah, NJ: Lawrence Erlbaum & Associates.

Mayer, J. D., Caruso, D., & Salovey, P. (1999). Emotional intelligence meets traditional standards for an intelligence. *Intelligence, 27,* 267–298.

Mayer, J. D., & Cobb, C. D. (2000). Educational policy on emotional intelligence: Does it make sense? *Educational Psychology Review, 12,* 163–183.

Mayer, J. D., DiPaolo, M. T., & Salovey, P. (1990). Perceiving affective content in ambiguous visual stimuli: A component of emotional intelligence. *Journal of Personality Assessment, 54,* 772–781.

Mayer, J. D., Roberts, R. D., & Barsade, S. G. (2008). Human abilities: Emotional intelligence. *Annual Review of Psychology, 59,* 507–536.

Mayer, J. D., & Salovey, P. (1993). The intelligence of emotional intelligence [Comment/Reply]. *Intelligence, 17,* 433–442.

Mayer, J. D., & Salovey, P. (1997). What is emotional intelligence? In P. Salovey & D. J. Sluyter (Eds.). *Emotional development and emotional intelligence.* (pp. 3–31). New York, NY: Basic Books.

Mayer, J. D., Salovey, P., & Caruso, D. R. (2000). Models of emotional intelligence. In R. J. Sternberg (Ed.), *Handbook of Intelligence* (pp. 396–420). Cambridge, UK: Cambridge University Press.

Mayer, J. D., Salovey, P., & Caruso, D. R. (2004). Emotional intelligence: Theory, findings, and implications. *Psychological Inquiry, 15,* 197–215.

Nisbett, R. W., & Wilson, T. D. (1978). Telling more than we can know: Verbal reports on mental processes. *Psychological Review, 84,* 231–259.

Panksepp, J. (1998). *Affective neuroscience: The foundations of human and animal emotions.* New York, NY: Oxford University Press.

Pessoa, L. (2012). Beyond brain regions: Network perspective of cognition–emotion interactions. *Behavioral and Brain Sciences, 35,* 158–159.

Ramsey, W. (2012). Eliminative materialism. In E. N. Zalta (Ed.), *The Stanford Encyclopedia of Philosophy.* Retrieved from http://plato.stanford.edu/archives/fall2012/entries/materialism-eliminative/

Ravenscroft, I. (2010). Folk psychology as a theory. In E. N. Zalta (Ed.), *The Stanford Encyclopedia of Philosophy*. Retrieved from http://plato.stanford.edu/archives/fall2010/entries/folkpsych-theory/

Salovey, P., & Grewal, D. (2005). The science of emotional intelligence. *Current Directions in Psychological Science, 14,* 281–285.

Salovey, P., & Mayer, J. D. (1990). Emotional intelligence. *Imagination, Cognition, and Personality, 9,* 185–211.

Scherer, K. A. & Ellgring, H. (2007). Are facial expressions of emotion produced by categorical affect programs or dynamically driven by appraisal? *Emotion, 7,* 113–130.

Simon, H. A. (1987). Making management decisions: The role of intuition and emotion. *Academy of Management Executive, 1,* 57–64.

Thagard, P. (2000). *Coherence in thought and action.* Cambridge, MA: MIT Press.

Thagard, P. (2006). *Hot thought.* Cambridge, MA: MIT Press.

Thagard, P., & Nerb, J. (2002). Emotion gestalts: Appraisal, change, and the dynamics of affect. *Personality and Social Psychology Review, 6,* 272–282.

Wagar, B. M., & Thagard, P. (2003). Using computational neuroscience to investigate the neural correlates of cognitive–affective integration during covert decision-making. *Brain and Cognition, 53,* 398–402.

Walter, F., Cole, M. S., & Humphrey, R. H. (2011). Emotional intelligence: Sine qua non of leadership or folderol? *The Academy of Management Perspectives, 25,* 45–59.

Winkielman, P., & Berridge, K. C. (2004). Unconscious emotion. *Current Directions in Psychological Science, 13,* 1–5.

Witherington, D. C., & Crichton, J. A. (2007). Frameworks for understanding emotions and their development: Functionalist and dynamic systems approaches. *Emotion, 7,* 628–637.

Zeidner, M., Matthews, G., & Roberts, R. D. (2004). Emotional intelligence in the workplace: A critical review. *Applied Psychology: An International Review, 53,* 371–399.

Zeidner, M., Roberts, R. D., & Matthews, G. (2010). Can emotional intelligence be schooled? A critical review. *Educational Psychologist, 37,* 215–231.

PART III

Complexity and Decision Making

6

ON-THE-JOB DECISION MAKING: UNDERSTANDING AND EVALUATING HOW LEADERS SOLVE PROBLEMS

Viviane Robinson and Rozanne Donald

Introduction

The primary objective of this chapter is to address two questions that are fundamental to using research to advance leadership practice in the areas of problem solving and decision making. The first question asks, "How can the process of real world decision making and problem solving be explained?" The reference to "real-world" is important as there is a substantial difference between the accounts of decision making provided by classical decision-making (CDM) theorists and the accounts provided by those in the more recent naturalistic decision-making (NDM) tradition. While the models of the former are based on analytic models of choice processes, the models of the latter are grounded in descriptions of the thinking and action of experienced practitioners making on-the-job decisions (Klein, 2008; Meso, Troutt, & Rudnicka, 2002).

The second question is a normative one and asks, "How can the quality of decision making and problem solving be judged?" The guidance that researchers give practitioners about how to make decisions should be based on explicit normative assumptions. We offer standards for the evaluation of both the problem-solving process and the adequacy of the solution.

Throughout this chapter we refer to both problem solving and decision making as we see the former as encompassing how people perceive and understand a situation, as well as how they decide on an appropriate course of action. A narrow focus on decision making may prevent examination of the perceptual and cognitive processes that shape how situations are understood and, therefore, what course of action is taken (Lipshitz, Klein, Orasanu, & Salas, 2001).

We begin with a brief account of classical and naturalistic approaches to decision making before positioning our account for investigating decision making, which we call problem-based methodology (PBM), within the naturalistic tradition (Robinson, 1993, 1998). We outline this methodology and explain how we used it in an original investigation of the adoption and implementation of a new curriculum in an urban K–12 school. PBM addresses our second normative question about the quality of problem solving by offering four meta-level criteria for evaluating the adequacy of problem formulation and solution.

Classical and Naturalistic Accounts of Decision Making

In very broad terms, one can summarize the history of decision-making research as moving from a model of optimal rationality that made unrealistic assumptions about the availability of complete information about decision alternatives and about human capability to process such information, to a model based on bounded rationality that acknowledged the necessity of more limited search and choice processes (Simon, 1973). In the late 1980s, both these classical models of decision choice were challenged by the emergence of naturalistic decision-making models, which questioned whether even the limited rationality (satisficing) model was either descriptively accurate or normatively useful (Rasmussen, 1997).

The classical approach conceptualizes decision-makers as choosing between alternative courses of action based on their calculation of the probability of each alternative satisfying their preferences. While the scope of the search for and evaluation of options varies, the core idea is that decision making involves a deliberate and analytic process based on a relatively thorough information search (Lipshitz et al., 2001). This classical model was seriously mismatched with both the complexity and uncertainty of real-world problem solving and the cognitive capacities of human decision-makers. In his well-known "satisficing" model of decision making, Herb Simon and his colleagues addressed these limitations by proposing a more limited rather than comprehensive search for alternatives. In addition, they argued that the loosely structured nature of many problems meant that they could be solved in chunks rather than all at once and that such chunking would enable solving of complex problems despite the bounded rationality of human beings (Newell & Simon, 1972; Simon, 1973).

While the satisficing model acknowledged the limitations of human cognitive capacities, it still included the key features of rational decision making. Decisions were the result of means-ends calculation of the probability that certain, albeit limited, courses of action would deliver preferred outcomes. In other words, satisficing was a necessary pragmatic compromise, which preserved the conception of rationality as an analytic calculation of the factual relationship between means and ends. Furthermore, the inputs into such calculations were restricted to matters of fact. Values, feelings, and emotions were treated as distortions to a truly rational approach to decision making. Such exclusion creates a massive gap between the CDM model and the real world, for every leader makes decisions on the basis of conscious or unconscious perceptions of the emotional implications of certain courses of action—indeed one could argue that failure to do so is unethical. Recent evidence from cognitive neuroscience suggests that, far from distorting rationality, emotion may be strongly integrated into, rather than separate from, our reasoning processes and send important signals about the likely bodily consequences of certain courses of action (Lakomski & Evers, 2010).

According to Klein (2008), it was fairly clear by the late 1980s that people did not make decisions by generating alternative options and comparing them on the same set of evaluative standards. Even when presented with relatively simple tasks that did not tax bounded rationality, people deviated substantially from the decision processes and outcomes prescribed by the CDM model. Part of the continuing debate between CDM and NDM researchers is whether such evidence signals how bias and other cognitive limitations lead fallible decision-makers to deviate from what is normatively desirable, or whether it raises more fundamental questions about the validity of rational choice models.

The account of decision making provided by those in the naturalistic tradition is based on descriptive evidence about how experienced practitioners such as fire commanders, naval officers, chess players, design engineers, and commercial pilots make on-the-job decisions. Rather than choose between options, experienced decision-makers recognize situations as having a family resemblance to existing categories, schemas, or prototypes that are associated with a particular course of action (Sternberg & Horvarth, 1995). The cognitive schema or prototype enables people to make a quick match between the situation and what they have already learned about how to deal with it. If the situation is recognized as at least partially familiar, people may not generate alternative courses of action, relying instead on the one that first comes to mind. While the "first to mind" strategy enables swift action, it may not lead to a quality solution, so the question of how possible courses of action are evaluated is still important (Mann, 2001). NDM researchers have used interviews and think-aloud methods to probe the mental rehearsal strategies that decision-makers sometimes use to test whether they need to adapt their intended course of action to the requirements of their current situation (Lipshitz et al., 2001).

The many strands of the naturalistic approach to decision making share some common features. Perhaps the most important is the one already discussed—its grounding in the thinking and action of practitioners making real on-the-job decisions. A second common feature is that decision making is conceptualized as a process of pattern matching rather than choice making. If a situation is recognized as of type S, then A is done because experience suggests that is what is appropriate for situations of that type. Since prototypes and schemas are the cognitive product of prior learning and experience, the explanation of decision making and problem solving requires investigation of the particularities of how a situation has been understood and how that understanding has produced the action taken. Generic accounts, as in CDM, of the scope of the search for alternatives and the thoroughness of their evaluation do not address the knowledge and meanings that shape the perceptual processes that produce a particular course of action. Finally, in naturalistic accounts of decision making, descriptive and normative research are closely connected. Accounts of how experienced practitioners make decisions constrain the normative models and tools that are being developed to improve decision making.

The debates between adherents of CDM and NDM approaches indicate unresolved issues about the methodological rigor of NDM research and its approach to the quality of decision processes and outcomes (Roelofsma, 2001). We will have some more to say on these matters in the subsequent introduction to PBM.

A Fit for Purpose Model of Problem Solving and Decision Making

In this section, we describe an approach to the explanation and evaluation of problem solving that has its origins in the constraint inclusion account of problem solving of the philosopher of science Thomas Nickles (1981, 1988). In his paper, "What Is a Problem That We May Solve It?" he defines a problem as a "demand that a goal be achieved, plus constraints on the manner in which it is achieved" (1981, p. 111). Nickles argues that problems arise through demands that they be solved and that, without such demands, a problem does not exist. For example, even though an elementary school may have 50% of its children performing at below-age-related benchmarks in reading comprehension, it does not have a problem unless there is a demand, from either inside or outside the school, that something is done about it.

Constraints are conditions that define what counts as an acceptable solution to the problem. They constrain in the sense that they rule out solutions that would otherwise be acceptable. Constraints on any given solution could include relevant values and beliefs, material conditions such as resource levels, and other practices with which any proposed solution must articulate.

The constraints on the solution may or may not be explicitly formulated. In social contexts like the reading example introduced above, constraints are likely to become clear during staff discussion of the issue. Teachers may argue that any new approach must be more effective than what has already been tried, supported by a dedicated literary coach, strongly focused on reading comprehension, and involve parents. In addition, teachers may insist that any new initiative must not add unduly to staff stress levels. Notice that these five constraints do not identify the solution itself—they specify the conditions that an acceptable solution must meet to some extent. Constraints are not obstacles to be overcome but conditions that enable problem solving, for, without them, an infinite number of solutions are possible. The more numerous and specific the constraints set on the solution, the narrower the space in which to search, and the more well structured the problem becomes.

Problems are solved by discovering or designing practices that adequately integrate the constraints that have been set on the solution. The more tension between the various constraints, the more difficult it is to find a solution that satisfies the principles that underlie all the constraints. There may be a considerable tension in our hypothetical example between the requirement to reduce teacher stress, involve parents, and do something that is effective. If too much weight is given to the stress constraint, it may be hard to satisfy the effectiveness and the parent involvement requirements. On the other hand, if too much weight is given to parent involvement, staff might react defensively rather than be open about learning more effective literacy teaching practices.

The example clearly illustrates how practical problem solving (and decision making) is a holistic process of trying to satisfy multiple, frequently conflicting requirements. In Nickles' terms, one seeks to satisfy an interacting set of constraints, rather than a single goal. While one could claim that improved reading comprehension is the goal, that is not the only consideration in formulating an adequate solution. The problem-solving process is not a means-end calculation about the relative probability of different literacy programs delivering better comprehension. While this information should be taken into account, the leader also needs to take teacher stress and cynicism seriously because, without teacher commitment, she will not be able to implement any new reading strategy. If models of problem solving are to have utility and validity they need to address the challenge of weighting and integrating multiple conflicting solution requirements.

The combination of actions taken, the constraint set that explains those actions, and the intended and unintended consequences of those actions, constitutes a theory of action for a particular problem (Argyris & Schön, 1974, 1996). By treating problem solving as theory formulation, one can inquire into the conceptual structure of a problem by probing the thinking and emotions that explain why one particular solution was preferred over other obvious alternatives. In addition, this account of problem solving enables us to address the question of the adequacy of a problem solution, and it is to that question we turn next.

Evaluating Problem Solving

An account of problem solving that is useful for the improvement of practice must address the critical question of how to evaluate the quality of the process and outcome of problem solving. While constraint sets provide the standards against which solution alternatives are evaluated for any particular problem, meta-level evaluative criteria are needed to adjudicate between competing theories of action. Four such criteria are used in PBM: accuracy, effectiveness, coherence, and improvability (Robinson, 1993, 1998).

Theories of action contain many empirical claims—hence the importance of accuracy. In the reading example, such claims include the reading comprehension levels of students, perceptions of the level of teacher stress, and their willingness to commit to another attempt to improve reading. Checking the accuracy of such claims is critical to the quality of problem solving, as inaccurate claims can shape constraint formulation and integration in ways that rule out solutions that would be otherwise admissible. If, for example, the administrator did not directly check the level of stress experienced by her teachers, she could over- or underestimate the weighting she needed to give this constraint and thus not satisfy her desire to find a reading strategy that did not unduly stress her staff.

The second effectiveness criterion asks whether the theory of action achieves what was intended from the point of view of the practitioners. Information about consequences is particularly critical to this evaluation as it enables discernment of the extent to which actual consequences actually match those intended.

The coherence criterion brings an evaluative stance that steps outside the self-referential constraints, including goals, set by the problem-solvers themselves. One of the limitations of goal-based evaluation is that it excludes critique of goals (Mark, Henry, & Julnes, 2000; Scriven, 2001). Even though particular solutions may sufficiently satisfy the constraints set on the solution, the constraint set may be limited by omission of an important consideration or by inappropriate weighting. This would normally be argued on the basis that the practices employed to solve one problem make it harder to solve other problems that are within the responsibility of those involved in the situation. Too much weight on teacher stress, for example, may contribute to a teacher culture in which adult needs come to take precedence over those of the students.

The fourth criterion of theory adequacy, improvability, is important because the uncertainty and complexity of practical problems, plus the need to adapt constraints to changing conditions, means that theories of action need to be open to revision (Argyris, 1976b; Argyris & Schön, 1996). This standard evaluates the extent to which the theory includes processes of inquiry and evaluation, such as the collection of evidence and review cycles, so key assumptions in the theory can be tested. Does, for example, the school's solution include feedback loops that enable learning about not only whether the theory is effective in its own terms (single loop learning), but also whether key constraints have been appropriately weighted or whether additional ones need to be included (double-loop learning) (Argyris, 1976a)? An improvable theory of action includes planning, review, and feedback processes that question the reasoning that underpins the theory.

Using PBM to Explain Curriculum Decision Making

In this section, we outline how we used PBM to infer and evaluate the theories of action involved in the introduction of a new curriculum in a large urban single-sex high school. We describe the actions taken by key decision-makers and then identify the constraints sets that explain those actions and their intended and unintended consequences.

Setting and Context

This case documents the adoption and implementation of a curriculum innovation in a New Zealand school located in a wealthy urban area. The focus of this study is on a curriculum intervention in Years 7 and 8 (students aged approximately 11 and 12) called Integrative Curriculum (IC). IC is an interdisciplinary approach to curriculum planning. Instead of planning the curriculum in terms of traditional subjects such as math, science, and English, it is organized into thematic topics, which may draw on elements of all three through a thematic unit on a topic such as natural disasters. The term IC is sometimes used interchangeably with curriculum integration (Vars, 1991; Vars & Beane, 2000). What distinguishes IC from curriculum integration is the method of structuring the curriculum around the personal and global concerns of students (Brazee & Capelluti, 1995) framed in questions such as, "What would happen to where I live in a natural disaster?"

IC was adopted at Silver School during 2007. Prior to that time, the school had already adopted the Reggio Emilia (RE) approach for the Years 1–4 levels. This is relevant to the study because the senior manager who made the decision to adopt IC did so because of IC's resonance with her deeply held commitment to RE as a curriculum model. RE is a philosophy of education for early childhood education (ages 0–6) originating from the northern Italian town of Reggio Emilia. RE principles include teachers learning alongside the children and responding to their interests and questions (New, 2007). IC was implemented as the curriculum model for teaching English and social sciences in Years 7 and 8. The subjects formally known as social studies and English were merged and became known as "topic" or "integrative study" and the curriculum was derived from the questions and concerns of students. Years 5 and 6 retained a traditional approach to curriculum planning as the curriculum leader in that area of the school held strong beliefs about curriculum, and her student achievement data were excellent.

In New Zealand, the national curriculum is largely conceptual and allows much freedom and flexibility. Schools are actively encouraged to interpret and plan to suit their particular learners and contexts. A recent Education Review Office report (the agency charged with school inspection in New Zealand) commented that, "every school's curriculum should be a unique and responsive blueprint of what they and their community consider is important and desirable for students to learn" (Education Review Office, 2012, p. 3). The Education Review Office's position is indicative of the educational environment in New Zealand, where self-managing schools are expected to take advantage of the flexibility offered to them by developing their own way of implementing the curriculum. The relative freedom with which schools in New Zealand are able to make decisions on curriculum design makes it all the more important to understand how these decisions are made. In such an environment, improving decision-making processes can have a direct and positive effect on student outcomes.

Method

The design and analysis of the case study is underpinned by PBM, which provides a data collection framework and a method for evaluating the case. We sought to answer three research questions. Each question was linked to a component of the theory of action practitioners developed to solve the problem of selecting and implementing IC as a curriculum innovation.

- What factors explain the adoption of IC?
- What explains how IC was implemented?
- How adequate are their theories of action for adoption and implementation?

The first and second research questions seek to reveal the constraints that explain the adoption and implementation of IC. The last question is evaluative and is designed to appraise the adequacy of the entire theory of action. Each research question and its connection to a component of the theories of action provided direction for designing the research. The collection methods for gathering data about each component are identified in Table 6.1.

TABLE 6.1 The Relationship Between Research Questions and Research Design

Research Questions	Requirements for Research Design	Data Collection Methods
What factors explain the adoption of IC?	A description of IC (definition from the literature review)	Interviews with two senior managers (responsible for Years 1–8) and 7 teachers (teaching in the Years 7–8 area)
	A description of how IC was adopted (actions)	Examination of school documentation
	Inquiry into and discovery of the factors that led to the adoption of IC (constraints)	
What explains how IC was implemented?	A description of IC (definition from the literature review)	Classroom observations of five teachers to observe IC in practice
	A description of how IC was implemented (actions)	Meeting observation
	Inquiry into and discovery of the factors that affected the implementation of IC (constraints)	Examination of school documentation
		Interviews with two senior managers and seven teachers
How adequate are their theories of action for adoption and implementation?	Identification of consequences of the theory of action	Interviews with three senior managers about consequences and evaluating IC
	A full and accurate constraint set by which to judge if the theory of action achieved what was intended	Student data analysis and discussion of student data with senior managers
	Proposed additional constraints	Established from all of the above data collection methods and data analysis
	Knowledge of the participants' interest in feedback about their theory of action and its consequences	Established from the literature review
		e.g., student achievement data
		Gathered from the feedback to key participants of the initial findings

Establishing an accurate account of practitioners' theories of action presents a methodological challenge because interviewees are frequently unaware of the constraints on their actions. A number of steps were taken during data collection and analysis to ensure the accuracy of our accounts of others' theories of action. For example, although our interview of one senior manager suggested that the decision to adopt IC was made by her alone, we needed to confirm her account by cross-checking it with the accounts given by those teachers charged with implementation. Our interviews of teachers about the adoption of IC confirmed that they were not involved in the decision and helped us to understand why this had happened.

Repeated probe questions, framed around the links between possible constraints and actions, were critical to understanding the relevant theories in action. In an effort to reduce confirmation bias, disconfirming evidence was sought and alternative explanations were explicitly considered. The process was iterative as we tested the validity of each constraint against the evidence, utilizing what Evers and Wu (2006) call "inference to the best explanation" (p. 315). Where there was conflicting information, or the data were unclear, a variety of possible explanations were explored to establish which one had the strongest evidence. Vague constraints were eliminated or made more specific to ensure they actually served to explain the actions.

As the findings emerged, they were represented on one-page diagrams showing the links between constraints, actions, and consequences. The diagrams, representing our accounts of others' theories in use, were checked with those whose reasoning and action they purported to describe in a series of member checks (Robinson, 1993). Often, that was a disconcerting process for the participants as the researchers highlighted possible constraints that they had not nominated. Through careful and open examination of the evidence, the authors were able to establish the validity of each component and whether there was any evidence for changing the content or weighting of constraints.

Findings

The findings are summarized as three theories of action relating to senior managers' adoption and implementation of IC, and teachers' implementation of IC in their classrooms. The actions box in Figure 6.1 summarizes how the decision to adopt IC was made by the senior manager in charge of Years 1–8 at Silver School.

IC was adopted subsequent to the appointment of a new teacher who had raised the idea of IC at her job interview. The senior manager held strong beliefs about the effectiveness of RE, and when she heard about IC from the new teacher, her response was, "Of course, this fits with our approach anyway, it fits with Reggio."

The senior manager made no link between the adoption of IC and solving any problems relating to student boredom. Concerns about student engagement were raised but only by a few teachers and they were never put forward as a rationale for adopting any curriculum changes. Having made the decision to adopt IC, the senior manager was faced with solving the problem of how to get teachers to

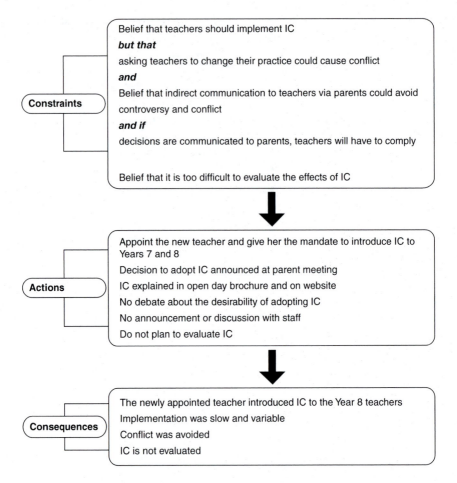

FIGURE 6.1 In Use Theory of Action for Adopting Integrative Curriculum

implement the approach. Figure 6.2 outlines the constraints driving the decisions she made about how to do this.

The belief that conflict should be avoided seemed to pervade all the actions taken by the senior managers and acted as a powerful constraint on their practice. This was particularly evident in senior managers' indirect communication to teachers regarding the decision to adopt IC. One senior manager described a "meet-the-teacher" evening for parents as a key method for getting information across to teachers about, "What I would expect to be seeing in classrooms." The other senior manager verified this approach of communicating with teachers via publications and events for parents. When asked about how the expectation to implement IC was communicated to teachers, she said:

It's in all our language. There is no other option. We don't do social studies and English and something or other else. Even putting it on our

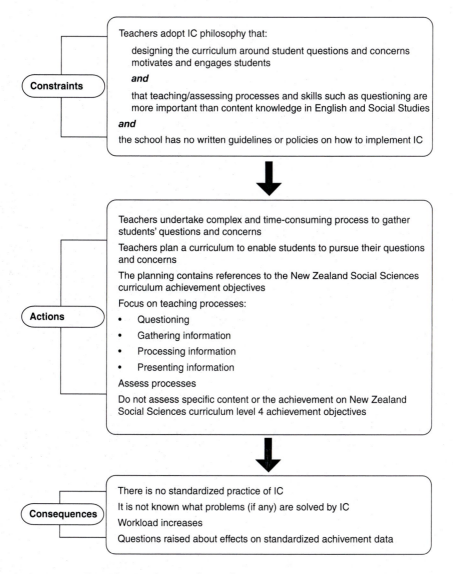

FIGURE 6.2 In Use Theory of Action for Implementing Integrative Curriculum (Senior Managers)

curriculum overview for the parents to read, we publish information about it. We talk about curriculum in the newsletters and the College Ties so the parents are getting information. And so, if the teacher isn't up with the play and the children are coming home saying, "Well, we're doing x, y, z in our class," but they're doing much more interesting stuff—that sort of subtle pressure plays a big role in a place like this, huge role.

From her perspective as a manager, she felt that IC "just sort of crept in. It's one of those things that just sort of crept in and took over." A comment from one of the curriculum coordinators confirms this description: "I don't ever remember a session where all the Years 7 and 8 teachers were sat down and said [*sic*], this is the way we want to move forward because . . . No, it was a lot more subtle than that."

The senior managers' actions had consequences for the teachers and affected how they experienced the adoption and implementation of IC. Figure 6.3 summarizes how the teachers made sense of IC and how they translated their understanding into their classroom practice.

The absence of any written guidelines resulted in varying teacher understanding of IC, which in turn affected their practice. The key contrast between the IC and more traditional methods of planning the curriculum is that the IC approach

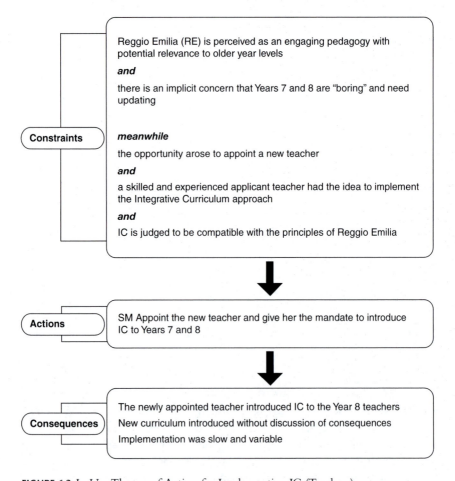

Constraints

Reggio Emilia (RE) is perceived as an engaging pedagogy with potential relevance to older year levels

and

there is an implicit concern that Years 7 and 8 are "boring" and need updating

meanwhile

the opportunity arose to appoint a new teacher

and

a skilled and experienced applicant teacher had the idea to implement the Integrative Curriculum approach

and

IC is judged to be compatible with the principles of Reggio Emilia

Actions

SM Appoint the new teacher and give her the mandate to introduce IC to Years 7 and 8

Consequences

The newly appointed teacher introduced IC to the Year 8 teachers

New curriculum introduced without discussion of consequences

Implementation was slow and variable

FIGURE 6.3 In Use Theory of Action for Implementing IC (Teachers)

allows for exploration of students' ideas and concerns. Instead of defining and assessing key ideas that students should understand, the IC approach involved assessing the processes that students used to explore their questions and concerns. Many teachers embraced IC, believing that increased student engagement is a result of its implementation. However, recent value-added analyses of student learning across math, English, and science have begun to raise questions about the effects of IC on Years 7 and 8 achievement. Although the relationship between the introduction of IC and the recent, largely downward, trend in achievement in these subjects may be correlational rather than causal, there is reason to examine the efficacy of the approach in this context.

Theory Evaluation

All three theories of action (the senior managers' theories of adoption and implementation and the teachers' theory of implementation) were judged to be effective because they achieved what they intended to achieve. IC was adopted and implemented with minimal conflict.

Where the three theories fall short of the criteria provided by PBM is in their lack of coherence and improvability. The decision to adopt IC and the teachers' methods of implementation could have caused negative unintended consequences for students, but the extent of these effects is unknown because the impact of IC on achievement or engagement was not evaluated. The decision to adopt IC was made unilaterally and without consideration of its merits in comparison with alternative curriculum models. As the teachers solved the problem of how to implement IC, they were guided by the belief that processes of inquiry are more important than content knowledge. We found no evidence that that belief was subject to any critical scrutiny either before or after the decision to adopt IC.

The remaining criterion for judging the adequacy of theories of action poses the question as to whether they are improvable. For a theory to be improvable it must be evaluated, which means that a connection needs to be made between a problem and IC as the solution. The task of evaluating IC and its effects on student engagement and achievement is made much harder by the lack of any identified desired outcomes prior to implementation. In the absence of criteria proposed by the practitioners, we propose that any curriculum intervention should be evaluated first and foremost in terms of its effects on student achievement. Engagement is also an important factor and these two aims should not be seen as mutually exclusive. The implementation of IC at Silver School has not been reviewed, largely because both senior managers and teachers at Silver School saw IC as too complex to be able to measure its effects. While the difficulty of evaluating the efficacy of IC is discussed in the IC literature (Bahr, Bahr, & Keogh, 2005; Gehrke, 1998), such complexity should not prevent a school from learning how to examine the intended and unintended consequences of its introduction. At present, none of the theories of action are improvable because problems are not discussed as they arise, and the assumptions and beliefs driving practice are not tested.

Discussion

This case study of curriculum change at Silver School offers an explanation of the decision to adopt a new curriculum for Years 7 and 8 that bears little relationship to the models offered by CDM. Only one alternative was considered by the senior manager and no information about its probable consequences was sought because it was recognized as akin to a pedagogical approach with which she already had considerable positive experience. IC became a solution to the hitherto unrecognized problem, at least in the public sense, of how to spread the RE approach and increase the engagement of students. While the RE prototype drove the adoption decision, the conflict avoidance prototype best explains the implementation process. The conflict avoidance constraint was weighted so heavily that no announcement was made to teachers, there was no staff discussion and no written guidelines were provided.

PBM enabled us to reveal these constraint sets despite their implicit and taken for granted nature. Repeated probe questions, constantly anchored in observed or unobserved actions, combined with careful cross-checking and disclosure of initial analyses, were essential to enable us to get beyond rationalization and closer to the reasoning that explained actions. We came to understand the particularities of these decisions, by which we mean how particular understandings, interests, and emotions shaped both the actions that were taken and those that were avoided. It is this detailed field work, designed to detect how a pattern of constraints shaped problem solutions, that links PBM most closely to the NDM tradition. PBM adds to that tradition by linking it to the constraint inclusion account of problems and the idea of problem solving through the formulation of a theory of action.

Some critics of NDM have criticized its reliance on experts for its normative benchmark for judging decision quality (Roelofsma, 2001). We would agree that a normative account is needed that is independent of the reputation of particular decision-makers. That is why PBM includes the four criteria of theory adequacy we have outlined. We prefer to speak of the adequacy of theories of action rather than of error, for the latter notion invites a focus on the decision outcome rather than on the relationship between the outcome and the reasoning that produced it. While we are critical of the decision to adopt the IC curriculum and could agree that it constitutes an error, since it was made without any consideration of evidence of its efficacy, we are much more critical of the theory of action that produced this decision. While the beliefs that IC cannot be evaluated and that conflict must be avoided remain, a theory of action that affects a dozen teachers and hundreds of students cannot be publicly examined or improved.

There are important implications of this work for the preparation of school administrators. The current texts on administrator decision making and problem solving present a variety of rational approaches to problem solving and decision making and are silent about the challenges that have come from NDM. The most popular of such texts presents six different versions of decision making (Hoy &Tarter, 2008) and a contingency table that guides decision-makers about when to use which one. It advises, however that, in contexts of uncertainty, "administrators must settle for a satisfactory decision rather than the best one. Thus, satisficing is the strategy of choice for most rational administrative decisions" (Hoy & Tarter, 2008, p. 86). As far as we are aware, there is no empirical evidence of the distinctiveness of these models. Indeed, a recent factor analysis of administrator responses to a questionnaire that was based on the Hoy and Tarter models showed that a single factor, which the authors called leadership, accounted for most of the variance in the data (Denig, Polka, Litchka, Calzi, & Brigano, 2011). Thus, the construct validity of the Hoy and Tarter models of decision making has yet to be established. Rather than a complex contingent approach to decision making that is mismatched to features of human cognition and emotion, we advocate that administrators learn about theories of action, constraints, and the tools that enable them to reveal, evaluate, and progressively improve the theories of action that determine individual and organizational problem solving.

Finally, we note the strong role of emotions in the three theories of action employed in the adoption and implementation of IC at Silver School. This constraint was so strongly weighted that it ruled out the very practices required for collaborative and critical examination of curriculum decisions. Our evidence, along with dozens of empirical examples reported by Argyris (1990), supports the call of Lakomski and Evers (2010) for inclusion of emotions in accounts of problem solving and decision making. We also agree, as suggested by these authors, that emotional reactions should be treated as a kind of early warning system to prompt reconsideration of initial plans. We are concerned, however, that using negative emotional cues as signals to avoid certain courses of action could severely limit the epistemically progressive problem-solving trajectory that Lakomski and Evers advocate. Such avoidance led to unilateral and unexamined curriculum change at Silver College and will continue to produce self-sealing theories of action, until a nondefensive and open-minded examination of the causes of the negative emotion are publicly discussable (Argyris, 1990). The avoidance of actions associated with negative emotions is protective in the short term but can also be a major barrier to high quality individual and organizational problem solving. Administrators need the skills to examine the cause of their anxiety and to reframe the situation so their cognitions and actions are not controlled by their emotional history. Some of the educational tools for such reframing are available in the work of Argyris (1990) and NDM researchers (Klein, 2008).

References

Argyris, C. (1976a). Single-loop and double-loop models in research on decision-making. *Administrative Science Quarterly, 21*(3), 363–375.

Argyris, C. (1976b). Theories of action that inhibit individual learning. *American Psychologist, 31*(9), 638–654.

Argyris, C. (1990). *Overcoming organizational defenses: Facilitating organizational learning.* Boston, MA: Allyn and Bacon.

Argyris, C., & Schön, D. (1974). *Theory in practice: Increasing professional effectiveness.* San Francisco, CA: Jossey-Bass.

Argyris, C., & Schön, D. (1996). *Organizational learning II: Theory, method and practice,* Reading, UK: Addison Wesley.

Bahr, N., Bahr, M., & Keogh, J. (2005). Interdisciplinarity vs. disciplinarity: Developing knowledge for problem-solving in middle years of schooling. Paper presented at The Australian Curriculum Studies Association Biennial Conference: Blurring the boundaries, sharpening the focus, University of Sunshine Coast, Queensland, September 2005.

Brazee, E., & Capelluti, J. (1995). *Dissolving boundaries toward an integrative curriculum,* Columbus, OH: National Middle School Association.

Denig, S. J., Polka, W. S., Litchka, P. R., Calzi, F. F, & Brigano, M. O. (2011). Problem-solving and decision-making: The ongoing influence of Wayne Hoy. In M. F. DiPaola & P. B. Forsyth (Eds.), *Leading research in educational administration: A festschrift for Wayne K. Hoy* (pp. 147–161), Charlotte, NC: Information Age Publishing.

Education Review Office. (2012). *The New Zealand curriculum principles: Foundations for curriculum decision-making.* Education Evaluation Reports. Wellington, NZ: Education Review Office.

Evers, C. W., & Wu, E. H. (2006). On generalising from single case studies: Epistemological reflections. *Journal of Philosophy of Education, 40*(4), 511–526.

Gehrke, N. J. (1998). A look at curriculum integration from the bridge. *Curriculum Journal, 2*(9), 247–260.

Hoy, W. K., & Tarter, C. J. (2008). *Administrators solving the problems of practice* (3rd ed.). Boston, MA: Pearson.

Klein, G. (2008). Naturalistic decision-making. *Human Factors, 50*(3), 456–460.

Lakomski, G., & Evers, C. W. (2010). Passionate rationalism: The role of emotion in decision-making. *Journal of Educational Administration, 48*(4), 438–450.

Lipshitz, R., Klein, G., Orasanu, J., & Salas, E. (2001). Taking stock of naturalistic decision-making, *Journal of Behavioral Decision-making, 14*(5), 331–352.

Mann, L. (2001). Naturalistic decision-making: Still finding its way. *Journal of Behavioral Decision-making, 14*(5), 375–377.

Mark, M. M., Henry, G. Y., & Julnes, G. (2000). *Evaluation: An integrated framework for understanding, guiding, and improving policies and programs.* San Francisco, CA: Jossey Bass.

Meso, P., Troutt, M. D., & Rudnicka, J. (2002). A review of naturalistic decision-making research with some implications for knowledge management. *Journal of Knowledge Management, 6*(1), 63–73.

New, R. S. (2007). Reggio Emilia as cultural activity theory in practice. *Theory into Practice, 46*(1), 5–13.

Newell, A., & Simon, H. A. (1972) *Human problem-solving.* New York, NY: Prentice Hall.

Nickles, T. (1981). What is a problem that we may solve it? *Synthese, 47*(1), 85–118.

Nickles, T. (1988). Questioning and problems in philosophy of science: Problem-solving versus directly truth-seeking epistemologies. In M. Meyer (Ed.), *Questions and questioning* (pp. 43–67). Berlin, Germany: Walter de Gruyter.

Rasmussen, J. (1997). Merging paradigms: Decision-making, management, and cognitive control. In R. Flin, E. Sala, M. Strub, & L. Martin (Eds.), *Decision-making under stress: Emerging themes and applications* (pp. 67–84). Aldershot, UK: Ashgate.

Robinson, V. M. J. (1993). *Problem-based methodology: Research for the improvement of practice.* Oxford, UK: Pergamon Press.

Robinson, V. M. J. (1998). Methodology and the research-practice gap. *Educational Researcher, 27*(1), 17–26.

Roelofsma, P. H. M. P. (2001). Evaluating ten years of naturalistic decision-making: Welcome back in the lab! *Journal of Behavioral Decision-making, 14*(5), 377–379.

Scriven, M. (2001). Goal-free evaluation theories. In E. R. House (Ed.), *School evaluation: The politics and process* (pp. 319–328). Berkeley, CA: McCutchan.

Simon, H. (1973). The structure of ill-structured problems. *Artificial Intelligence, 4*(1), 181–201.

Sternberg, R. J., & Horvarth, J. A. (1995). A prototype view of expert teaching. *Educational Researcher, 24*(6), 9–17.

Vars, G. F. (1991). Integrated curriculum in historical perspective. *Educational Leadership, 49*(2), 14–15.

Vars, G. F., & Beane, J. A. (2000). Integrative curriculum in a standards-based world. *ERIC Digest* (ERIC Document Reproduction Service No. ED 441 618).

7

REVISIONING DECISION MAKING IN EDUCATIONAL LEADERSHIP

Peter P. Grimmett

Introduction

Decision making in such settings involves a strong commitment to understanding the role that myths, rituals, and ceremonies play in an organization, how they are used to envelope the mission and purpose at the heart of the school's culture, and how remystification is used to affirm and revision a desirable, normative professional culture. Hence, while experience in teaching and decision making will be valued and regarded as central to education, it will not be seen as sufficient; rather, experience will be purposefully examined to understand its complexities and nuances. Such understanding will be mediated through discourse in a manner in which decision-makers attend to how they frame its events and conditions. Leaders will thus study the specifics of context to focus on how meanings and a sense of agency are culturally constructed through language in social settings. In this way, they can avoid the trap of monolithic understanding to focus on how our beliefs and values influence the decisions we make, all of which need to be grounded in principle and embedded in policy.

Revisioning Decision Making in Educational Leadership

Whenever one writes about decision making in educational leadership, there is always good and bad news. The good news is that all schools are enmeshed in politics that affect teaching and learning. The bad news is that leaders need to have the aptitude and capability to transform the potential negativity and sometimes toxicity of such politics into a positive pedagogical force. How one can embrace politics in a manner that transforms educators' actions into a positive force for good is what I want to address in this chapter.

This chapter is written with a basic premise, namely, that in decision making, leaders always act on a theoretical basis. By theory I do not mean an abstract framework that somehow has to be applied rationalistically to practice; rather, I mean the deeply held understandings that both drive and lie hidden in every practice that must be searched for and grasped. If we are to revision decision making in educational leadership, then, we need to become aware of the theoretical frames that undergird the decisions and the choices we are making.

My colleagues and I (Grimmett, Dagenais, D'Amico, Jacquet, & Ilieva, 2008) recently concluded a major cross-Canada study looking at the impact of education policy on conditions of teaching and learning in schools. We found contrasting discourses at work in the teachers and principals that we interviewed and observed. On the one hand, there was a strong *political* discourse about the policy changes and how they constrained what educators could do in their work in classrooms and schools. On the other hand, there was an equally powerful *pedagogical* discourse that emphasized ways of working professionally to bring about optimal learning conditions within the parameters of the new policies.

The apparent contradictions in educators' discussions about the conditions of their work, particularly their contrasting reports of feeling satisfied with their working environment, yet worried about issues related to workload and recognition, can be viewed as different discourses that emerge at a deep level of practice. These discourses express conflicting emotions about teaching and teachers' identity struggles in a context of rapid policy changes. We found that there were two distinct discourses, the political and the professional, at work in the minds of teachers in Greater Vancouver. The political discourse was framed around a partisan response to policy changes and takes on trappings of despair. The professional discourse focused on engagement in satisfying educational activities.

Political Discourse: Emotional Despair

At one level, educators viewed the policy changes affecting their workload and professional recognition with suspicion. This suspicion translated into a discourse of despair about the lack of resources and support contributing to the impossibility of being effective in their work as professional educators. But this discourse seemed at the time to correspond more to rhetoric and likely constituted a political reaction to what educators perceived as the intention behind the policy changes.

When educators in British Columbia perceived changes affecting schooling as emanating from New Right government policies, they tended to engage a partisan reaction that bred a political discourse bordering on apparent despair. The basis of this despair was a fear that what has happened elsewhere in the Anglophone world (in the United States, the United Kingdom, and Australia, etc.) might come to British Columbia. This may or may not be true.

While the trends in other education systems might not have been prevalent in British Columbia, local educators did know about them. This knowledge contributed to creating a discourse of despair among educators that was essentially a form of political resistance to the changes taking place locally. At the same time, educators also engaged in a parallel professional discourse that was markedly different from the political and was not apparent in other jurisdictions.

Professional Discourse: Emotional Satisfaction

At another level, educators were positive about their school environment and the challenge and independence of their work. This translated to a discourse of satisfaction on the rewarding aspects of their professional activities, such as the relationships established with colleagues in schools and the stimulating nature of their daily work. This discourse centered on action that falls within the limits of educators' locus of control. In a context of increased policy changes, fragmentation, difficult conditions, and the disruption of professional identities, it may be that the discourse of satisfaction served as a counter-text to the discourse of despair. By idealizing the local workplace, they were discursively positioning themselves and their work in a more positive light. This discursive practice might even have served to manage negative trends and reconcile them to their situation for it reminded them—and others—that, notwithstanding the policy agendas and the way they might have been constructed by the media and the public, the core of their work centered around curriculum, learning, and relationships, and it was meaningful and rewarding for a number of reasons. The frame of reference for this discourse of satisfaction was more local as it focused on pedagogical actions and relationships at the level of the school.

What Did We Make of These Contrasting Discourses?

A survey conducted by the British Columbia Teachers' Federation in 2001 identified multiple sources of stress in teachers' work life (Naylor, 2001). Three key areas of stress were (1) increasing difficulty and complexity of teaching and relating to students; (2) the volume of work during a teacher's day; and (3) lack of time, resources, support, and respect. The report concluded that teachers in British Columbia experience high workload stress with its many negative effects that need to be addressed through collective bargaining.

While the Grimmett et al. (2008) study confirmed these findings, it also proffered a different conclusion. It suggested that, whereas teachers were very aware of outside pressures and policy changes to the point of engaging in a frequently partisan critique of those changes through a political discourse, they nevertheless tempered that critique with a professional discourse that was shaped by pedagogical concerns in the local context. This concern with the local classroom context enabled them to focus their energies on constructing their sense of professional identity and pedagogical expertise. Whereas the former discourse had trappings of despair, the latter contained glimpses of hope.

Our 2004–2006 data led us to speculate that the professional discourse was currently untouched by the political, but we did not know whether or not such a trend would hold over time. I personally now believe that there are instances in 2013 that indicate that the pedagogical is no longer untouched by the political, something I find deeply disturbing.

Theorizing the Prioritizing of Pedagogy Over Politics in School Cultures

Let me introduce to you, then, a theoretical basis on which administrators can act as leaders in these situations to transform the political into a positive pedagogical force.

Recently, my personal circumstances have provided me a unique opportunity to learn a good deal about cancer. Each cancer tumor has its own context. Each context is different. Some cancer tumors, because of their context, are treated by chemotherapy. Other cancer tumors, because they don't respond in females to hormones, are treated not by chemotherapy, but only by radiation. Yet, with other tumors where the context is so different and the cancer so aggressive, the treatment involves chemotherapy, radiation, surgery, and the works. And the scourge for women is that breast cancer is becoming more and more prolific as time goes on. But this is the aspect I have found so indelibly impressive. Within each cancer context, a tumor normally and surprisingly comprises both cancerous and immune cells. The latter are there to battle the former. However, in some tumor contexts, these immune cells lose their way and become deceived. Thus, instead of fighting the growth cells that are cancerous, they become dysfunctional and actually, and mystifyingly, work to help them grow. Cancer researchers do not know how or why this happens, and the one thing they are trying to fathom is how to get the immune cells to revert to their original immunological function.

I think this is analogous to leadership and decision making in the public school system. I am not here suggesting that politics is a cancer; rather, I am suggesting that we need to find a key that unlocks the positive power of politics to revert it to its original function of serving pedagogy. When politics trumps pedagogy, we have dysfunctional schools, making our jobs as educational leaders extremely difficult and tempting us to think the system is broken. But when politics serve pedagogy, we find that teachers are responsibly accountable and students engage in assiduous study. How, then, do we fathom how we can address this situation so that we can right the potential imbalance in the system. Specifically, how do educational leaders engage in the kind of decision making that nurtures a culture that encourages teachers to be responsibly accountable and students to engage in assiduous study?

Study as the Site of Education

I want to add an aside here, because I think that a good deal of the emphasis on learning is misplaced. Recently, I came across Pinar's (2006) *The Synoptic Text Today and Other Essays: Curriculum Development After the Reconceptualization*. It contains a seminal idea that sheds light on responsible curriculum making, in a manner that nourished and invisibly repaired my mind.[1] "Study [not learning] is the site of education" (Pinar, 2006, p. 120). We acquire knowledge and insight through the struggle of study for which every individual has the capacity, though not necessarily the will. Teaching and learning may disseminate knowledge, but study enables understanding. Study arises not from compliance with instructions but from an aspiration to understand the shifting vicissitudes between self and circumstances. Here, Pinar is rectifying Tyler's distorted emphasis on learning technology.

As Pinar declaims, "Not instruction, not learning, but study constitutes the process of education" (2006, p. 112). Study, then, is central to self-formation. Self-formation arises from our appropriation of what is around us in the world; study builds our capacity for making choices, for developing focus, for exercising critical judgment that is so central to a well-formed character. I maintain that the absence of seeing school subject matter as a living culture, as distinct from a set of works to be received could be explained by the fact that our conception of education is not guided by curriculum theory. There is still far too much social engineering present. As Pinar says, "if only we make the right adjustments—in teaching, in learning, in assessment—it will hum, and transport us to our destination, the promised land of high test scores" (p. 109). The equivalent in music, for instance, is we will know the notes but not have musicality.

Tying learning to assessment and instruction creates, according to Pinar, two traps: (1) the intellectual trap that makes students dependent on teachers for learning, and (2) the political trap, that holds teachers entirely responsible for student learning (Pinar, 2006, p. 120). Equally, in leadership, when we bring teachers into innovative content and pedagogy using instrumentalist techniques, we place false expectations on teachers by introducing irresponsible curriculum designs.

Thus, Pinar's seminal idea about study's central place in education shows how current policy and practice in K–12 schooling and educational leadership violate the attainment of learning through its misplaced and instrumentalist direct focus on learning in and of itself. Here permit me to juxtapose learning with happiness. We all want to be happy in some shape or form, and I dare say that all students want to learn. But the direct pursuit of them makes their attainment elusive. In other words, to focus narrowly and directly on either learning or happiness is to miss out because both sneak up on us when we least expect it. Happiness occurs when we become absorbed in meaningful activities and relationships; likewise, learning occurs, as Dewey (1997) has said, as a by-product of meaningful activity, that is, when we embrace the hard work of wise study and eschew a vacuous focus on learning, so central to the current neoliberalist audit culture that reifies the Tylerian cage.

So, Where Does Pedagogy Fit With Study?

When we grapple with what it is that teachers need to do in order to nurture appropriate curriculum conditions that propel all students in differentiated ways toward assiduous focused study to expand their minds through the understanding of new ideas, we are enacting pedagogy. Pedagogy consists of teachers engaging in a complicated conversation about how their students' and their own subjectivities can be potentially reconstructed through activities framed around the subject matter content that is central to teaching. Dewey (1997) puts it like this:

> When the parent or teacher has provided the conditions which stimulate thinking and has taken a sympathetic attitude toward the activities of the learner by entering into a common or conjoint experience, all has been done which a second party can do to instigate learning . . . [When teachers] give the pupils something to do, not something to learn; and the doing is of such a nature as to demand thinking, or the intentional noting of connections; learning naturally results . . .
>
> (pp. 160, 154)

For Dewey, then, when teachers and educational leaders focus directly on learning (as the neoliberalist audit culture exogenously compels them to do), rather than on the conditions and intentional activities that foster learning, they miss the point of pedagogy and their students miss out on learning opportunities. As he says so trenchantly, "frontal attacks are even more wasteful in learning than in war" (p. 169). Hence, the aim of pedagogy is to foster student engagement, reflection, and experience through carefully thought-out activities that promote study. Nowhere is this more salient and appropriate than in the work that leaders do in schools.

What I am arguing for is for a conception of pedagogy in teaching that addresses the content *indirectly*. This goes beyond Pinar in claiming that, while the stimulus for thinking about educational activities always arises from the curriculum, the actual making or *design* of those activities in keeping with the curriculum aims and content is also an important focus in itself. And my claim is that this important focus constitutes pedagogy. In teaching, a more technical discourse of pedagogy constructs the world of institutional text, thereby determining what teachers *do*. I argue that, if we are interested in how and what school students learn and particularly keen to change the institutional context in which teachers learn to teach, then we need to understand how teachers create the educational activities that they use to enact the curriculum. Why is this important? It is important precisely because a pedagogical perspective enables the enactment of redirective practices when teachers do not fully integrate the curricular aims they are working toward with the activities they choose. Hence, a pedagogical focus differs from a curriculum one in that it encompasses both how teachers can address the curriculum indirectly and also how their practices can be redirected when they attempt a potentially disastrous "frontal attack" on learning, that is, ignoring meaningful activities, that often leads them into the instrumentalist trap. I consider these distinctions absolutely vital for educational leaders to understand their work.

My position, then, is that educational leaders and teachers need to live in the tension between curriculum understanding and curriculum enactment that I am calling pedagogy. Living in the tension involves not falling into the trap of aligning design with Tyler's rationalist cage, but rather understanding how inappropriate decisions around approaches to learning can be redirected to practices framed around study-promoting educational activities.

Premise

Hence, I want to argue in this chapter that most attempts at school reform, particularly those relating to leadership and educational decision making, have failed because they do not take account of how the principles, policies, and practices on which the reform is based frequently become co-opted and reframed by the micropolitics that exist in the local organizational setting. I want to examine this situation in order to suggest that effective decision making and educational leadership in organizational settings necessitate symbolic and cultural forms of leadership that use decision making and legal-rational power to *infuse the work of teaching with value, meaning, passion, and purpose.* Leaders are indeed invested with power. But it's power *for,* not power *over.* And the purpose of power *for* is to infuse the work of teachers with value-added meaning. Such forms of leadership relate closely with the development of an organizational culture that binds and bonds people together in professionally productive ways to promote conditions for students to study.

Making Teachers' Work Significant

Exercising leadership as infusing the work of teaching with value, meaning, passion, and purpose will engage us in examining the role that myths or stories play in the organizations we inhabit. Understanding how organizations are storied is a very powerful way of leading. For instance, when one goes into a school or a university department, as I did three years ago, particularly units that have had all sorts of inter-colleague difficulties, there are always deeply held stories that influence how people judge situations and hold a key to understanding what possibly determines their actions. A leader's job is not only to understand those stories, but also to engage in a process called "remystification." That is what leaders have to do to engage teachers, students, and parents in discussions about the mission, vision, and the purpose that are at the heart of any school culture. Not only do the mission, vision, and purpose define success—but also, and much more importantly, they define the school's significance. In today's world, we are frequently measured by our successes. I want to suggest a different way in which we need to be accountable. We need to be accountable for what is *significant* in what we do.

Let me give you an example. Educators teaching in a multicultural context make thousands of different curriculum and pedagogical decisions on a daily basis. And I am suggesting that how they actually deal with the multitudinous contextual variables they face in these situations is, for me, one of the significant aspects of what teachers do in today's public education system. We need to focus on how in the public system (where there is no selection, teachers must deal with students of all levels of aptitude and ability) we actually see a school's vision and purposes being worked out. This is a more rigorous and honest way of holding ourselves accountable by looking closely at the significance of what we do and, in so doing, examining the significance of the role of the school in society. For instance, we would look closely at the ways in which, in Canada, the policies of official bilingualism and multiculturalism get played out through our schools, which is an essential aspect of their significance to our country's culture. It seems to me that this form of accountability is much more important than how students potentially represent their knowledge on standardized tests.

Another aspect of examining the significance of what we do is to look at the relationships that teachers have with the various and diverse student groups in their classrooms, and the way in which they take their content and transform it to teach engaging concepts about, for instance, issues of social justice, issues of oppression, and issues of historical significance that affect our lives in today's world. This will involve leaders in encouraging teachers to work pedagogically in an inter-disciplinary way that does not neglect the rigors of the disciplines but uses discipline-based understandings to study real-world issues as cross-disciplinary problems.

For example, if in Canada we present the history of Louis Riel only from the dominant White colonialist perspective of the time, we do not only a disservice to students' understanding of history but also an offence to the large non-White and First Nations' people of Canada, thereby forfeiting a glorious opportunity to connect learning to important contemporary issues of social justice in our understanding of Canada's formation. Instead, we need to create opportunities for firsthand encounters with historical and current education policy documents that might inform students' understanding of the current multicultural context. Specifically, we could use artistic, musical, literary, mathematical, scientific, or social cultural documents in our teaching to help students learn how to relate and work more effectively with other persons whose cultural, racial, religious, and economic backgrounds are different from their own. That is, we could work toward cultivating a disposition toward encountering artistic, musical, literary, mathematical, scientific, or social cultural knowledge (e.g., in the form of archival documents and narratives) not only as artifacts from the past but also as something that makes ethical demands on us here and now.

Or in choral music when the composer has thrown in an *appoggiatura*—a type of ornamental grace note that clashes with the melody to create a dissonant sound—between the altos, tenors, and basses, and none of the voices wants to enter into the crunch for they fear the lack of consonance, thereby denying themselves and the piece a richness in its tonality and its harmony. These notes are mere semitones apart. For singers, it is very difficult to go there when they are singing, because it just does not feel natural, it does not feel right. Singers think the choral composer is forcing an unbearable form of musical tension on them, and the tendency is not to want to enter the crunch. However, when singers embrace the tension, they actually come to realize the beauty of the music. Similarly, when we are dealing with diversity, it is not enough to pronounce with manufactured normative authority, "Oh we have to embrace diversity." To students, it means nothing. But if teachers could understand the idea of diversity in terms of embracing the tension of something toward which they do not naturally lean and act like singers who want to recognize the depth and beauty that comes out of the choral manifestation of an *appoggiatura,* then the teaching of music provides an avenue that connects them pedagogically to why we need to embrace diversity in a multicultural society because it demonstrates that difference is, in fact, a very real strength. This, then, constitutes a wonderful opportunity to teach the benefits of embracing diversity for the richness that engaging with the "other" in honest, ethical ways brings to our lives.

My point here is that the work of teaching takes on significance when teachers go beyond teaching mere subject matter content to recognize the significance they achieve when they use that content to introduce students to the richness of the world in all its aspects. The significance of such work is that teachers are opening up students' eyes to an enlarged vista on the world, which suddenly becomes a very exciting place for them. And it becomes exciting because their teachers have infused their work with value, passion, and purpose; which teachers tend to do when they have educational leaders who know how to encourage such an approach. That is, they have come to understand the complex and delicate relationship that exists between values, beliefs, assumptions, and professional norms.

The Relationship Between Values, Beliefs, Assumptions, and Professional Norms

When educational leaders focus on infusing the work of teaching with value, passion, and purpose, they begin to grapple with questions such as:

*   What are values, beliefs, assumptions, and norms? How do they make up a school culture?
*   What role do myths and historical artifacts play in organizations?
*   How are mission and purpose at the heart of school culture? How do they define success? How do they define significance?

Schein's (2010) book, *Organizational Culture and Leadership,* set out to transform the abstract concept of culture into a tool that leaders could use first to map and then to shape the dynamics of organization and change. He defined culture in terms of the norms, values, behavior patterns, rituals, and traditions that pervade an organization as it grapples with how to adapt to external forces and to integrate its various component parts internally. As such, culture provides a form of structural stability because of its implied institutional patterns and integration that arise from the accumulated learning over time from shared myths and historical artifacts. It plays a vital role in the derivation and constitution of the organization's mission and purpose, which in turn determines how members define success and, more importantly, how they define the significance of their work. Culture is a hidden but powerful feature of an organization that leaders ignore at their cost. Either they understand its power, becoming acutely attuned to the way values, beliefs, sentiments, and norms covertly define what is acceptable organizational behavior, or their misfortunate obliviousness results in their leadership being seriously undermined by its subtle force. Leo and Wickenberg (2013) studied the role of principals in the derivation of school norms and found that professional norms are set when principals and teachers experience expectations from each other, from students, and from policy documents, concluding that the school principal plays a crucial role in norm-setting processes.

In pursuing questions about values, beliefs, and assumptions, educational leaders who are sensitively attuned to school culture also assume that they are dealing with people who are self-motivated and professional. Yet even self-motivated and professionally responsible people have to be governed. But they cannot be governed by fiat; leaders cannot successfully govern professionals in an enabling culture by unilaterally laying down explicit expectations or rules for their behavior. Responsible and self-motivated teachers are governed by professional norms. Norms are unwritten laws of practice that build over time in an institution to govern professional action. When norms emerge within a school, professional expectations around practice then flow not from the leader's dictate but from a principle-based policy context that is perceived as the co-construction of the present community's interaction with the institution's history and culture.

How does this happen? Let me share an example. This particular one involves a remystification and restructuring of something that we were already doing at Simon Fraser University (SFU). It comes from a time when I was helping a committee to bring about a revisioning of teacher education. Our intent was to integrate the idea of practice more deeply into the teacher education program in theoretically sensitive ways. We wanted the SFU teacher educators, both old and new, to understand that the program was not framed around a rationalistic theory-into-practice model (as some had interpreted it when their teaching was observed), nor an anticipatory-socialization model wherein teacher educators gave students answers to questions they had not yet confronted; rather, we wanted to emphasize that it constituted a social constructivist grappling with practice. Thus, we attempted to consolidate the place of practice as a central focus in the program but not in an a-theoretical way. Hence, we negotiated through the following assumptions that gradually changed the ways in which people acted, and which in turn changed the normative context within which professors and seconded teachers worked in the education of teachers:

- The role of experience in learning is central to education but it is not enough. Experience must be purposefully examined to understand its complexities and nuances. Understanding is mediated through discourse in which we attend to how we frame its events and conditions.
- Teaching is socially constructed. We must understand the specifics of context and how meanings and a sense of agency are culturally constructed through language in social settings.
- Education is complex, hence we avoid the trap of monolithic understanding to focus on how our beliefs and values influence the choices we make.
- When difficulties occur in learning and understanding is resisted we attempt to make sense of such detours with appropriately nuanced understandings of difference. No person is viewed as a deficit.

(Committee for the Re-Visioning of Teacher Education, 2007)

Although it took a long time for the committee to agree on the articulation of these assumptions about what we were doing in teacher education, the deliberative process itself was an important part of the remystification. Once we had concluded the process, it changed the way in which people began to think about their work. We had established that teaching is socially constructed. In other words, SFU teacher educators had agreed that it is important to understand both the specifics of context and how meanings and a sense of agency are culturally constructed and constrained through interpersonal interaction in social settings. We had also established the central place of practice in teacher education but with the corollary that practice and experience must always be purposefully examined to understand its complexities, and that such understanding is inevitably mediated through discourse wherein we focus closely on how we construct the events and conditions of experience and practice. Hence, we agreed to frame difficulties in learning as detours, asserting the principle that no person is to be viewed as a deficit.

This example thus shows how the deliberative process used in articulating these assumptions remystified in a generative way the meaning and purpose in which teacher educators continued to develop their sense of value and vision for the education of teachers. It amounted to a theorizing of practice that, in turn, connected with the existing body of theoretical knowledge that can be used to interpret teaching-learning situations that teachers typically face. How, then, do professional and cultural norms emerge in a school?

Theorizing the Emergence of Professional Norms

If we are to understand how norms are formed, then we need to look closely at the kind of sentiments that people hold about some of the interactions they have with their colleagues around specific activities. In 1995, I characterized this process by associating it with restructuring and reconceptualization:

> Back in 1950, George Homans documented how changes in activity structures produce ripple effects throughout the human group. These changes affect the nature of the interactions that take place, which, in turn, influences the sentiments that people derive from their work. And these sentiments typically take on a normative force, governing what people may or may not do. Using today's language, Homans would have said that restructuring inevitably leads to some form of reconceptualization. In other words, even blunt forms of restructuring (the kind that is used euphemistically to describe corporate-style firings) provokes people to think about their work in different, though not always innovative, ways. Although it is possible to restructure in an adventitious and ultimately dysfunctional manner, the process nevertheless brings about some form of rethinking. The question thus becomes not one of whether restructuring occurs without reconceptualization but whether the kind of reconceptualization that restructuring precipitates is appropriately rigorous and purposeful.
>
> (Grimmett, 1995, p. 204)

This puts a different slant on what we were attempting to do in the SFU example. In this characterization, we were using a process that was established to renew and restructure the teacher education program to bring about a reconceptualization derived from a careful examination of the program's principles and assumptions that undergirded its emerging practice. In so doing, we were addressing the relationship between assumptions and professional norms.

So why do leaders when they begin a position first meet informally with each member on an individual basis? Is it to create a good impression? Partially. But far more important is that it gives them an opportunity to trace the professional normative context in which they are expected to give leadership. Frequently, leaders map the context well but then commit a very common mistake. They come across a professional norm governing the practice of teachers in their school that they find undesirable and in need of change. Mistakenly, they then decide to send out a missive about the considered unacceptable professional behavior, stating strongly that this practice will cease and desist. Let me illustrate. In the early 1970s, I was a teacher in a school in which a new principal discovered that many of us teachers were coming in at 7:00a.m. in the morning and staying at school until about 6:00 or 7:00p.m. in the evening, while a few others were arriving just before the bell at 8:30a.m., and when the bell went at 3:30p.m., they were disappearing very quickly. He understood the disgruntlement of those of us who chafed at the lack of professional commitment (a tendency to "coast" to retirement) on the part of some of our older colleagues, so he decided to act. He sent out an administrative memorandum stating that this professional practice was unacceptable in his school; moreover, he added that, in future, all teachers must be present in school at least 30 minutes before the first bell and must not leave school until 30 minutes after the final afternoon bell. Guess what happened! Everyone (myself included) began arriving at 8:00A.M. and leaving at 4:00P.M., whereas previously most of us had been arriving far earlier and staying much later. The principal had meant well. He wanted to challenge and change the professional norm by addressing it directly, but in the process of creating what he thought of as a floor for professional practice, he created a ceiling. Before, he had about 80% of his teachers who were working phenomenally long hours and doing magnificently productive work. Yet, because he attempted to hit the norm head on, his action produced the opposite effect. And one of the things that I have learned over the many years I've been in education (I started my first job teaching in 1967) is that if you make the mistake of hitting an unacceptable norm head on, it has the opposite effect to what you desire. That is because the people who are working extremely hard and typically comply with appropriate norms are struck by fear when leaders unilaterally define acceptable professional practice, and those for whom the desired change is required always find ways of getting around a dictate from above.

How then can leaders change unacceptable norms without unwittingly producing the opposite effect of reinforcing them? As in pedagogy where, for teachers, "frontal attacks are even more wasteful in learning than in war" (Dewey, 1997, p. 169), educational leaders need to understand the folly of hitting the norm head on, because it frequently guarantees the opposite effect. The key is to come at changing the norms *indirectly*. This approach takes time; but it is a case of where going slower amounts to making faster progress, as distinct from "more haste, less speed." First, leaders change the activities. This produces different interactions among the personnel involved. The close connection between activities and human interaction is key here. The changed activity affects the nature of the interactions. That is the beginning of the ripple effect throughout the human group that Homans (1950) theorized. Leaders continually nurture the environment in which teachers do their work so that the changed human interactions around different activities have a positive effect on the sentiments that they derive from and about their work. And these sentiments typically take on a normative force over time, governing what people may or may not do as professionals. The aim, of course, is to produce positive sentiments among teachers about their work and the school environment that eventually over time become norms that constrain their professional action and behavior. It is a slow but steady process, typically taking about at least two years to change the normative context of a school.

This approach is consistent with what I was saying about learning. We live in a current age where the norm of learning successes are so important to the neo-liberalist policy-makers that, in matters of pedagogy, they insist on teachers hitting that norm of "learning" head on. And what they apparently do not to understand is that they are actually achieving the opposite of the success they crave. But if educational leaders encourage teachers to work through the activity of study and the interactions that occur around it (often with parents and with colleagues, students), we then find that the sentiments derived from such a pursuit, particularly if the ones thus nurtured are positive, eventually turn out to change the norms as they affect student engagement with content. While this may be a strangely simple way of looking at things, we must not be deceived by its simplicity. It is very, very profound and hugely complex undertaking that is deeply anchored in the assumptions we make. Hence, what educational leaders assume about teachers and what teachers assume about students is very important to nurturing significance in the work we do in schools.

Another way of nurturing a more appropriate normative context in schools is to practice what the late Ted Aoki (2005/1986) called "public pedagogy." In my own institutional context, I took over a fractious department three years ago and set out to turn it into one of the best academic units of its kind in North America. But I could not state it so directly because, coming as a statement from the head, it would lack the normative power to be convincing and compel appropriate action. I have had to come at it indirectly. Hence, I tell stories, stories that are embedded in myths and poetry that open up generative discussion about what is important. An example of this comes from my practice of sending an encouraging email to all members on the first day of every term. Recently, I sent the following email on January 1, 2012:

Colleagues,

Happy New Year to you all!

Although some of us were back at work yesterday, today represents the first day of classes for this new term and I want to welcome you back and to wish you all a most productive and fulfilling year in 2012. As a unit, we will be engaging this term in setting strategic direction for the department for the next four years or so. But, although the official rhetoric calls that process "strategic planning," I would prefer us to think of it as engaging in a complicated conversation (as befits a department of curriculum and pedagogy) about examining Department of Curriculum and Pedagogy's past to consider our future as we mobilize the present. I'll be sharing specific details of the process in ten days or so but I want you to understand that the intention is not to make this an add-on activity; rather, we will use an hour in each of the three department meetings (January, February, and March) to begin that conversation. The aim is to produce a sketch of possibilities that could serve as a framework for a retreat in May that would enable us to deliberate on our priorities and direction for the next four years or so. As I said, more details will follow in about ten days.

In the meantime, you may take time to read one of Tolstoy's stories titled "Three Questions." This is a story that I use to keep myself grounded and present (but not presentist) in the important work we do as educators. It goes as follows:

> One day a king decides that, henceforth, he would never fail at anything if only he could get an answer to three questions: *What are the most important things to do in life? When is the right time to undertake them? and Who are the right (and wrong) people to deal with in so doing?* He promised a large reward to any person who could provide him answers. But the learned people who came to him from far and wide offered conflicting advice, which confused and annoyed the king and so he heeded none of it. Instead, he disguised himself as a peasant and went into the woods to visit an old hermit renowned for his insight. He found the hermit digging a garden. Noticing the man's frailty and fatigue, the king took over the digging. He dug for hours. All the while the hermit said nothing in reply to his questions. Suddenly, just as the sun was setting, an injured man staggered out of the forest. He had been stabbed in the stomach. The king tended his wound and carried him into the hermit's hut. After settling him in, the tired king fell deep asleep. The next morning he awoke to find the now healing stranger gazing at him intently. The man confessed he had been lying in ambush to kill the king for injuries to his family the king's men had inflicted years before. The man had waited and waited in the woods, but the king never returned from the hermit. When he went looking for him, he stumbled on the king's soldiers, who recognized him and wounded him before he got away. The man begged for reconciliation, which the king was happy to grant. Finally, before taking his leave, the king once more asked the hermit his three questions. The hermit, bent over while sowing seeds, looked up at him. "You have already been answered," he said calmly. The king was dumbfounded. The hermit continued:

> Had you not taken pity on my weakness yesterday and dug these beds for me, instead of turning back alone, that fellow would have assaulted you, and you would have regretted not staying with me. Therefore, the most important time was when you were digging the beds; I was the most important man; and the most important pursuit was to do good to me. And later when the man came running to us, the most important time was when you were taking care of him, for if you had not bound up his wound, he would have died without having made peace with you; therefore he was the most important man, and what you did for him was the most important deed. Remember then: there is only one important time—*Now.* And it is important because it is the only time we have dominion over

ourselves; and the most important man [sic] is *he* [sic] *with whom you are,* for no one can know whether or not he will ever have dealings with any other man [sic]; and the most important pursuit is *to do good to him* [sic], since it is for that purpose alone that man [sic] was sent into this life.

(Grimmett, 1997, pp. 460–461, emphasis in original)

I would only add that to enjoy the "now" fully, we have to appreciate how our past has formed us. My hope is that we can now engage in a complicated conversation as a form of respectful dialogue that examines our past as a department to arrive at an understanding of which things we need to conserve and which ones we need to move beyond as we embrace the uncharted terrain of the future together.

I wish you all a happy new year.

Peter

The purpose of leaders practicing public pedagogy is to nurture a positive normative context by symbolically embedding messages of significance and hope in poetry and story. The above message was about the need to be very clear about what we are doing as a community and why the work that we do is important. The subtext is that, when we understand the importance of our work and do it well, we excel in a manner that makes others sit up and take note. But it also notes the requirement for us to understand how the past has shaped us, and not to see historical lore as something to be denied, but something to be investigated and brought into the present and sometimes re-storied. In some rare but specific instances, we may have to remystify the history, particularly when members have been at each other's throats, as it were, and not known how to act with rigorous and respectful collegiality. Thus, this cultural form of leadership aims supportively to motivate and inspire teachers by enunciating the kind of symbolic messages that provoke questioning and discussion about the normative context and priorities governing the work of schools. In this way, leaders are signaling the importance of the organization's cultural roots, while continually infusing value, purpose, meaning, and direction into the work of teaching.

A further example of public pedagogy I have practiced in nurturing an enabling culture comes from sharing a quotation and a poem by Homer and a poem by Dante. The Homer quotation I used is in the *Odyssey*: "Oars are wings that make ships fly" (Homer, 1980, 11, 138–149, 800B). The purpose is to generate discussion about how oars can become wings that make ships fly; that is, to fathom what can act as catalysts in nurturing a community of educators that is both rigorous in its tasks and respectful in its relationships. The discussion usually gets us into a distinction between reflexivity and reflection. Reflexivity is where the reflection is turned inward and we look then at how consistent we are in our own actions and decisions with the things we say we stand for and value. Sometimes it becomes a case of learning to let the oars go so that we can discover other possibilities in making the ships fly, that is, other ways in making communities sing.

The poem reflects the darkness experienced by Dante:

> Just halfway through this journey of our life
> I re-awoke to find myself inside
> A dark wood, way off course, the right road lost.
> How difficult a task it is to tell
> What this wild, harsh, forbidding wood was like
> The merest thought of which brings back my fear;
> For only death exceeds its bitterness.
> But I found goodness there.
>   (Dante, 1888, Canto 1, 1–8)

Despite the dark experience, Dante found goodness there. I used the poem to generate discussion about having an experience like being trapped in a dark wood, where one feels particularly vulnerable and exposed, facing a challenge toward which one does not warm but nevertheless has to dig deep in one's inner resources to overcome and move on. This specific form of public pedagogy is particularly suited to organizations that have become somewhat destabilized, whose culture is dysfunctional. It enables them to face the darkness they are experiencing as a group while also challenging them to plumb the depths of their problems to articulate how they "found goodness there," how they have been able to transform a difficult situation into a gift.

I have faced this over the last year in my personal circumstances. For almost a year from August 2012, I have been severely tested by the unexpected onset of cancer in my soul mate. But I am now at the point where I can see that even cancer is a gift, because nothing sharpens your priorities than the knowledge at how evanescent life actually is. And leaders must live in the moment, as well as strategize for the future. And the decisions that leaders make are always in the moment. We always have to take account of the past, and project in a strategic way for the future. But we must always be present in the moment. Sometimes the moments we experience in educational leadership are very difficult. But a leader who practices symbolic, cultural leadership will find ways of transforming immense difficulties into gifts, into opportunities. How one deals with values, beliefs, norms, rituals, ceremonies, organizational history, stories, organizational lore, informal networks, and organizational symbols is absolutely paramount in its importance because decisions around these key factors often determine the success and significance of educational leadership.

Conclusion

Recently, I came across this poem by Ken Gire about a dream dancer that sums up what I have been saying about educational leaders revisioning their decision making:

> Stop then
> from the staid and somber line.
> Move out in dancing
> into dreams so daring;
> without them you will settle for the road
> that wanders by and winds to nowhere.
>
>   (Gire, 1996, p. 154)

In 2008, I was crossing a divided highway in Australia with an American colleague who had lived there for some time. As we got to the median, I looked right and began to step out. Abruptly, my colleague grabbed me, hauling me back to the median, just in time for a car that was speeding from the left to miss me. I was looking the wrong way! Those of us involved in the public school system need to look another way. We need to turn politics on its head by making it subservient to pedagogy. We need to use our decision making to *infuse the work of teaching with value, meaning, passion, and purpose* by nurturing an organizational culture of strong professional norms that binds and bonds people together in pedagogically productive ways. As educational leaders, we need to move out into visions of pedagogical leadership so daring that, without them, we will settle for the uninspiringly staid road that wanders by and winds to nowhere!

Note

1. See my article on this theme in the forthcoming *Journal of Action, Criticism, and Theory for Music Education* (2014, in press).

References

Aoki, T. T. (2005/1986). Teaching as indwelling between two worlds. In W. F. Pinar & R. L. Irwin (Eds.), *Curriculum in a new key: The collected works of Ted T. Aoki* (pp. 159–165). Mahwah, NJ: Erlbaum.

Committee for the Re-Visioning of Teacher Education at Simon Fraser University. (2007, November). Report to the Faculty forum. Burnaby, BC, Canada: Simon Fraser University.

Dante, A. (1888). *Inferno* (transl. by Henry Wadsworth Longfellow). London, UK: George Bell.

Dewey, J. (1997). *Democracy and education: An introduction to the philosophy of education.* New York, NY: Free Press.

Gire, K. (1996). *Windows of the soul.* Grand Rapids, MI: Zondervan.

Grimmett, P. P. (1995). Reconceptualizing teacher education: Preparing teachers for revitalized schools. In M. F. Wideen & P. P. Grimmett (Eds.), *Changing times in teacher education: Restructuring or reconceptualizing?* (pp. 202–225). London, UK: Falmer Press.

Grimmett, P. P. (1997). A search for hope in teaching and teacher education during changing times. *American Journal of Education, 105*(4), 458–477.

Grimmett, P. P. (In press, 2014). Help me if you can, I'm feeling down: The best lack all conviction while the worst are full of passionate intensity. *Journal of Action, Criticism, and Theory for Music Education, 13*(2).

Grimmett, P. P., Dagenais, D., D'Amico, L., Jacquet, M., & Ilieva, R. (2008, published online, June 7, 2007). The contrasting discourses of educators in Vancouver, Canada. *Journal of Educational Change, 9*(2), 101–121. Retrieved from www.springerlink.com/content/j24 8x577r1489436/?p=d4f7f22e429c4700b8b0da9676b718f5&pi=0

Homans, G. (1950). *The human group.* London, UK: Routledge & Kegan Paul.

Homer. (1980). *Odyssey* (transl. by Walter Shewring). Oxford, UK: Oxford University Press.

Leo, U., & Wickenberg, P. (2013). Professional norms in school leadership: Change efforts in implementation of education for sustainable development. *Journal of Educational Change,* 14(4), 403–422.

Naylor, C. (2001). What do British Columbia teachers consider to be the most significant aspects of workload and stress in their work? Analysis of qualititative data from the BCTF Worklife of Teachers Survey Series, 1: Workload and Stress [Research report]. Vancouver, Canada: BCTF. Retrieved from https://www.bctf.ca/publications/ResearchReports.aspx?id=5570

Pinar, W. F. (2006). *The synoptic text today and other essays: Curriculum development after the reconceptualization.* New York, NY: Peter Lang.

Schein, E. H. (2010). *Organizational culture and leadership.* San Francisco, CA: Jossey-Bass.

8

PRINCIPALS' PERCEPTIONS ABOUT RESISTANCE TO IMPLEMENTING MAJOR DECISION FOR CHANGES

Karen Starr

Introduction

Decision making is inextricably linked to change with major decisions incurring significant modification and adjustment in their implementation. Research evidence suggests, however, that schools are slow to transform, that many individuals are resistant to implementing major change, and that school reforms are often cursory or short lived. Principals are pivotal players in decision making for major educational reform, and governments hold them accountable for leading and managing significant change for school improvement (Hargreaves & Fink, 2006). The stakes are rising for principals to produce measurable improvements, while disincentives for failure are also heightening. This chapter discusses the experiences of Australian principals implementing major decisions in the context of rapid structural and policy reform—a critical issue because performance appraisal is tied to measureable change for school improvement.

Despite the proliferation of literature on the topic, the processes of decision making and change are still shrouded in mystery since obstacles and set backs are the norm (Grey, 2005). It is not easy for organizations of any kind to change, but schools have particular characteristics that militate against implementing decisions for major change (Evans, 1996; Hargreaves & Fink, 2006). The enormous complexity of schools, their numerous stakeholders with competing interests and conflicting ideologies, constant policy change and political intervention, unfavorable media commentary, an increasingly diverse student population, and the messy quotidian of expected and unexpected events makes implementing major change difficult. These difficulties are exacerbated in the context of ongoing educational restructuring and reform (Beck, 1999).

Nearly all reforms and restructuring efforts by Australian governments over the past two decades have been second order in intent (see Cuban, 1988; Watzlawick,

Weakland, & Fisch, 1974), with mandated, externally imposed reforms often being extrinsic to a school's self-determined decisions for change and competing with or contradicting other reforms (Packer, 2001). Second order change refers to transformational exercises such as organizational restructuring, curriculum or pedagogical reform, or fundamental shifts in goals, beliefs, values, cultures, and procedures, entailing radical departures from usual practice. In comparison, first order change modifies or adjusts existing practices without significant alteration (Cuban, 1988).

Recently, educational researchers have investigated the political behaviors and activities behind decision implementation processes in schools (see, for example, Blase, 2005). To date, however, there has been little research about these processes in Australian schools or of the experiences and perceptions of principals. Hence this chapter takes a "behind-the-scenes" look at what actually happens in schools undergoing major change, focusing on principals' experiences of resistance to reform decisions and their perceptions about the catalysts for opposition in the context of rapid policy reform. Since the implementation of major decisions nearly always fail in schools (Sarason, 1990), exploration as to why this is the case is important when successful change is a professional imperative. This chapter particularly focuses on exploring how resistance to renewal is recursively linked with broader principles and issues related to neoliberal restructuring and reform within the global economy (Smyth, 2006). It closes with suggestions for future research and leadership practice.

Resistance to Change

Resistance is a common theme in research about schools implementing major change, but usage of the word is much contested. Micro-political activity intensifies during periods of major change, making decision implementation efforts both complex and messy (Blase, 2005). Blase (1991) defines micro politics as "the use of formal and informal power by individuals and groups to achieve their goals in organizations" (p. 11). Micro-political structures and activities involve both convergent and divergent processes, with resistance encapsulating the latter. As the word is most commonly used, resistance usually refers to "negative" actions and nonaction, ill will and resentment, and defensive or confrontational dispositions. For example, Jermier, Knights, and Nord (1994) define resistance as "a reactive process where agents embedded in power relations oppose initiatives by other agents" (p. 9). The authors argue that resistance stems from desires to challenge, disrupt, and/or overturn organizational practices, discourses, and power relations. Similarly, Bordo (1993) defines resistance as "all behaviours, events and social formations that challenge or disrupt prevailing power relations and the norms that sustain and reproduce them" (p. 199).

Follett (in Graham, 1995), Watson (1982), and Evans (1996) argue, however, that it is human nature to resist change if the individuals who have to implement change decisions and live with their effects are not involved in its creation. Major change requires implementers giving up feelings of comfort, long-held values or beliefs, and established routines. It entails new thinking, extra time, and effort (Strebel, 2006). For sanity and safety's sake, individuals try to retain comfort and quell confusion through practicing caution, constraint, and subversion, thus protecting the status quo (Barth, 2007).

Abelson (1995) augments these views by suggesting that individuals are defined by their strongest beliefs as much as they are by their most valued possessions, so when major decisions challenge attitudes, values, or assumptions, they become a threat to identity, making resistance inevitable. Self-interest motivates everyone (Machiavelli, 1998), hence reforms perceived as being disadvantageous to an individual or group are construed as threats to be contested (Shapiro, Lewicki, & Devine, 1995).

Rogers (1995), recognized for his work on the diffusion of innovation, argues that homophilous organizational systems such as schools (with staff from similar backgrounds achieving cultural convergence through adherence to norms and values), are those where change implementation is more likely to be met with skepticism and suspicion. Further, Rogers's bell curve of adoption responses suggests that the most resistant group—"laggards"—represent approximately 16% of the population. Rogers has his critics, however, who point to problems with post facto definitions and suggestions that individuals (or organizations) fall into one particular change adoption category irrespective of context (e.g., de Jager, 2005).

There are further criticisms about the notion of "resistance to change," with some rejecting implicit hegemonic, hierarchically biased assumptions about virtuous, holistic, visionary leaders advocating change in contention with myopic and self-interested opponents who disrupt achievement of organizational goals (e.g., Ball, 1987; Blase, 1990; Dent & Goldberg, 1999; Higgs, 2009; Merron, 1993). Resistance is derived from various intentions and motivations, not all of which are bad (e.g., Foy, 1985; Lawrence, 1954; Mawhinney, 1999; Piderit, 2000). Resistance to change could be motivated by desires to reform, shift, critique, or ignore change intentions (Thomson, 2008). For example, some researchers (e.g., Smyth, 2006) seek to stimulate overt dissent in light of "the diseased reasoning behind the corruption of our educational institutions" (p. 302) as a principled stance. From such a perspective common, negative conceptions of resistance marginalize employees and foreclose comprehensiveness in decision making for change. Similarly, compliance may be coerced or the result of self-interest or cowardice due to the high stakes consequences of noncompliance, especially within the principalship. Compliance might disguise what is really going on, with external change mandates being heavily mediated and altered, especially by principals as the gatekeepers of decision-making agendas (Thomson, 2008). Questions about the drivers of change and the interests they serve can easily be ignored, stripping initiatives of their implicit values, political imperatives and processes.

There are criticisms that failure to probe the roots of resistance necessarily elides "taboo" subjects, thereby skewing change data (Gabriel, 1999). Others argue that the micro politics of power and agency are commonly overlooked in research on decision making for major change (Follett in Graham, 1995; Blase, 2005), as are the possible benefits of attitudinal ambivalence (Piderit, 2000).

Hence, the concept of resistance is complex, and oversimplifying arguments via an "obedient or disobedient" (Piderit, 2000) dichotomy is unhelpful. Perhaps a compliance/simulation/resistance conception comes nearer the mark (Thomson, 2008), but it would still not fully capture the range of political complexities that are at play. Suffice to say, resistance may not be a negative or "bad" thing—depending on one's perspective. Here the stance of Krantz (1999) is accepted, which concedes there are deleterious conceptions of resistance, but acknowledges the predictable political phenomenon of opposition to change as worthy of legitimate research without resort to instruments of irrational "blame and self-idealization" (p. 44).

This chapter and the research from which it emanates focuses on school principals only, so in light of the above discussion, it is important to note that the views of other stakeholders are not canvassed. As principals are powerful social actors in the dynamics of school decision-making and change processes, this must be born in mind. Resistance may take particular forms in specific contexts, where the principal's own behaviors and use of positional power in decision making have an impact on the reactions of others, as would the dominant culture and ethos of the school. Hence, others involved in the implementation of major decisions may contradict the principals' comments in this chapter.

The Research

The data emerged from a three-year study into the learning requirements of school principals. Both newly appointed and very experienced principals from across Australia were interviewed to explore each group's perceptions about the essential learning required to conduct their role successfully. It was assumed that inexperienced principals would be able to recollect recent "steep learning curves" they had encountered in their new role, while experienced principals would possess wisdom from long experience. Principals from all levels of schooling, all schooling sectors (government, Catholic, independent), and metropolitan and rural locations were involved. Data collection occurred through intensive, semistructured interviews with one hundred principals (some conducted face-to-face and others via telephone), and through discussions recorded as field notes. Forty-one respondents were in the first two years of the principalship; others had been in the role from eight to twenty-eight years. The research investigated all aspects of the role, but this chapter refers specifically to experiences and perceptions about implementing major decisions for change.

The research was an exercise in grounded theory building (Glaser & Strauss, 1967). In this approach, theory emerges from the data through an inductive process whereby emerging research insights are analyzed and continually tested, producing further evidence and/or new theoretical insights (Corbin & Strauss, 2008). Grounded theory building supports examination of individual standpoints within complex and interconnected contexts and considers the inextricability of the macro, meso, and micro. Real life experience is taken as a starting point that connects individual agents corporeally and emotionally to the structural, the social, and the historical. In other words, large-scale social structures affect tangible realities that are inseparable from contextualized practice or from the historicity of the period (Ball, 1994). In this case, for example, micro-level experience is where the effects of power are sensed and resistance instigated, with school-based experience being influenced by local, systemic, national, or global decisions and events. Hence the iterative processes of developing claims and interpretations within a grounded theory approach is responsive to research situations and the multiple layers of meaning produced by the people in them (Gray, 2009).

Following is a distillation of principals' discussions about the forms of resistance to implementing change they encountered in schools and their perceptions about its causes. Their views are recorded under headings that encapsulate the main themes that emerged from interviews. The sorts of decisions for major changes that principals mentioned included curriculum reforms, school restructurings and amalgamations, the introduction of new pedagogies or technologies, a reshuffling of senior staff roles and titles, preparation of a radically different industrial agreement with staff, policy revisions (e.g., the staff performance appraisal policy), and the sweeping transformation of a school timetable.

Forms of "Resistance" Experienced and Perceptions About Causes

Without exception, all principals viewed implementing major decisions as a complex and situated process emanating from their desire or need to solve problems or make improvements. All principals experienced many forms of opposition when initiating major change, no matter where the school or how long they had been in the job. No one cited a problem-free second-order change process (Cuban, 1988).

Principals' perceptions about the motivations behind change resistance reveal two main underlying drives: to block the goals behind major decisions and to undermine the authority of key change agents. The individuals that principals mostly categorized as resistors were described as "loud" and "self-righteous" people who often claimed authority as spokespeople for others (see Holland, 2010). From principals' experiences, resistance behaviors all fell into the negative, "bad" conceptions of the word. Every principal described resistance to major decisions for change in derogatory terms with the most obdurate resistors being constructed as troublemakers or "difficult" people.

Resistance to implementing major decisions, as principals discussed it, covered a spectrum of behaviors from the aggressive and violent to the defensive, passive, or silent. The most distressing stories concerned illegal activities: One principal received death threats and was living with 24-hour security protection. A few had personal property vandalized; others experienced professional sabotage (e.g., papers stolen or files destroyed). Some stories concerned blows to professional identity, for example, staff in one school delivered a vote of no confidence in the principal to the governing council, while another principal confronted heated delegations of staff and parents demanding reversal of a major decision. Most principals had experienced undermining through exclusion, being aware of clandestine caucusing going on behind their backs (see Burns, 1961), or the withholding of information. Bad behaviors included temper tantrums and physical outbursts such as door slamming. Interviewees also cited behaviors such as "nit-picking" whereby dissidents tried to find fault in the principal's actions or words, demanded precise information even before detailed planning had commenced (see Alvesson & Sveningsson, 2003), or demanded answers to difficult questions designed to embarrass them in public. Principals reported being the subject of slanderous rumors or disingenuous remarks, experiencing "back-stabbing," "white-anting," or receiving anonymous letters and blackmail. Principals had come to accept negative behavior as an unpleasant but expected aspect of the principalship, as the following comment suggests:

> . . . the "anti-principal" gossip is designed to discredit you personally and professionally, but it's hard to know how to stop it. You hope your results speak for themselves. . . . Confronting enemies seldom improves relationships, but you can't ignore bad behaviour. It's nasty and nerve wrecking, but it's part of the job.
>
> (Principal, South Australia)

The micro politics of implementing change were often reported in combative terms; a "battle of wills," "a blood sport," "a fight to the death," being "stabbed in the back." Principals were troubled by extremely irrational and destructive behaviors from "difficult" people; the "bulldogs," "anarchists," "trouble-makers," "the old guard" (suggesting age-related resistance), the "thorn in my side," "workplace psychopaths," "swamp-dwellers," "swashbucklers," "doomsayers"—those seen to hold up change processes and a school's progress and waste vast amounts of principals' time. The following quotations reveal principals' experiences:

> No matter how much I do, how thorough . . . or convincing the argument, whether we have any choice in the matter or not . . . change upsets the apple cart. Some . . . dig their heels in . . . stress goes up and down the line . . . tempers fray . . . there's rudeness or professional inertia so things won't get done. The atmosphere's unpleasant . . . The bigger the change, the greater the resistance.
>
> (Principal, Western Australia)

> There's a high price to pay . . . at every turn 'doomsayers' defend the status
> quo . . . The longer I'm in the job, the more rapid [is] the change and the
> higher [are] the expectations. It never gets any easier.
>
> (Principal, South Australia)

Principals suggested that destructive resistance behaviors are often dressed up as
professionalism being performed in the best interests of students and the school.
One principal said:

> It's self-interest . . . They're holding the school back . . . It's a game . . . to
> make you jump through hoops and stymie progress. If it was really about
> the kids, they'd be all for change.
>
> (Principal, Queensland)

There are times, however, when oppositional "group speak" is unsuccessful
and resistors are found to represent only a handful of staff, even when their tumult
creates a far bigger impression. Several spoke about the "silent majority" of staff
whose opinions can be relied upon to come to the fore to enable the implementation of major decisions to occur:

> There's always the wisdom of the silent majority. Sometimes you feel embattled
> but eventually you find most staff are actually on your side and support change.
>
> (Principal, Victoria)

> Opponents can be loud but often they're a minority.
>
> (Principal, South Australia)

> Staff voting is confidential here. Nobody has to justify their preference. . . .
> A ballot in favor of change doesn't stop resistance but it helps.
>
> (Principal, Victoria)

One of the most difficult situations occurs when factionalism and divisions
appear within a staff. Then there is more at stake for those holding strong views
one way or another and the sense of common purpose or collective vision can
evaporate. As one principal put it:

> Insurgents become more defiant and rebellious . . . [it's] safety in num-
> bers . . . but a splinter-group situation spells disaster because people are
> *deliberately* working at cross-purposes and whatever you're trying to do, fails.
>
> (Principal, New South Wales)

Staff resistance was viewed as misguided and a nuisance by principals if accompanied by unprofessional behaviors, whereas people demonstrating courtesy were

accorded more respect. In other words, principals' perceptions of resistance often concerned how people went about it. This is interesting, especially when many principals also spoke openly about their own opposition to particular policy interventions or accountability procedures.[1] The principals in this study saw that open resistance on their part would yield highly negative results (such as having professional repercussions—see, for example, Grattan, Tomazin, & Harrison, 2008).

Principals in their first appointment and experienced principals working in a new school experienced the severest forms of resistance to change (see also Duke & Salmonowicz, 2010). In comparison, long-standing principals cited fewer major difficulties the longer their tenure. This indicates that school communities may experience difficulty in coming to terms with a new leader, new ideas, and an unfamiliar modus operandi whereas, over time, a respected leader's views and processes become known "and don't frighten the horses as much" (Principal, Victoria). Principals also cited their initial years in schools as those in which the most radical reform programs are undertaken, which may also explain this phenomenon. However "if you fail to win the hearts and minds of staff over time, change won't happen" (Principal, New South Wales).

While many common perceptions and experiences were recounted in this research, the data revealed some notable differences. First, large schools exert more resistance forces against change than smaller schools, which may be understandable given their larger numbers of people. However, small school principals complain that having less assistance in their role from deputies, assistant principals, and business managers makes for very difficult times when dealing with change resistance. In these cases, principals cited resorting to confiding in other small school principals (see for example, Starr & White, 2008) or to seeking professional support through regional education offices or mentors. Second, the nature of the change itself affects outcomes. Generally, the greater the change, the greater the resistance to it. Third, the longer the principal has been in the role, the more confident he or she appears to be about the major change processes and outcomes. While they appear to have learned to expect the worst, they understand it's a wave to ride that will eventually subside. Experienced principals unanimously saw resistance as part of the change territory, although initial experiences often make way for periods of greater equilibrium when the change decision has been implemented for a period of time. Some comments reveal a learned patience on the part of experienced principals:

> I've learnt that even the worst initial upheavals calm down eventually—and there've been times when the opponents of change come to see the change was an improvement. I had one woman really concerned about us changing where we had the book room that she operated. She created no end of opposition. The union intervened and we had to send her on courses and stick to the times she had always worked. . . . In the end she was much happier and all the fuss was for nothing. You get a few experiences like this over

the years, which helps you put it all in perspective. It's rare that disruption lasts forever.

(Male secondary principal, Victoria)

The more you make changes, the more you learn two things. First, change rarely brings out the best in some people who like things the way they are—so you expect some agitation. And second, if the change has been a good one, as the dust settles, the people settle down and in the best of all worlds, you think it's all been worthwhile.

(Male principal, Preparatory to Year 12 school, Victoria)

Principals had many explanations about the causes of resistance, although the three most commonly expressed grounds concerned widespread disenchantment about policy directives and the rapidity of decision mandates brought about through neoliberal reform and restructuring; a negative cathexis associated with leadership and leaders, including gendered cathexis; and a growing culture of complaint, protest, and litigation. These are discussed in turn below.

The Effects of Unpopular Policy and Procedure

External policy intervention and increasingly complicated workloads are viewed as the most significant causes of teacher dissatisfaction and antagonism against implementing change (see also Fink & Stoll, 2005). Rapid policy and political change has created a work culture that is fast moving, demanding, and stressful. Dissensus is heightened and goal achievement is reduced as coercive "power over" influences collide with "power with" or cooperative political aspirations in schools (Ball, 1987; Blase, 2005). The nonparticipation of school-based educators in policy formulation fuels resilience to renewal (Starr, 2009; Yap & Chrispeels, 2004). The principals perceived that work overload and uninspiring compliance and accountability requirements exacerbate resistance behaviors. Some believed teachers feel a lack of support, appreciation, trust, and loyalty from employing bodies, (a feeling not entirely absent in the principalship), which explains why some work against rather than with principals who are leading change. Principals suggested that too many externally imposed changes in policy and practice were seen as unnecessary and interfered with school-based decisions for change that were far more important to students, learning, and teaching. For example:

Teachers would say the best thing the [Education] Department could do is leave us alone. Seriously, they're getting in the way. Teachers are sick of it—they feel their professional judgment is totally undermined. "Just let us get on with the job" sums up the general mood.

(Principal, Victoria)

> Let teachers teach! That's the issue . . . Another policy arrives and they just groan and dig their heels in.
>
> (Principal, Victoria)

Principals were more understanding of resistance to externally imposed change than they were to changes devised through decisions made at the local level to deal with internal problems, but that adds to change dilemmas. Given the rapidity of change and the short-lived nature of many educational policies, long-standing teachers are often custodians of stories about the unintended, unanticipated, negative consequences or side effects of change (Evans, 1996). Policy changes are viewed as cyclical—they've "seen it all before," "tried it and it didn't work"— producing cynicism and disengagement. Grey (2005, p. 97) sums up thus:

> New techniques are announced with a great fanfare, and presented as the unproblematic solution to previous problems, but disillusion soon sets in . . . the everyday experience of people in organizations is that one change programme gives way to another in a perennially failing operation: nirvana is always just on its way.

Principals believe the shifting values implicit in recent policy regimes have increased resistance behaviors. They are acutely aware of the values shift that has occurred through neoliberal policies that unproblematically ignore broader social geneses of educational outcomes and that stand in opposition to previous social democratic agendas that championed social justice and equity. Competition among schools for enrollments, resources, and rankings is an unwelcomed outcome. Most teachers are opposed to standardized testing and league tables as educationally unfair and unwarranted—they know what students have learned and which schools will appear in the lowest rankings. These are sources of frustration for many teachers and their unions, which fuels opposition (see Clarke, 2001):

> Teachers know when something's unfair and won't go along with it if they don't believe in it. A lot of the trouble is politicians announcing changes without consulting the profession—they know how unpopular their policies actually are.
>
> (Principal, South Australia)

Perceptions are that policy fails to account for school-based narratives, contemporary research findings, or historical evidence (see for example, Callaghan, 2011). The professional wisdom of practitioners is largely ignored, and macro and meso structure is privileged over school-based agency, with schools bearing resultant obstruction.

The changing nature of the principalship and underlying policy values are seen to hinder reform. The intensification of principals' work, a systemic emphasis on managerialism, regulation, and accountability, and the subsequent reduction of personal time for engagement with students, classrooms, and curriculum frustrate change implementation. Being increasingly consumed with management tasks (Hoyle & Wallace, 2005), principals become less visible, and teachers grow more skeptical and less trusting of decisions being pursued. It is problematic when teachers no longer know what principals actually do, as one principal summed up:

> They have no idea what I do—not even the Assistant Principals know. Everyone is busy . . . they don't see what anyone else is doing but assume no one's as busy as them . . . distrust and dissatisfaction increase when people feel isolated and overworked . . . They don't know what they don't know.
>
> (Principal, Victoria)

Principals perceive that their own status and power in the educational hierarchy has been reduced, with their involvement in broad policy decision making curtailed and their work redefined, more controlled, and intensified. The neoliberal state exercises power and control through audits, compliance, accountability, and testing regimes, by cross-school comparisons, standardized regulation, and testing (see Smyth, 2006). Principals unanimously believe that this "tyranny of transparency" (Strathern, 2000) dramatically affects morale, through the creation of core (central) and peripheral (school) power structures:

> I think the [Education] Department thinks we're a nuisance. We don't help in the "doing" and "deciding." We're "done to" and "done over." That's what people think.
>
> (Principal, Victoria)

A further concern is that principals must tread a cautious path in leading the implementation of major change, having to ensure support and agreement from those who have power over their employment, while assessing reactions from within the school and making further decisions about how to address them. Hence for principals, implementing second-order change involves professional vulnerability, with resistance spelling danger of failure and negative professional consequences.

Negative Connotations About Leadership

Principals report subtle changes in the behaviors of others when they became a school leader. Psychologically, perceptions alter, and while most people appear ambivalent, a few attach negative connotations to leadership and leaders, especially if the leader is a woman (Starr, 1999). The interviewees in this study found this phenomenon was less noticeable when they became assistant principals or leading teachers, but that it became undeniably perceptible when they entered the school's top job. Six women cited their gender as a factor, with one calling it "an ingredient in the resistance recipe that just makes it all the nastier." There is no space to pursue the complexity and enormity of the gender factor here, but it is important to note that both motivations for, and forms of, resistance may also derive not only from a negative cathexis about leaders, but also about the sex of the leader, compounding opposition and antagonism.

One of the severest and irreconcilable learnings for newly appointed principals appears to be coping with these unexplained changes in the perceptions and behaviors of colleagues. Experienced principals were used to the fact that some teachers did not regard them as "one of them," which exacerbated opposition to major change, as the following comments reveal:

> . . . you're an animal who's changed his spots . . . they distrust you . . . give you a wide berth. It's hard to get anyone but the Deputy to sit next to you at the Xmas dinner! It can be lonely at the top but that's not entirely of your own making. Leadership creates a mental and physical separation that makes it very hard to work alongside those who won't 'connect' with you personally . . .
>
> (Principal, New South Wales)

> The biggest shock was how hostile some people can be towards principals. There's sexism and racism and ageism and much more wrapped up in this . . . some people aren't going to accept you . . . "Principal" equals "Enemy" . . . and if you're a woman, well! Say no more!
>
> (Principal, South Australia)

> [For some people] . . . even transparent, collaborative decision-making [can be] viewed with skepticism if I'm involved. The best strategy is to co-opt influential teachers . . . to get support for change.
>
> (Principal, Victoria)

Some interviewees perceived new work practices and the changed role of principals as having exacerbated the separation between principals' and teachers' work, which fuels an "us and them" situation. There is also a view that resistance is not always caused by the nature of the proposed change, but it can be a deliberate personal power struggle against a leader and his or her intentions (see Starr, in press). This may explain similarities in leaders' experiences over the decades and in different countries, institutions, and work contexts (e.g., Coch & French, 1948; Lawrence, 1954; Mintzberg, 1983). New principals are distressed by this phenomenon and fail to comprehend why it happens. One said, "You can cope with the 'what,' and the 'how, but can't understand 'why.'"

In some instances, principals cited institutional problems that created or exacerbated resilience to change implementation, such as a lack of leadership, team cohesion (more common than might be expected), high staff turnover, or insufficient agreement about long-term strategy or vision—all of which feed off each other. In such contexts, productivity decreases and disenchantment increases along with applications for transfer to other schools (see also Shapiro et al., 1995; Tucker, 1993).

A Culture of Complaint and Litigation

Experienced principals look back over many years in education and believe that, in the past, their decisions were more readily accepted, especially by students and parents. Now a greater range of stakeholders is perceived to have higher expectations and an increased appreciation of consumer rights. A number of principals believed they had witnessed a growing culture of complaint, whereby legal or procedural rights were pursued to procure desired outcomes, with complainants being more convinced of the effectiveness of these strategies. For example, some particularly militant parents can activate a formal complaint or legal action against a principal, or instigate media attention. As one interviewee said:

> If someone wants to, they can go to great lengths to work against you to get what they want. There's [sic] many avenues they can take . . . you're led a merry dance, having to justify what you do. Gone are the days of easy decision making.
>
> (Principal, Queensland)

School leaders bear the brunt of such overt opposition that incurs additional work to restore reputations, calm, and order—tying context and feeling with the social act (see Hochschild, 1983). For example:

> We've all experienced it—having to remain calm and civil while some out-of-control, bad-tempered, abusive adult has a go at you . . . [Our] feelings don't matter—it's all about the other person and what they want you to do . . . it's about learning the art of courteous combat.
>
> (Principal, NSW)

According to principals, threats of litigation are more common than actual cases, but formal complaints to external education authorities are increasing. Protestors increasingly seek restitution through power brokers such as school councils, district superintendents, or others within school leadership teams in the belief that they can override the principal's intentions by disrupting their support networks and discrediting them in the eyes of peers or superiors. All the while, principals have to put on a brave face and deal with opposition in rational ways. While staff members can express a range of emotions, principals feel constrained to act confidentially, diplomatically, and courteously at all times:

> You can't go into the staffroom to complain about someone . . . but teachers do . . . A principal has to be above all that . . . conversations are confidential and who cares about your feelings?
>
> (Principal, Victoria)

Despite experiencing blows to their esteem and confidence, principals have to be adept at appearance management, hiding their true feelings to present a steady, "bullet-proof" persona, which is not always easy:

> Staff took a vote of no confidence in me to the school council . . . I'd stood down a teacher but couldn't tell staff why. They assumed I had a vendetta . . . I couldn't believe they would do this . . . I thought they knew me better . . . I was devastated.
>
> (Principal, Victoria)

Hence principals perceived that opponents of change have considerable formal means of resistance available to them—means enhanced through localized knowledge and cultural resources, engagement of strategic external agencies, or the protection of secure employment and union membership.

Principals say that they can't get rid of bad teachers. They see unions supporting poor performers as part of the union contract with little or no consequence for bad behavior. One principal said:

> The union's holding us back from getting improvements . . . protecting teachers who are past their use-by date, giving power to . . . the wrong people. It's students who suffer in the end.
>
> (Principal, South Australia)

Ironically, principals are often in the same union as the teachers but feel their leadership role discounts their union membership. Some principals reported that resistant teachers in their schools were more likely to enlist union support against them instead of dealing with a dispute in-house and in person (see also Collinson, 1994). Such formalized resistance strategies increase principals' workload through meetings, negotiations, deputations, formal documentation, procedural compliance, even court appearances. The processes are stressful but effective in delaying or allaying the implementation of unpopular decisions.

Blame is a common theme in conversations about resistance—principals blame staff members (or others such as parents or school council members)—for disrupting plans. In turn principals understand that others blame them and "the system" for not understanding their position, the nature of their work, making jobs more difficult or reducing their professionalism through unpopular policies. Such a stance creates distrust and a gap between principals and teachers. Blame is a two-way street, with everyone claiming their position is not appreciated by other parties, but effective decision implementation requires a focus on cooperation for learning and continuous improvement, which often gets lost through micro-political maneuvers in change resistance. Change then often fails proving resistance tactics worthwhile.

The culture of complaint is seen to have superseded an era of greater compliance and is viewed as an outcome of consumer choice, competitive individualism over collectivism, political and media appeals to parents as consumers of education, and an emphasis on market forces that emphasize responsiveness to consumer power. After all, if stakeholders are not happy with one school, they can go to another.

Conclusion

Politics and decision making for major change are fundamental aspects of school life and leadership (Blase, 2005), with resistance and political game playing occurring in every school, and experienced by every principal in every context in this study. Overwhelmingly principals viewed resistance as a negative, disruptive phenomenon stemming from self-interest, in much the same vein as definitions cited earlier by Jermier et al. (1994) and Bordo (1993). Principals unanimously perceive leading implementation of major change as one of the most difficult aspects of their jobs—along with managing difficult people—with the two often being interlinked.

In this study, principals' reflections about obstacles to school change implementation gave rise to three major themes that are philosophical, psychological, and cultural in nature. Leaders believe that they are viewed as purveyors of unpopular policies and procedures at the basis of externally imposed neoliberal change. Subsequently principals perceived psychological barriers in communications with those who harbor negative views about leadership, leaders, and/or decision-making agendas (where other factors such as gender also take part). And principals have noticed increased resistance through formal, official complaint and litigation. Resistance tactics are deployed because they often have the desired effect. These power struggles, political intrigues, ideological differences, and the maneuvering of knowledge and personal agendas make for micro-political messiness in school life and often thwart change implementation (Punch, 1996).

Undoubtedly school leaders require political astuteness to implement major decisions successfully, yet many researchers reveal the lack of essential knowledge and skills of school leaders as the cause of change failure (Blase, 2005; Evans, 1996). Opposition to change can come from any area within or outside the school and must be anticipated and acted upon, which is more difficult than it sounds because resistance is exercised in myriad overt and covert ways. Principals ponder the causes of resistance that are often unclear, and tell cautionary tales about ignoring divergent micro politics and groundswells of resistance at their peril. They also explain, however, that sometimes they do not know what to do in these difficult and emotionally charged circumstances. Too often micro-political issues are considered "undiscussable" (Argyris, 1998)—too uncomfortable for open conversation because they reflect badly on leaders (Watson, 1982).

Governments respond to global forces to ensure national economic competitiveness, releasing some "dark" micro repercussions for school leaders. The principals cite ongoing external interventions, intensified workloads, insufficient resources, the timing, nature, volume, and disruption of externally imposed initiatives, and union objection as hindrances to change that exacerbate resistance and antagonism when implementing major decisions (Gronn, 2003; Yap & Chrispeels, 2004). Further concerns were a lack of agreement about policy or direction; increased stress and burnout, widespread disenchantment and disengagement; rapidly changing student populations; and a lack of professional learning, preparation, and induction for principals focused on decision making, change implementation, micro politics, and resistance. The study also emphasizes a desire for a returned focus on learning and teaching with more democratic, collaborative, cooperative decision-making processes operating in schools.

The study demonstrates the need for further research into the political machinations of school renewal and the essential political skills and understandings required to lead and manage major change. There is also a strong need for more research focusing on principals' experiences, reactions, and reflections on resistance—its causes, manifestations, and effects—and, importantly, principals' own resistance to change.

As governments place more emphasis on measurable performance outcomes, implementing change will become even more important for principals, with concomitant implications for their selection, appraisal, and longevity in the job. As Buchanan and Badham (2008) argue, the imperative for major change implementation in leadership preparation, induction, professional learning, and support simply is this: "the change agent who is not politically skilled will fail" (p. 18).

Note

1. The subject of principals' resistance was raised several times, with many principals feeling they would be viewed as disloyal or lacking in commitment if they openly criticized or complained, but who get around the problem by mediating and adapting change/policy initiatives. Compliance, even if simulated, is a conscious agential act (Blase, 1990), but one that may not stem from honesty or integrity, as resistance may.

References

Abelson, R. P. (1995). Attitude extremity. In R. E. Petty & J. A. Krosnick (Eds.), *Attitude strength: Antecedents and consequences*. Mahwah, NJ: Lawrence Erlbaum Associates.

Alvesson, M., & Sveningsson, S. (2003). Good vision, bad micro-management and ugly ambiguity: Contradictions of (non-)leadership in a knowledge-intensive organization. *Organization Studies, 24*(6), 961–988.

Argyris, C. (1998, May–June). Empowerment: The emperor's new clothes. *Harvard Business Review,* pp. 98–105.

Ball, S. J. (1987). *The micro-politics of the school: Towards a theory of organization.* London, UK: Methuen.

Ball, S. J. (1994). *Education reform: A critical and post-structural approach.* Buckingham, UK: Open University Press.

Barth, R. S. (2007). Risk. In *The Jossey-Bass reader on educational leadership* (2nd ed., pp. 211–218). San Francisco, CA: John Wiley and Sons.

Beck, J. (1999). Makeover or takeover? The strange death of educational autonomy in neo-liberal England. *British Journal of Sociology of Education, 20*(2), 223–238.

Blase, J. (1990). Some negative effects of principals' control-oriented and protective political behavior. *American Educational Research Journal, 27*(4), 727–753.

Blase, J. (1991). *The politics of life in schools: Power, conflict, and cooperation.* Newbury Park, CA: Sage.

Blase, J. (2005). The micropolitics of educational change. In A. Hargreaves (Ed.), *Extending educational change: International handbook of educational change* (pp. 264–277). Dordrecht, The Netherlands: Springer.

Bordo, S. (1993). Feminism, Foucault and the politics of the body. In C. Ramazanoglu (Ed.), *Up against Foucault: Explorations of some tensions between Foucault and feminism.* London, UK: Routledge.

Buchanan, D. A., & Badham, R. J. (2008) *Power, politics, and organizational change: Winning the turf game* (2nd ed.). London, UK: Sage.

Burns, T. (1961). Micropolitics: Mechanisms of institutional change. *Administrative Science Quarterly, 6*(3), 257–281.

Callaghan, R. (2011, September 15). Survey shows division over reform agenda. *Education Review.*

Clarke, P. (2001). Feeling compromised—the impact on teachers of the performance culture. *Improving Schools, 4*(3), 23–32.

Coch, L., & French, J. R. P. (1948). Overcoming resistance to change. *Human Relations, 1*(4), 512.

Collinson, D. (1994). Strategies of resistance: Power, knowledge and subjectivity in the workplace. In J. M. Jermier, D. Knights, & W. R. Nord, (Eds.), *Resistance and power in organizations.* London, UK: Routledge.

Corbin, J., & Strauss, A. (2008). *Basics of qualitative research* (3rd ed.). Thousand Oaks, CA: Sage.

Cuban, L. (1988). A fundamental puzzle of school reform. *Phi Delta Kappan, 69*(5), 340–344.

de Jager, P. (2005). The danger of the "early adopter" myth. Retrieved from www.techno bility.com/docs/chapter032.htm

Dent, E. B., & Goldberg, S. G. (1999). Challenging "resistance to change." *The Journal of Applied Behavioral Science, 35*(1), 25–41.

Duke, D., & Salmonowicz, M. (2010). Key decisions of a first-year "turnaround" principal. In *Educational Management, Administration and Leadership, 38*(1), 33–58.

Evans, R. (1996). *The human side of school change: reform, resistance, and the real-life problems of innovation.* San Francisco, CA: Jossey-Bass.

Fink, D., & Stoll, L. (2005). Educational change: Easier said than done. In A. Hargreaves (Ed.), *Extending educational change: International handbook of educational change* (pp. 17–41). Dordrecht, The Netherlands: Springer.

Foy, N. (1985). Ambivalence, hypocrisy, cynicism: Aids to organizational change. *New Management, 2*(4), 49–53.

Gabriel, Y. (1999). Beyond happy families: A critical re-evaluation of the control-resistance-identity triangle. *Human Relations, 52*(2), 197–203.

Glaser, B., & Strauss, A. (1967). *The discovery of grounded theory.* Chicago, IL: Aldine.

Graham, P. (Ed). (1995). *Mary Parker Follett—prophet of management: A celebration of writings from the 1920s.* Boston, MA: Harvard Business School Press.

Grattan, M., Tomazin, F., & Harrison, D. (2008, August 28). School v school: PM's rule. *The Age,* p. 1.

Gray, D. E. (2009). *Doing research in the real world* (2nd ed.). London, UK: Sage.

Grey, C. (2005). *A very short, fairly interesting and reasonably cheap book about studying organizations.* London, UK: Sage.

Gronn, P. (2003). *The new work of educational leaders: Changing leadership practice in an era of school reform.* London, UK: Paul Chapman Publishing.

Hargreaves, A., & Fink, D. (2006). *Sustainable leadership.* San Francisco, CA: Jossey Bass.

Higgs, M. (2009). The good, the bad and the ugly: Leadership and narcissism. *Journal of Change Management, 9*(2), 165–178.

Hochschild, A. R. (1983). *The managed heart: The commercialization of human feeling.* Berkeley: The University of California Press.

Holland, B. (2010, February 16). *Leading through change: Managing the change process.* Keynote address delivered at the Leading through teaching conference, Swinburne University, Hawthorn, Melbourne, Victoria, Australia.

Hoyle, E., & Wallace, M. (2005). *Educational leadership: Ambiguity, professionals and managerialism.* London, UK: Sage.

Jermier, J. M., Knights, D., & Nord, W. R. (Eds.). (1994). *Resistance and power in organizations.* London, UK: Routledge.

Krantz, J. (1999). Comment on "Challenging 'resistance to change.'" *The Journal of Applied Behavioural Science, 35*(1), 42–44.

Lawrence, P. R. (1954). How to deal with resistance to change. *Harvard Business Review, 32*(3), 49–57.

Machiavelli, N. (1998). *The prince.* Chicago, IL: University of Chicago Press.

Mawhinney, H. B. (1999). Re-appraisal: The problems and prospects of studying the micropolitics of leadership in reforming schools. *School Leadership and Management, 19*(2), 159–170.

Merron, K. (1993). Let's bury the term "resistance." *Organization Development Journal, 11*(4), 77–86.

Mintzberg, H. (1983). *Power in and around organization.* New Jersey, NJ: Prentice Hall.

Packer, M. (2001). *Changing classes: School reform and the new economy.* Cambridge, UK: Cambridge University Press.

Piderit, S. K. (2000). Rethinking resistance and recognizing ambivalence: A multidimensional view of attitudes toward an organizational culture. *The Academy of Management Review, 25*(4), 783–794.

Punch, M. (1996). *Dirty business: Exploring corporate misconduct—analysis and cases.* London, UK: Sage.

Rogers, E. (1995). *The diffusion of innovation.* New York, NY: Free Press.

Sarason, S. (1990). *The predictable failure of educational reform.* San Francisco, CA: Jossey Bass.

Shapiro, D. L., Lewicki, R. J., & Devine, P. (1995). When do employees choose deceptive tactics to stop unwanted organizational change? A relational perspective. *Research on Negotiation in Organizations, 5,* 155–184.

Smyth, J. (2006). The politics of reform of teachers' work and the consequences for schools: Some implications for teacher education. *Asia-Pacific Journal of Teacher Education, 34*(3), 310–319.

Starr, K. E. (1999). *That roar which lies at the other side of silence: An analysis of women principals' responses to structural reform in South Australian education.* Unpublished Ph.D. thesis, University of South Australia, Adelaide, South Australia.

Starr, K. E. (2009). Pressing issues in the new context of Australian educational leadership. In L. Ehrich & N. Cranston (Eds.). *Australian educational leadership today: Issues and trends.* Bowen Hills, Queensland: Australian Academic Press.

Starr, K. E. (2014). Interrogating conceptions of leadership: School principals, policy and paradox. *School Leadership & Management,* published online 16 April. Available at: http://www.tandfonline.com/doi/pdf/10.1080/13632434.2014.905466

Starr, K., & White, S. (2008). The small rural school principalship: Key challenges and cross-school responses. *Journal for Research in Rural Education, 23*(5), 1–12.

Strathern, M. (2000). The tyranny of transparency. *British Educational Research Journal, 26*(3), 309–321.

Strebel, P. (2006). Why do employees resist change? *Harvard Business Review on Change* (pp. 139–157). Boston, MA: Harvard Business School Press.

Thomson, P. (2008). Headteacher critique and resistance: A challenge for policy, and for leadership/management scholars. *Journal of Educational Administration and History, 40*(2), 85–100.

Tucker, J. (1993). Everyday forms of employee resistance. *Sociological Forum, 8*(25), 25–45.

Watson, T. J. (1982). Group ideologies and organizational change. *Journal of Management Studies, 19*(3), 259–275.

Watzlawick, P., Weakland, J., & Fisch, R. (1974). *Change: Principles of problem formation and problem resolution.* New York, NY: Norton.

Yap, M., & Chrispeels, J. H. (2004). Sharing leadership: Principals' perceptions. In J. H. Chrispeels (Ed.), *Learning to lead together: The promise and challenge of sharing leadership.* Thousand Oaks, CA: Sage.

9

TRUSTING OUR SCHOOLS: THE "SOFT" SIDE OF DECISION MAKING

Dean Fink

Introduction

This past week, I fired my lawn care company, visited my tax accountant, stopped by my local car dealership to inquire about a new car, wrote a rather strident letter to my local member of parliament, and arranged a 50th wedding anniversary cruise for my wife and me. What do these seemingly innocuous activities, which are of absolutely no interest to anyone but me and perhaps my wife, have in common? They all involve decisions that contain elements of trust or distrust. For example, my lawn care company is supposed to ensure that my lawn is not the scandal of the neighborhood, yet I have a wonderful crop of dandelions. When I complained to the company, its representative tried to sell me much more expensive products, then he told me that I had watered my lawn too much, and when that didn't work, a few days later he informed me that their "expert" has discovered that my soil was too dry. From my point of view, they can't be trusted—they are incompetent, devious, and have no particular interest in me, or my needs. Similarly, I wrote a letter to my local member of parliament because his government has gone back on promises related to educational policies. My argument had to do with trusting the integrity of a government that said one thing to win an election and hypocritically does the opposite once it was elected. Conversely, a long-time friend, who I trust implicitly, recommended an accounting firm to me, and I have had them do my income tax returns for over 20 years. They are competent, honest, transparent, and when Revenue Canada came calling some years ago, they provided all kinds of support. My local car dealer has also earned my trust. I have bought four vehicles from him over time, each one was priced fairly, trouble free, and serviced economically and well. Finally, a happy fifty-year marriage not only requires mutual love, understanding of the other's needs, and shared commitments, but an abundance of trust. Trust issues pervade virtually every social relationship and decision that we make throughout our lives. It would be impossible to drive a car unless we trusted that other drivers followed the rules of the road. How could you submit to the ministrations of a doctor, dentist, beautician, or barber without a certain element of trust? We trust the mail arrives on time, pharmacists (chemists) fill our drug prescriptions accurately, pilots land our planes safely, and our opponents at golf or cards play by the rules. We trust others competence, integrity, honesty, transparency, and commitment to the task at hand. Trust is the glue that binds our societies together or, sadly in many cases, distrust is the toxin that divides individuals, organizations, and in the extreme, nations. Trust makes or breaks governments, businesses, and social organizations like churches and schools. It is the element that creates the confidence among individuals within a society, or individual organizations that accelerates change, or the suspicion that slows it down, or in the extreme, buries it (Covey, 2012). It is a central tenet of civil democratic societies. In the words of Tom Friedman of the *New York Times,*

> You can't have a democracy without trust and you can't have citizens without trust—without trust that everyone will be treated with equality, no matter who is in power, and without trust and shared vision in what kind of society people are trying to build.
>
> (Friedman, 2012, p. 14)

My 30 years as an educational leader in many different capacities have taught me that trust, or lack of it, is also a key ingredient in educational decision making—trust in others' judgments, trust in my own judgments, trust that decisions resulting from these judgments will be carried out, trust that the calculations that went into decisions are accurate, trust that the data used to make a decision are factual, timely, and honest, trust in the policies and procedures that our organizations have developed over time. In my view, the latest mantra about data-driven decision making is just one more technocratic myth designed to reduce the human element in educational decision making. Accurate, intelligible data should inform our judgments by providing evidence to support decision making, but at some point in the decision-making process, a human has to be trusted to make a decision the data doesn't.

While much that happens in schools and districts is amenable to rational, linear, and logical decision-making models, many events in schools and districts are not predictable and easily anticipated and reducible to a set of policies and procedures. Researchers, politicians, and other alleged experts who base their findings of schools and districts on cursory observations and engagements underestimate the serendipitous nature of educational leadership. Well-conceived, logical, and evidence-based plans that dutifully attend to all stages of rational decision-making invariably fall prey to "Black Swans"—those events and situations that make leadership unpredictable. "Black Swan logic makes what you don't know far more relevant than what you do know" (Taleb, 2007, p. xix). The logical unfolding of a school improvement plan can unravel quickly in the face of a car crash that takes the lives of six young people and traumatizes an entire community, or the sudden death of a beloved teacher, or the very public attacks of a radical evangelical preacher on virtually any library book other than the Bible, or the arrival in school of eight "out-of-control" teens from a group home that springs up unannounced to any school official over the summer. These are the Black Swans I encountered in my first year as a secondary school principal. I coped, and so did the school's staff, but I have to admit I had to trust in their collective wisdom and professionalism, the moral support of my wife and a local clergyman who rallied the community behind the school to confront the attacks on contemporary literature, and the help and encouragement of my network of colleagues in the district office and other schools to get through that first year. Many of my decisions and those faced by school leaders every day fit Stephen Covey's category of urgent and important (Covey, 1989). These are the Black Swans that seldom show up in any of the glossy leadership frameworks or decision-making models that try to formulate precisely the nature of educational leadership. These models, often borrowed from business, fail to comprehend that schools are very complex places that must attend to multiple purposes and satisfy numerous and often conflicting constituencies. While all leaders like to feel they are in control, there are days and situations in which trust in colleagues, systems, and support groups is all a leader has to cling to. Pressure to turn schools around in a few months, for example, is, for the most part, nonsense. To change schools you have to change people who, in many jurisdictions due to declines in student enrollment, are middle-aged and often set in their ways. For leaders to build authentic, sustained school improvement, they need the time to develop relationships of mutual trust with colleagues, demonstrate respect for each individual, provide hope and optimism, and act with integrity and intentionality.

Sadly, powerful and efficacious concepts such as trust, respect, optimism, intentionality, commitment, and compassion no longer permeate the discourse on educational leadership. These unfashionable words and ideas are now considered soft, "touchy-feely," left-wing, "wussy," and effeminate and should not obscure the tough judgments necessary to oblige reluctant teachers and principals to change their ways and function in more utilitarian ways. The problem for the technocrats who claim to live in the "real world" or "in the trenches" who now seem to dominate educational policy in many nations, is that the "soft" words and concepts like trust are hard to quantify or codify; nor are they compatible with military and business metaphors. In place of words that speak of healthy and productive human interactions, we get a steady drumbeat of market-based words, phrases, and concepts that describe rigorous, demanding, and macho forms and functions like "accountability," performance management, "bottom line," and "more bang for the buck." In this production paradigm of how education should work, teachers are human resources not professionals to whom society entrusts its children's education; principals are managers of the productivity of this "workforce," not leaders of learning, and the results of these efforts are neatly and simplistically codified into easily understood and manipulated numbers based on the bottom line—students' test scores. Like the stock market or quarterly reports, a school's success goes up or down dependent on these numbers and, in more recent times, particularly in the United States, teachers and principals' salaries fluctuate with these numbers. As Michael Fullan has indicated, this model of educational change emphasizes multiple and often fragmented change initiatives, perseverance on accountability at all levels to drive and verify change among individual teachers, leaders, and schools, and massive investment in blind confidence that "the wonders of the digital world will carry the day v/s instruction" (Fullan, 2011). Evidence from nations such as the United States and the United Kingdom that have bought into this change model, indicates that these drivers of change and the "low-trust" paradigm upon which they are based, are clearly not working.

High trust nations,[1] like Finland and Canada have adopted an alternative approach that employs a different set of change strategies—capacity building, group work among staff members, a focus on pedagogy, and systemic solutions. But the "glue that binds the effective drivers together is the underlying attitude, philosophy or theory of action." (Fullan, 2011, p. 5) If we examine these nations as examples of high trust systems and the U.K. educational system under new Labour and the present U.S. system as exemplars of low trust and conditional trust systems,[2] using the results of the 2009 Programme for International Student Assessment, we can conclude that high trust systems produce far superior student achievement,[3] more resilient students,[4] more equitable results,[5] and greater efficiency[6] in terms of money and time. Both Finland and, particularly, Canada have responded to changing immigration patterns more effectively and more quickly than either the United States or United Kingdom (Organisation for Economic Co-operation and Development [OECD], 2010a), and both high trust nations show considerably less variance in student achievement based on socio-economic status (OECD, 2010a), than either the United Kingdom or the United States, with lower per-pupil expenditures (OECD, 2010a). If, as Finland, Canada, and other high-trust nations demonstrate, trust in teachers and school leaders to make the best judgments on behalf of the children in their care produces superior results defined not only in terms of achievement but also equity and efficiency, then it follows that trust is a powerful ingredient in decision making within school districts and, most importantly, within schools themselves.

"Empirical evidence has . . . shown that several aspects of trust—benevolence, reliability, competence, integrity, openness, and respect—are strongly connected with school performance and student outcomes" (Daly & Crispeels, 2008, p. 30). For example, Bryck and Schneider (2002) state that "We have learned, based on school reform in Chicago that a broad base of trust across a school community lubricates much of a school's day to day functioning and is a critical resource as local leaders embark on ambitious school improvement plans" (p. 40). Viviane Robinson (2011) concludes, after her analysis of the change literature that "there is compelling evidence that the level of trust among the members of a school community makes an important difference to the way they work together and to the social and academic progress of students" (p. 34). Additionally, there is a burgeoning business literature that ties levels of trust to corporate success (Covey, 2012; Hurley, 2011). From a broad array of evidence, we can conclude that highly successful schools and school districts and provincial, state, and national school systems build strong bonds of trust between and among policy-makers and policy implementers. Conversely, policy-makers in less successful schools and school systems tend to foment distrust, anxiety, and in some situations, downright hostility and fear among the very people who must implement policies. In turn, policy implementers such as teachers and principals in low-trust environments respond by overtly or covertly sabotaging change efforts, gaming verification systems, or engaging in militant union activities (Hargreaves & Fink, 2006).

Let me hasten to add, that this discussion is not about "blind trust," or Pollyanna trust or "look-the-other-way" trust, but trust in people, policies, and procedures that ensure deep and lasting learning for all students. *Blind trust* implies that policy-makers trust policy implementers in virtually all circumstances, and no one bothers to verify whether this trust is appropriate. Investors in Bernie Madoff's Ponzi scheme learned something about "blind" trust, as did home owners who signed up for subprime mortgages in the United States, and so did Barings' when Nick Leeson destroyed the company. It was American president Ronald Reagan who made the phrase "trust but verify" famous. The challenge for those interested in educational decision making is to find the right balance between trust and verification. Too much trust leaves policy-makers vulnerable politically and professionally, and too much or injudicious verification strips policy implementers of their autonomy and stifles creativity and innovation.

To this point I have used the terms *judgment* and *decision making* somewhat interchangeably, but when we examine what leaders actually do, we can define judgment as the long-term process that precedes action—a decision. My firing of my lawn care company, for example, took time and a series of disappointments before I actually decided to discontinue their service. A series of judgments over time led to my trust in my accountant and my car dealer that resulted in decisions to continue to deal with them. Trust in a long-term marriage *involves* judgments over time through the vicissitudes of the relationship. Covey connects trust to judgment when he asserts that "smart" trust is "judgment." "It is a competency and a process that enables us to operate with high trust in a low-trust world. It minimizes risk and maximizes possibilities. It optimizes two key factors (1) propensity to trust and (2) analysis" (Covey, 2012, p. 57). It is this ability both to trust *and* verify at all levels of an educational system that creates the context for positive growth and change and for effective judgments and decisions.

To develop these themes, the remainder of this chapter examines trust from three perspectives within an educational organization—interpersonal or *relational trust* between leaders and colleagues, *institutional trust* between schools, districts, and their communities, and *self-trust,* the ability of leaders to make judgments and, ultimately, decisions with confidence, courage, and when necessary, decisiveness, especially when they have to deal with the Black Swans of educational leadership.[7]

Relational Trust

The rather mundane anecdotes of trust or a lack of trust with which I introduced this chapter are all examples of interpersonal or relational trust[8]—my relationship with the lawn company, government, accountant, car dealer, and my wife. Themes of honesty (or dishonesty), transparency, competence, and respect for others define relational trust and the judgments and decisions that result. The same sequence follows in virtually all our interpersonal engagements. Whenever we have entered into a new relationship, whether it was our first day in school and we met our new teacher, or encountered our boss on our first job, the unspoken questions in our minds were—do I trust this person, do I have confidence in his or her leadership, what will my relationship with this person become? How will I respond? Similarly, relational trust answers such implicit questions that staff members have of their leaders as "How well do you know me and care about me as a person? Do you truly respect me? What do you know about my interests, my family, my aspirations, my fears, and the support I may need to do my job well? Do you really listen to me at a deep level? Are you open to influence or do you just pretend to be interested? Do you treat me with civility and friendliness? Are you with me for the long haul or are you using me to advance your own career?"

The degree to which relational trust exists in a school, a district, or even a school jurisdiction will determine staff members' willingness to commit time and energy beyond their contractual obligations to provide extra help to students, coach teams, organize students' events, festivals, concerts, and attend to the myriad of activities outside the classroom that make schools vibrant and engaging places for students. Similarly, teachers' commitment to engaging in collegial efforts that contribute to enhanced student performance is directly correlated to their feelings of efficacy and well-being derived from relational trust. Not surprisingly, leaders require followers, or they are not leaders. We base decisions to follow the leadership of others on relational trust in that person's competence, dedication to shared purposes, and integrity. Elsewhere I have defined leaders of learning as "ordinary people who through commitment, effort, and dedication, have become extraordinary and have made the people around them exceptional" (Fink, 2005, p. xvii). I came up with this definition after a half-day visit with Elena, the principal of a small village school is Piscu in Romania.

Elena was in her late forties, perhaps early fifties, very plainly, indeed drably dressed, quite soft-spoken, and not the sort to stand out in a group—the antithesis of the charismatic leader. As we toured her school, I watched her closely, and without my understanding the language, observed how teachers and students responded to her. She was like a ballet dancer floating from student to student, teacher to teacher, with a word of encouragement here, a suggestion there, each evoking smiles and nods as she progressed. I don't know if she had an office; if she did she rarely visited it. Everywhere we went in the school, we were met with displays of children's work, even in the boy's washroom. With the help of my interpreter and my many years of experience observing children's work, I would have to say the work of the children in Elena's school was of very good quality. As I went from classroom to classroom, I found that most children past the age of 10 could converse with me in passable English. They, of course, asked about Canada, and they all knew about Niagara Falls. I was then ushered into a meeting of the staff that included the head of their parent's council who happened to be Elena's predecessor as principal. The staff had the usual complaints one might hear in any staff meeting anywhere about government mandates, insensitive inspectors who knew nothing about the challenges of rural schools, and deteriorating working conditions. They made very sure I knew how much they appreciated and trusted Elena. What made this school and staff different from most, however, is that this faculty hadn't been paid in two months. In addition, any repairs or upgrades to the school had to come from the local community. This preindustrial village had collected the money and provided the manpower to put a new roof on the school and lay new carpet throughout, because the World Bank and International Monetary Fund would only provide loans to the central government if it tightened expenditures. In order for the government to create a climate for Western corporate investment, these international agencies required it to squeeze the public services and, in the process, totally undermined the most basic element of trust between a government and its employees—the arrival of a pay check. Yet, here was this little school located at the heart of a poor agricultural village in which the teachers continued to work industriously and effectively with only vague promises of a payday. Why? They trusted Elena as their leader of learning. This very ordinary woman had built up, over time, strong, sustainable bonds of trust with her teaching staff and community. You can't bottle it, nor can you measure it, but trust is the ingredient that enables high trust schools, like Piscu, and other high trust organizations to flourish in low trust environments. As the financial tycoon Warren Buffet has observed "Trust is like the air we breathe. When it is present no one really notices. But when it is absent, everybody notices" (Covey, 2012, p. 12).

As anyone who has followed sports knows, coaches and managers don't suddenly lose their knowledge of the game or its strategies during a failed season. What they lose however, is "the room." In other words, the team collectively loses its trust and confidence in the manager's competence, dedication, or commitment. Similarly teams and sports leagues, like other organizations and institutions, can very easily lose the trust of their most ardent supporters. It took a long time for baseball and ice hockey to recover their fan bases after prolonged players' strikes. Similarly, perennially popular teams like baseball's Los Angeles Dodgers and the Liverpool football club in the British premier league lost a great deal of "institutional" trust because of their ownerships' disregard for the needs of the fans of the teams.

Institutional Trust

Institutional trust refers to the degree to which an organization's various constituencies continue to have confidence in its competence, integrity, sustainability, and future. Automobile companies don't order expensive recalls of defective vehicles out of altruism, but rather to maintain customer loyalty and trust. Similarly, companies spend millions in advertising to assure potential customers that they are concerned about the environment (even if they are not) to maintain institutional trust. The most egregious examples lately of a loss of institutional trust at renowned, indeed, revered institutions, relate to the scandals over child sex abuse among Catholic priests and, more recently, by a well-known football coach at Pennsylvania State University. In each case, it was not the crime with all its seriousness that has shaken the communities' trust in the institutions, because one can rationalize that every large institution will have a few bad characters, but it was the cover up by these institutions that considered the good reputation of the institution more important than the welfare of victims and potential victims of child abuse.

In *Sustainable Leadership*, Andy Hargreaves and I outlined five action principles to ensure sustainability in practice. With a little adaptation, these action principles provide some useful rules for building institutional trust (Hargreaves & Fink, 2006, p. 256). The first rule of institutional trust is *transparency*—open, honest communication of the good news and the bad. Cover ups come undone in time and the repercussions are far worse than an up-front disclosure of problems. Richard Nixon would have finished his term in office if he hadn't orchestrated a cover up of the Watergate burglary. The second rule of institutional trust is *vigilance*. Organizations maintain institutional trust by verifying with its important constituencies that they continue to maintain their trust in the organization's mission, competence, and integrity. Effective leaders who spend their time on problem seeking expend considerably less time later on in problem solving. I found it useful as a principal to spend a great deal of time in the community and to encourage my staff colleagues to participate in community activities. I needed eyes and ears in the community. For example, I made a point of inviting parents in small groups into my school so that we could address issues of concern before they became problems. Similarly, I enrolled the local clergy, politicians, and various other community leaders in my search for Black Swans. These "critical" friends proved invaluable in identifying potential issues that are not always apparent from the principal's office.

Activism is the third rule of institutional trust building. Leaders not only read and respond to their environments, they actively go about influencing them in ways that benefit the school and its students. If this involves addressing environmental issues in a community, or taking on political challenges that impinge on the school, then activist leaders make sure that their school's perspective is front and center. Similarly, schools and districts need to get out front with their stories, tell the world how they are pursuing excellence in all aspects of their operation, and explain how they are addressing contemporary approaches to student learning and, if necessary, acknowledge missteps and actively address their solutions publicly. Building trust not only requires active engagement it also requires immense *patience*. Policies and practices designed to build relationships between the school and its communities require sustained, perseverant, and consistent implementation over time, from one year to the next, from one leader to the next. A school's reputation takes a long time to build and a short time to destroy.

Finally, trust is built and maintained and enhanced "by systems that are personalized for people's use and that are compatible with human capacity" (Hargreaves & Fink, 2006, p. 262). For example, attention to the *design* of a school's communication mechanisms must address what Vicente (2003) calls the "human factor." Websites that require a Ph.D. from MIT[9] to decipher, unappealing, wordy, and lengthy newsletters, phone recording systems that may save money but lose the caller in a myriad of choices, not only fail to communicate, they often antagonize and undermine institutional trust. Institutional trust is the result of multiple decisions within schools and school districts that have at their heart a "theory of action" that places the needs of its students and their parents at the center of every decision its leaders make.

Self-Trust

At some point in the decision-making process someone has to say yes or no to a course of action, or at least acquiesce to the actions of other individuals or groups. Like the message communicated by President Harry Truman's famous sign on his desk "The Buck Stops Here," someone ultimately has to take responsibility for decisions made on behalf of a school or district. This is the hard part of decision making because there are no "sure fire" rules, no "how-to-do-it" templates, for successful decision making, especially when facing decisions in uncharted waters, working with incomplete information, or confronting Black Swans. How then does a leader acquire the self-trust or confidence to make tough decisions? As a former history teacher, I find history instructive and biography particularly useful to understand the factors that impinge on individual decision making and the thought processes of decision-makers who have had to face issues of monumental importance.

Why, for instance did, an inexperienced president, John Kennedy, trust his own judgment and hold back from a direct attack on the missile sites the Russians were constructing in Cuba in 1962 when most of his senior advisors and his military leaders advocated a direct attack. By trusting his own judgment over the advice of more experienced and seasoned professionals he probably averted a potentially catastrophic conflict with the Soviet Union (Case, 2012). Why did Josef Stalin trust his own judgment and blindly ignore all the advice of his advisers and compelling evidence that the German's would attack Russia in 1941 and, as a result of his stubbornness, leave his country woefully unprepared when the attack eventually came (Beevor, 2012). Why did George III continue to trust policies that eventually led to the Americans breaking away from the British Empire in 1776 when every piece of evidence suggested that these policies were failing (Tuchman, 1984). The answer, I suspect, is wrapped up in the character of the decision-maker, the context in which they operated, and the degree of mutual trust that existed between these leaders and their closest advisers.

One of my favorite books, *Team of Rivals* by Doris Kearns Goodwin, is a detailed study of how Abraham Lincoln and his cabinet that included three of his rivals for the presidency in 1860, each of whom considered himself to be better suited for the highest office than the untested, somewhat ungainly, poorly educated law-yer from Illinois, navigated their way through the innumerable crucial decisions that led to a successful conclusion to the American Civil War. Kearns Goodwin explains that her book is a story about how Lincoln

> . . . possessed an acute understanding of the sources of power inherent in the presidency, an unparalleled ability to keep his governing coalition together, a tough-minded appreciation of the need to protect his presi-dential prerogatives, and a masterful sense of timing. His success in dealing with the strong egos of men in his cabinet suggests that, in the hands of a truly great politician, the qualities we generally associate with decency and morality—kindness, sensitivity, compassion, honesty, and empathy—can also be impressive political resources.
>
> (2006, p. xvii)

She goes on to explain that, in spite of great personal sorrow, innumerable mili-tary and political setbacks, and countless Black Swans, he persevered:

> When resentment and contention threatened to destroy his administration, he refused to be provoked by petty grievances, to submit to jealousy, or to brood over perceived slights. Through the appalling pressures he faced day after day, he retained an unflagging faith in his country's cause.
>
> Kearns Goodwin (2006, p. 749)

What was there about Lincoln's approach to decision making that provides guidance for today's leaders in schools and districts to make consequential deci-sions with confidence? At the very heart of Lincoln's decision making was "an indomitable sense of purpose that "sustained him through the disintegration of the union, and through the darkest months of the war . . ." His conviction that the United States was "one nation indivisible, 'conceived in Liberty, and dedicated to the proposition that all me are created equal,' led to the rebirth of the union, free of slavery" (Kearns Goodwin, 2006, p. xvii). As the Civil War evolved, he had come to the conclusion that the war was also about ending slavery as well as restoring the union, but he resisted pressure for quick action, and waited for the right time militarily and politically to issue the emancipation proclamation in 1863 that freed the slaves in the states in rebellion. Similarly, school and district leaders' decision making must be guided by an "indomitable sense of purpose" as leaders of learning. As I have written elsewhere, they must be "passionately, creatively, obsessively and steadfastly committed to deep learning for all students—learning for understanding, learning for life, learning for a knowledge society" (Fink, 2005, p. xvii).

Just as Lincoln had an "intuitive sense of when to hold fast, when to wait, and when to lead" (Kearns Goodwin, 2006, p. 501), school leaders need to develop a sense of timing as part of their decision-making approach. I suspect this awareness of the importance of timing develops with experience. Some leaders tend to rush to a decision to clear their desks of issues. Unfortunately, acting precipitously can often make matters worse. One of my mentors never acted on the first phone call, only when he received a second did he know that the call was important. While I don't advocate this technique, it is sometimes better to let an issue simmer for a while until it cools down and then act. John Kennedy waited an excruciatingly long time, in spite of considerable pressure to act decisively, to allow the Russians to contemplate the consequences of their actions in Cuba and find a way to back down (p. 468).

Like Kennedy, Lincoln surrounded himself with strong, thoughtful people who were not afraid to disagree with him, and to offer alternative approaches to decisions. He, in turn, was sufficiently open-minded to consider their advice. For example, while Lincoln had made the decision to issue an emancipation proclamation because it was politically, militarily, perhaps most important, morally right, he did listened intently to the various views of his cabinet colleagues, particularly to his Secretary of State, William Seward, and opted to postpone the declaration until after the North had achieved a military victory. As Lincoln later observed, "The wisdom and view of the Secretary of State struck me with very great force. It was an aspect of the case that, in all my thought upon the subject, I have entirely overlooked." Conversely, disagreeing with Stalin was not just a career ending move; it was often a life-ending decision. George III surrounded himself with like-minded people from the landed aristocracy, and collectively, their group-think lost the American colonies.

Perhaps, Lincoln's most powerful decision-making attribute was his ability to engender trust. When, Kearns Goodwin described him as possessing the qualities of "kindness, sensitivity, compassion, honesty, and empathy," she described a person whose leadership promoted trust and confidence. This ability was a powerful political tool that united his supporters, won him an election in 1864, and had he lived, might have rebuilt trusting relationships with the South. Sadly his premature death enabled less trusting and compassionate politicians to reverse his policy of "With malice towards none; with charity for all" and open the door for a century of division, racism, and distrust between and among the former protagonists. What, then, can we learn from Lincoln about self-trust? While not all of his decisions turned out successfully, many failed ignominiously although he was quick to accept the blame and take steps to rectify the situation; it was his dedication to a clear and transcendent moral purpose, his willingness to encourage divergent opinions among his advisors, his fine sense of timing, and his ability to engender trust, that provide an exemplary model for school and district leaders when they face consequential decisions.

Conclusion

Just as Lincoln's decision making sought to build bridges of trust with the people around him and with adversaries, policy-makers in successful school systems, like those in flourishing businesses[10] and successful democracies only succeed when their decisions create a climate of mutual trust with the people who must carry out their policies. High trust educational systems like Finland and Canada not only dramatically outperform low trust systems like the United Kingdom and United States, they do so with greater efficiency and equity. They ensure that educational professionals are well prepared, well paid, and given sufficient autonomy to use their creativity and expertise to enhance the educational experiences of all of the students in their care. At the same time high trust systems employ appropriate verification strategies to ensure that trust is appropriate and well placed. Finding a reasonable balance between trust and verification is at the heart of educational improvement. Blind trust can produce some highly creative and imaginative practices, but it can also result in inefficiencies, inequities, and a lack of professionalism. Verification systems should ensure quality, equity, and efficiency, but many become so intrusive they kill creativity and innovation and foster distrust and apathy.

These principles of trust and verification apply as well at the district and school levels. Schools and districts can maintain high trust even in low trust environments, as my story of Elena and Piscu illustrates, by building relational trust, institutional trust, and self-trust. High-trust environments encourage leaders to develop the confidence to make decisions with courage, decisiveness, and efficacy, even in situations involving Black Swans, by focusing on transcendent moral purposes in terms of students' learning, a willingness to encourage divergent opinions among colleagues, a sense of timing, and a concerted effort to develop bonds of trust within and outside the school and district.

Notes

1. Both Finland and Canada rate among the most trusted countries in the world. On the 2010 Corruption Perceptions Index, Finland scored 9.2 and Canada 8.9, whereas the United Kingdom scored 7.8 and the United States 7.1 (Transparency International [TI], (2010).
2. I characterize "conditional trust" systems as ones that trust some parts of their system but not others. For example, the policy of the present Cameron government in the United Kingdom is to trust academies and free schools but not state schools.

3. Canada and Finland significantly outperform the United States and United Kingdom in reading, mathematics, and science (Organisation for Economic Co-operation and Development [OECD], 2010b).

4. "Resilient students are those who come from a disadvantaged socio–economic background and perform much higher than would be predicted by their background." Canada and Finland are well above the OECD average while the United States and the United Kingdom are well below that average (OECD, 2010a, pp. 62–63).

5. Percent of variance in student performance explained by socio-economic status, Finland, 7.8%, Canada, 8.6%, United Kingdom 13.7%, and the United States 16.8% (OECD, 2010a).

6. Finland and Canada spend 3.6% and 3.5% percent of GDP respectively on nontertiary education, whereas the United States and the United Kingdom spend 4.0% and 4.4%, respectively (OECD, 2012).

7. The most important aspect of trust building within a school, of course, is with students. While this topic is beyond the scope of this chapter, I would suggest that the same relational principles described in the chapter apply to working with students. Moreover, leaders who build trusting relationships with colleagues within a school provide a powerful model for teachers and others within the school context for teachers to emulate with students.

8. Bryck and Schneider (2002) in their study of trust based on their work in Chicago connect four broad based trust themes that affect leaders' judgments and decisions. Robinson (2011, pp. 34–41) connects relational trust to her student-leadership model.

9. Massachusetts Institute of Technology.

10. Covey (2012) provides many examples of the importance of trust for business success.

References

Beevor, A. (2012). *The second world war.* New York, NY: Little Brown.

Bryck, A., & Schneider, B. (2002). *Trust in schools: A core resource for school improvement.* New York, NY: American Sociological Association.

Case, R. (2012). *The Years of Lyndon Johnson: The passage of power.* New York, NY: Alfred A. Knopf.

Covey, S. M. R. (2012). *Smart trust.* New York, NY: Free Press.

Covey, S. R. (1989). *The 7 habits of highly effective people: Powerful lessons in personal change.* New York, NY: Simon and Schuster.

Daly, A. J., & Crispeels, J. (2008). A question of trust: Predictive conditions for adaptive and technical leadership in educational contexts. *Leadership and Policy in Schools, 71*(1), 30–63.

Fink, D. (2005). *Leadership for mortals.* London, UK: Sage.

Friedman, T. (2012, February). The impulses behind freedom. *New York Times,* p. 14.

Fullan, M. (2011). Choosing the wrong drivers for whole system reform. *Seminar Series 204.* Melbourne, Australia: Centre for Strategic Education.

Hargreaves, A., & Fink, D. (2006). *Sustainable leadership.* Thousand Oaks, CA: Jossey-Bass.

Hurley R. (2011). *The decision to trust: How leaders create high trust organizations.* San Francisco, CA: Jossey-Bass.

Kearns Goodwin, D. (2006). *Team of rivals: The political genius of Abraham Lincoln.* New York, NY: Simon & Schuster.

Organisation for Economic Co-operation and Development (OECD). (2010a). *PISA 2009 Results: Overcoming social background: Equity in learning opportunities and outcomes (Volume 2),* OECD Publishing. Retrieved from http://dx.doi.org/10.1787/9789264091504-en

Organisation for Economic Co-operation and Development (OECD). (2010b). *PISA 2009 Results: What students know and can do: Student Performance in reading, mathematics and Science (Volume 1)*, OECD Publishing. Retrieved from http://dx.doi.org/10.1787/9789264091450-en

Organisation for Economic Co-operation and Development (OECD). (2012). *Education at a glance: OECD indicators*, OECD Publishing. Retrieved from http://dx.doi.org/10.1787/eag.2012.en

Robinson, V. (2011). *Student-centered leadership.* San Francisco, CA: Jossey Bass.

Taleb, N. N. (2007). *The black swan: The impact of the highly improbable.* New York, NY: Random House.

Transparency International (TI). (2010). Corruption perceptions index. Retrieved from www.locationselector.com/images/stories/featured_reports/CPI_report_ForWeb.pdf

Tuchman, B. (1984). *The march of folly: From Troy to Vietnam.* New York, NY: Ballantine Books.

Vicente, K. (2003). *The human factor: Revolutionizing the way people live with technology.* Toronto, Canada: Knopf.

PART IV
Ethical and Legal Issues

10

ETHICAL DECISION MAKING IN LEADERSHIP: A MORAL LITERACY PERSPECTIVE

Patrick M. Jenlink

Introduction

Educational leaders face dilemmas requiring ethical decisions on a daily basis and are often called on to make difficult choices between competing ethical demands and values. These conflicting demands take on a political or professional coloring; they may also reflect conflicts internal to the school organization or between the school and the bureaucratic ideology of the larger educational system (Cranston, Ehrich, & Kimber, 2006). Educational leaders often find achieving social consensus with respect to competing ethical demands difficult in considering the most appropriate solution and, ultimately, make a value-based decision (Begley, 1999; Cranston, Ehrich, & Kimber, 2003). Therein lies a compounding factor related to ethical decisions; that is, value-based decision, as Sims and Keon (1999) explain, are not purely rational and, therefore, present an ethical challenge in relationship to prevailing social factors and values.

Compounding the nature of ethical decision making, educational leaders are confronted daily with multiple occurring problems—dynamic in nature—that draw into specific relief the interrelated nature of theory and practice. In a sense, the complex and dynamic nature of problems may be described as a "problématique" (Warfield & Perino, 1999), a form of structural modeling that represents relationships among members of a set of problems. As well, it means the identification of power-relations and interests that are involved. For the educational leader confronted by multiple problems each day, the *problématique*[1] is used to connote that a question or problem needs analysis before it can be answered or addressed properly, because any question or problem tends to be more complex than might at first be thought.

With respect to the concept of ethical dilemma, problématique connotes a problem structure that is the beginning point from which an ethical decision or solution is generated. In particular for the educational leader, examining the structure of the dilemma in concert with power-relations and interests of those involved is of critical importance. With this thought in mind, what theories are most appropriate in decision making related to complex and dynamic problems is companioned with the need to discern the cognitive and contextual demands of education problems (Beachum & McCray, 2010; Dempster & Berry, 2003; Goldring & Greenfield, 2002; Langlois, 2004; Starratt, 2003). Formulating the complex nature of education problems and representing the various aspects of the problems educational leaders must address require an understanding of implicit and explicit aspects of decision making, and a high level of ethical responsibility.

The thesis of this chapter focuses on the ethical nature of education problems, in particular drawing on problématique as a frame for discerning the ethical issues in play and what cognitive and contextual resources are important to the decision-making process. The ethical nature of decision making speaks directly to the "dilemma-based" nature of many education problems. That is, there is often more than one answer or solution to a question or problem, respectively. Multiple decision paths create a challenge for the education leader, in particular, when considering the political, cultural, economic, and academic nature of the education context (i.e., school).

Ethical Dilemmas

Cranston et al. (2003) state, with respect to the nature of an "ethical dilemma,"

> [It] can be described as a circumstance that requires a choice between competing sets of principals in a given, usually undesirable or perplexing, situation. Conflicts of interest . . . are possibly the most obvious situations that could place school leaders in an ethical dilemma".
>
> (p. 137)

Ethical dilemmas require the educational leader to question his or her moral beliefs and theories, and to search for an understanding of what is going on below the surface.

A central and perhaps defining element of educational leadership and ethical decision making, in particular as it relates to problématique in education contexts, centers on the nature of ethical dilemmas that leaders are confronted with on a daily basis. Ethical dilemmas draw into specific relief the increasingly complex context in which education leaders work (Cooper, 1998; Cranston, 2002; Cranston et al., 2006). As well, ethical dilemmas draw into specific relief the values-based nature of education leadership (Walker, 2003). Hodgkinson (1991) further explains, "values, morals and ethics are the very stuff of leadership and administrative life" (p. 11). Goldring and Greenfield (2002), in their work on the "roles, expectations, and dilemmas of leadership," state that the "moral dimensions of educational leadership and administration" constitute one of the special conditions that make administering schools "different from such work in other contexts" (pp. 2–3).

Robbins and Trabichet (2009) are instructive in their discussion of an ethical dilemma:

> A dilemma is a situation where one has to choose between two options but does not know which side to take because both seem legitimate. This approach hides two possibilities: First, either the contradiction is only apparent because a superior or objective solution exists. In this case the problem is epistemic: the dilemma needs to be overcome to find the best outcome. Second, the contradiction is real and one needs to make a choice, but according to which norms? In either case the problem revolves around finding criteria for decision-making when faced with ethical dilemmas.
>
> (p. 52)

Concerning ethical decision making, Tuana (2007) has argued that, by being provided the relevant and necessary knowledge and ethical acumen requisite to recognizing (being sensitive to), assessing (reasoning through), and making a judgment (imagining a moral solution), the educational leader is then able to recognize, assess, and make a moral judgment in relation to an ethical dilemma. That is to say, the educational leader is prepared to examine the problématique—complex and dynamic nature—of an ethical dilemma. Ethical dilemmas are complex in that they rarely exist as a single or independent problem. Rather, ethical dilemmas are a complex set of interrelated problems, with lived history, multiple social actors, varying social factors, and conflicting values. And, ethical dilemmas are dynamic in that they are based on human interactions with social contexts defined by shifting political and cultural patterns and practices (Cranston et al., 2003).

Ethical Drift

There are many factors in today's educational system and its schools that challenge educational leaders in adhering to ethical values. Ethical drift is the erosion of ethical behavior that occurs in individuals below their level of self-awareness. Kleinman (2006) notes that ethical drift occurs when good people do bad things. Sternberg (2012a, 2012b) explains ethical drift as the gradual ebbing of standards that occurs in an individual, a group, or an organization as the result of pressures internal and external to the social content of an organization, such as a school. Drift typically occurs when there is intense competition for resources; people start to feel that they are in a zero-sum game; people perceive, or think they perceive, others acting in ways that are ethically compromised; or people see no other viable way out of the quandary; they feel they just can't leave the situation (Sternberg, 2012a, p. 59). Educational leaders are confronted with ethical dilemmas each day in the school setting, and they experience the ebb and flow of tensions that impact ethical decision making. With the ebbing of ethical standards in concert with the challenges of resolving ethical dilemmas, educational leaders are confronted with yet another challenge, that of ethical drift in the behavior of others who are primary to an ethical dilemma.

Kleinman (2006) explains that ethical drift is "an incremental deviation from ethical practice that goes unnoticed by individuals who justify the deviations as acceptable and who believe themselves to be maintaining their ethical boundaries" (p. 73). Often, ethical drift occurs below a level of awareness to the individual and to others, and "facilitates doing that which fosters self-serving needs" (p. 73). The educational leader working to resolve an ethical dilemma may find that the dilemma's point of origin and/or its intensity is predicated on or exacerbated by ethical drift in various social actors embedded in the problématique. The very essence of ethical drift is that it occurs before the seriousness of the dilemma takes shape or before the conflict is even perceived (Kleinman, 2006; Moore & Gino, 2013; Sternberg, 2012b).

Ethical drift can be interpreted as moving away from one's moral compass, so to speak. Given the political nature of education and the complex and dynamic nature of education problems, compounded by external tensions from government agencies (i.e., accountability and testing) and internal tensions (i.e., cultural resistance to value-based decisions), the decision-making process is subject to those tensions and therefore subject to ethical drift.

Critical Incident

Ethical dilemmas are animated by a critical incident that sets dilemma in play, creating the problématique that educational leaders are confronted with in the school or educational setting. In concert with the critical incident, as Cranston et al. (2003) explain, "is a set of forces, each of which has the capacity to illuminate the critical incident from its own particular bias or basis" (p. 141). Within and across this set of forces there are competing tensions. Cranston et al. (2003) identify nine competing forces: professional ethics; legal issues; policies; organizational culture; institutional context; public interest; society and community; global context; political framework; economic and financial contexts; and an unidentified force that might emerge at any time and generate an ethical dilemma (p. 141). For the educational leader, the eight identified forces are recognized as part of the defining nature of the day-to-day functions of the school. However, the unidentified force is the one that often creates an extreme tension, and for which there is no referent in experience.

Enomoto and Kramer (2007) draw forward that the importance of discerning "the sources of ethical tension in a dilemma is helpful in that it exposes the reasoning or logic that may be underlying the decision" (p. 16). The authors are worth quoting at length on the complexity of ethical decisions:

> . . . the nature of a dilemma is in the complexity of the choices if offers, the deliberation related to values or right and wrong, and the judgments

that one must make as a result of such choices. What might be a small problem to resolve for one person may be a tough decision for someone else. . . . The relative experience of the leadership, the perspectives of varied participants, and the cultural context all affect working the dilemma. These factors force us to probe for deeper understanding of the unique context of the situation.

(p. 91)

When educational leaders find themselves in perplexing situations that necessitate their choosing among competing sets of principles, values, beliefs, or ideals, ethical dilemmas emerge. Kidder (1995) maintains that many of the ethical dilemmas facing professionals and leaders "don't centre upon right versus wrong [but can] involve right versus right or wrong versus wrong" (p. 16).

Exemplars of Ethical Dilemmas

Dempster and Berry (2003) identified four primary categories of ethical dilemmas: those related to students, staff, finance and resources, and external relations. Begley (2005), in a study of school administrators, identified ethical dilemmas concerned with "the best interests of students," on conflicts with parents or community members, and on abusive and/or incompetent staff. As well, principals reported conflicts between organizational policies and the principal's own sense of professional autonomy. Accountability to the educational system and to others in both the Dempster and Berry and Begley studies were central ethical dilemmas faced.

Jenlink and Jenlink (2012), in a study of case-based pedagogy in a doctoral program, noted that dilemmas examined by the participants (practicing educational leaders) focused on difficult personnel and student issues. However, there were instances of personal ethical dilemmas that involved complex moral considerations that left respective participants emotionally charged. Specifically, conflict among the dimensions of ethical conduct and conflict emanating from blurred or competing accountability (Begley, 2005) seem to have been the most prevalent. An examination of the ethical dilemma cases authored by participants identified the following categories:

* Social arrangements
* Conflicts emerging when personal and professional boundaries are crossed
* Internal versus external relations
* Students, staff, finance, and resources
* Equity/inequity
* Accountability, both within the system and to others, and competing accountabilities between social groups

- Sexual orientation
- Social performance
- Politics—community, professional, cultural, etc.
- Teacher and student relationships
- Curriculum and programmatic issues

Ethical dilemmas, difficult ethical decisions are not necessarily the same as a decision that is difficult to make. An educational leader, in making a moral judgment concerning an ethical dilemma, may be faced with decisions that are right and wrong, right and right, or a variation of right and wrong options that are often value based, politically charged, and antithetical to social norms in the school community (Campbell, 2003). An ethical dilemma is perplexing and often leaves the educational leader in an ethical quandary as to what decision to make in consideration of consequential versus duty-bound ethics.

Ethical Frames in Decision Making

Various scholars including Begley (1999), Cranston et al. (2006), Nash (1996), Furman (2004), Shapiro and Stefkovich (2005), Starratt (1994, 2004), Strike, Haller, and Soltis (2005), and others have focused extensively on ethical frames. The derivation of the scholarly examination of different ethical leadership perspectives has resulted in a fairly constant framing of ethics that includes ethic of justice, ethic of care, ethic of community, ethic of critique, ethic of profession, and ethic of presence to note the more common occurring ethics of educational leadership. When examining case-based pedagogies and case methods (Cranston, et al., 2003; Strike et al., 2005) for leadership preparation, two specific philosophical perspectives emerge: consequentialism and non-consequentialism.

Consequentialist

Philosophical theories aligned with consequentialism, referred to as teleological, are often aligned with utilitarianism, or ends-based thinking. When the individual is attempting to determine what is right or wrong, consequentialist theories focus attention on the results or consequences of the decision or action. In the case of resolving an ethical dilemma, the educational leader as consequentialist is concerned with consequences his or her decision has in the larger social context.

Strike et al. (2005) explain that a consequentialist, in ethical decision making, holds that the rightness of an action can be determined based on consequences and a commitment to the "principle of benefit maximization" (p. 19). The best decision or choice is the one that results in what is intrinsically valuable or of the most good or the greatest benefit to the most people. Therefore, outcomes or consequences decide the morality of our actions.

However, consequentialism is often criticized because it fails to attend to the needs of the individual and its lack of focus on either short-term or long-term results (Duignan, 2006; Haynes, 1998; Jarvis, 1997). The consequentialist approach presumes that the greatest good can be discovered independently of any ideological or conceptual schema. Critics have rejected consequentialism because they believe we cannot always predict the outcomes of our actions; therefore the end is often unknown and uncertain. Therefore, the morality of an act cannot rely on its repercussions.

Freakley and Burgh (2000, p. 120) explain the consequentialist as an individual who takes the perspective that actions can only be justified with reference to the end or outcomes they achieve. A consequentialist would make a decision only after carefully weighing the foreseeable consequences and choosing the alternative that produces the better result.

Non-Consequentialist

Philosophical theories aligned with non-consequentialism, referred to as deontological, are guided by a duty-bound ethic. Such an ethic requires of the educational leader an application of human rationality and the same principle or moral law, universally. Kant (1993) argued that a duty-bond ethic is a compulsory rule or "categorical imperative" that, if applied to one person must be applied to everyone. This imperative states: "Act only according to that maxim whereby you can at the same time will that it should become a universal law" (Kant, 1993, p. 30).

The educational leader as non-consequentialist, in resolving an ethical dilemma and ethical decisions making, is concerned with treating others as ends rather than means, following the "principle of equal respect" by considering their welfare rather than our own gain, and considering that all people are free, rational, and responsible moral agents, therefore all deserving of equal treatment and opportunity no matter what our interests or ability (Strike et al., 2005, p. 17). The non-consequentialist is not oblivious to consequences; however, "the crucial point that makes an action a moral action is that the action taken gives first consideration to the value and dignity of persons" (p. 17).

Burke (1997) explains the non-consequentialist as an individual who lives his or her life "by an uncompromising, moral legalism which requires adherence to duty, principle or absolute truth, etc., as more important than consequences . . . in determining what is good, just, right and fair" (p. 15). The non-consequentialist makes ethical judgments based on duty, rights, laws, motive, intuition, or reason.

Virtue Ethics

Virtue or character ethics has its beginning with Aristotle's *Nicomachean Ethics* (2000). The virtue ethics perspective focuses, in large part, on the integrity of the moral actor, more so than on the moral act itself (the decision or behavior). A chief concern of virtue ethics is the obligation to transcend one's self-interest, to care for one's fellow citizens in community. Virtue ethics emphasizes the development of internal qualities of character, rather than obedience to moral rules (Hart, 1994).

MacIntyre (1981) defines virtue as "an acquired quality the possession and exercise of which tends to enable us to achieve those good which are internal to practices and the lack of which effectively prevents us from achieving any such goods" (p. 191). Freakley and Burgh (2000) explain virtue ethics as based on the assumption that morality is best understood in terms of individuals' inner traits (p. 124). The virtue ethicists argues "in favor of a connection between character and reasoning for without good character I may reason about what is right but still choose not do so" (p. 125). A virtue ethics perspective of educational leadership considers the leader's character, motivations, and intentions.

Motivations and intentions are important to ethical decision making in resolving a dilemma. For the educational leader working within the problématique of an ethical dilemma, it is important to ascertain professional standards of ethical behavior (i.e., decision making) (Rachels, 2003; Solomon, 1988). A virtue ethics perspective, for the educational leader, requires that the leader look to the community that holds him or her to the highest ethical standard and, as an educational leader, support his or her intentions to be a virtuous person. A virtue ethics approach to leadership is critical to professional ethics as "a just society depends more upon the moral trustworthiness of its citizens and it[s] leader than upon structures designed to transform ignoble actions into socially useful results" (Hart, 1994, p. 107).

A Moral Literacy Approach to Ethical Decision Making

Ethical decisions require moral judgments, and in turn moral judgment requires a moral literacy on the part of the individual rendering a judgment. Herman (1998), in her examination of the fundamental nature of moral literacy, explained it "is a culture-dependent, intentional process. To be literate in a domain is to have the capacity to recognize and perform at some specified level of competency" (p. 3). Moral literacy is defined as "a capacity to read and respond to the basic elements of a moral world" (Herman, 2007, p. 97). Simply stated, everyone has a fundamental yet minimal capacity for responding to moral facts as a kind of launching point in the development of one's moral character that assists an individual in being sensitive to moral tensions, and being able to reason through those tensions—to make the morally responsible decision.

Developing Moral Literacy

Moral literacy, in consideration of what it means to be a moral leader, relates to the conceptual and practical capacity of the school leader to make and encourage morally grounded decisions, decisions that take into consideration values and beliefs within the cultural setting of the school (Begley & Johansson, 2003). Educational leaders face increasingly complex and conflicting demands and, in turn, "leadership decisions are unavoidably complex as they are connected to and interconnected with different contexts simultaneously, contexts that are themselves shifting" (Walker, Haiyan, & Shuangye, 2007, p. 380).

Developing moral literacy is analogous to ongoing learning. Tuana (2003), in her examination of moral literacy, posited three basic components of moral literacy: becoming knowledgeable, cultivating moral virtues, and developing moral reasoning. With these components in mind, Walker et al. (2007) noted that development of moral literacy in leaders is made problematic when a leader's

> traditional socio-cultural orientations diverge from those of their school community . . . in intercultural schools . . . due to the interplay of the divergent cultural values, inequality of opportunity, and often, social disadvantage, carried by their students, teachers, and broader communities.
>
> (p. 381)

The morally literate leader enacts his or her leadership practice guided by critical self-reflective processing of what makes leading in an educational setting problematic.

Dimensions of Moral Literacy

Recent literature on moral literacy identifies three dimensions of ethical decision making as a form of moral literacy, which should guide educational leaders' practice in addressing the problématique of education problems and the ethical dilemmas that make such problems complex and difficult. These dimensions include: ethical sensitivity, ethical reasoning, and moral imagination and are drawn from the related literature on moral literacy (see Begley, 1996, 1999, 2005, 2006; Begley & Johansson, 1990; Langlois, 2004; Starratt, 1991, 1994, 2004; Stefkovich & Begley, 2007; Tuana, 2003, 2006, 2007), and their contemporaries.

These dimensions follow a philosophical argument for moral literacy in leadership practice, in particular drawing into specific relief the implications of decision making as an ethical, political, cultural, and intellectual responsibility. These three dimensions align with ethical decision making in resolving ethical dilemmas: ethical sensitivity and ethical reasoning necessary to examining and deconstructing the ethical dilemmas; identifying the nature of the problématique and ethical issues in play, as well as the human dynamics and contextual elements.

Tuana (2007), in her essay "Conceptualizing Moral Literacy," advances her framing of moral literacy, refining what she believes are the three basic components. These include ethical sensitivity, ethical reasoning, and moral imagination. Figure 10.1 presents a conceptual framing of Tuana's (2003, 2006, 2007), conceptualizing moral literacy, synthesizing the three components and a set of related

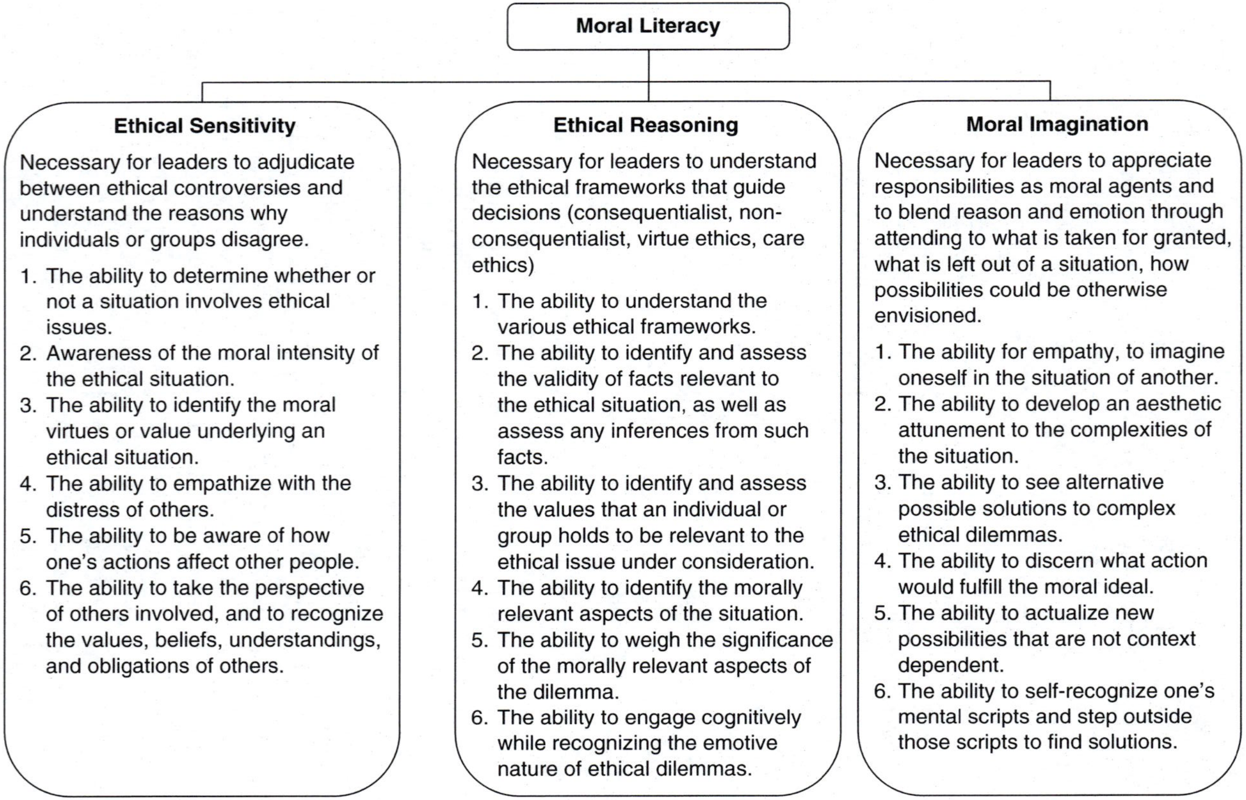

Moral Literacy

Ethical Sensitivity

Necessary for leaders to adjudicate between ethical controversies and understand the reasons why individuals or groups disagree.

1. The ability to determine whether or not a situation involves ethical issues.
2. Awareness of the moral intensity of the ethical situation.
3. The ability to identify the moral virtues or value underlying an ethical situation.
4. The ability to empathize with the distress of others.
5. The ability to be aware of how one's actions affect other people.
6. The ability to take the perspective of others involved, and to recognize the values, beliefs, understandings, and obligations of others.

Ethical Reasoning

Necessary for leaders to understand the ethical frameworks that guide decisions (consequentialist, non-consequentialist, virtue ethics, care ethics)

1. The ability to understand the various ethical frameworks.
2. The ability to identify and assess the validity of facts relevant to the ethical situation, as well as assess any inferences from such facts.
3. The ability to identify and assess the values that an individual or group holds to be relevant to the ethical issue under consideration.
4. The ability to identify the morally relevant aspects of the situation.
5. The ability to weigh the significance of the morally relevant aspects of the dilemma.
6. The ability to engage cognitively while recognizing the emotive nature of ethical dilemmas.

Moral Imagination

Necessary for leaders to appreciate responsibilities as moral agents and to blend reason and emotion through attending to what is taken for granted, what is left out of a situation, how possibilities could be otherwise envisioned.

1. The ability for empathy, to imagine oneself in the situation of another.
2. The ability to develop an aesthetic attunement to the complexities of the situation.
3. The ability to see alternative possible solutions to complex ethical dilemmas.
4. The ability to discern what action would fulfill the moral ideal.
5. The ability to actualize new possibilities that are not context dependent.
6. The ability to self-recognize one's mental scripts and step outside those scripts to find solutions.

FIGURE 10.1 Dimensions and Abilities Associated With Moral Literacy and Ethical Decision Making

literacy abilities to serve as a heuristic for examining moral literacy and applying the theoretical to ethical leadership practices.

While ethical sensitivity and ethical reasoning align with Tuana's earlier components of becoming knowledgeable, cultivating moral virtues, and developing moral reasoning, the emergence of moral imagination reflects a blending "of affective and rational components that contribute to the imagination" (Tuana, 2007, p. 374).

Ethical sensitivity focuses on the ethical issues, and ethical reasoning focuses on the questions and/or problems requiring analysis. In deconstructing the ethical dilemma, power-relations and interests are revealed and the role each plays becomes a part of the calculus of ethical decision making. The moral imagination dimension of ethical decision making focuses on leaders' responsibilities as moral agents and the cognitive and ethical presence to blend reason and emotion through attending to what is taken for granted, what is left out of a situation, and/ or how possibilities could be otherwise envisioned.

Simply stated, moral imagination is the ability to see alternative possible solutions to complex ethical dilemmas. Johnson (1993) who explained moral imagination as the "ability to imaginatively discern various possibilities for acting in a given situation and to envision the potential help and harm that are likely to result from a given situation" (p. 202). Moral imagination, as Werhane (1998) explains, requires: "(a) Awareness of one's context, (b) Awareness of the script or schema functioning in that context, and (c) Awareness of possible moral conflicts or dilemmas that might arise in that context, that is, dilemmas created at least in part by the dominating script" (p. 85).

Solving complex moral problems requires the educational leader to engage with a defined level of ethical and moral sensitivity to existing issues and problems. Equal importance to the leader's capacity to make moral judgments is the ability to engage in ethical and moral reasoning, deliberating on the moral nature of a dilemma, recognizing the different solution paths present and the ethical/ moral frame necessary to interpret the complexity of the issues in play. Finally, the educational leader must critically self-reflect, engaging his or her moral imagination to see a moral solution.

Werhane (1999) is instructive with respect to the importance of moral imagination as a form of moral consciousness. She defines moral imagination as:

> The ability to understand that context or set of activities from a number of different perspectives, the actualizing of new possibilities that are not context-dependent, and the integration of the process of evaluating those possibilities from a moral point of view.
>
> (p. 5)

Moral imagination enhances moral reasoning by encouraging the generation of novel or nuanced alternatives to resolve an ethical or moral dilemma. Moral imagination facilitates moral reasoning in that it "helps leaders step away from their typical mental scripts or schemas and to recognize the moral elements of events" (Johnson, 2012, p. 56). The importance of moral imagination lies in the realization that an educational leader's mental scripts or schemas are based on past experiences; the script or schema, when applied to current or new events, may leave out some of the moral elements that define the new event.

A Decision-Making Model for Ethical Leadership

The educational leader is confronted daily by ill-structured problems, ethical dilemmas for which there are no universal answers. Each leader works within a complex and dynamic educational setting. The intersection of ethical sensitivity, ethical reasoning, moral imagination, and moral judgment enables the educational leader to address the ill-structured problems in education. Importantly, moral judgments require continuous critical self-reflection to ascertain one's position, ethically, as an educational leader in juxtaposition with the daily challenges of ethical dilemmas, compounded by ethical drift and conflicting values.

The problématique with which the educational leader is confronted represents an interconnected set of all interactions between the elements of a complex ethical dilemma, the social actors or participants animating the dilemma and giving it life, the contexts (social, cultural, political, moral, legal, and professional), and the emergent value conflicts. As noted previously, the presence of ethical drift is also a factor that must be considered in making ethical decisions. Figure 10.2 presents an ethical decision-making cycle that demonstrates the interactive nature of a moral literacy approach to decision making. The cycle represents an analytic framework for making ethical decisions that are predicated on sound moral judgment.

The *initial phase* of the cycle begins with the educational leader's recognition that an ethical dilemma exits, which is termed ethical sensitivity (Tuana, 2006, 2007). Ethical sensitivity, as the beginning point for identifying an ethical dilemma, requires that the dilemma be stated as clearly as possible. Stating the dilemma, naming it, can best be done by formulating a sound moral question to guide the moral judgment of the educational leader. A moral question meets three

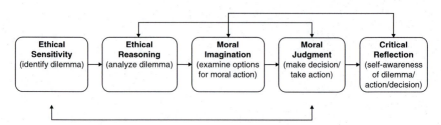

FIGURE 10.2 Ethical Decision-Making Cycle (adapted from Rest, 1986; Tuana, 2003, 2006, 2007; van de Poel & Royakkers, 2006).

conditions: (1) It must clearly state what the dilemma is; (2) it must state for whom it is a dilemma, and (3) it must articulate the moral nature of the ethical dilemma.

Taking direction from the moral question, ethical sensitivity not only requires the leader to discern that an ethical dilemma exits, it also requires that the leader critically and self-reflectively examine the nature of the dilemma, that is, examine the context(s) within which the dilemma exists, the human factors, perceived value conflicts, whether there is a conflict of interest on the part of the leader in relation to others, what makes the dilemma a dilemma, if there are multiple problems interacting to create the dilemma, the history of the dilemma (i.e., if the dilemma is of recent origin or has been in existence for a period of time, the potential issues that contribute to the dilemma, and whether a more experienced moral voice is required (see Johnson, 2012; Rest, 1986; Tuana, 2003, 2006).

The *second phase* of the ethical decision-making cycle is moral reasoning, which requires the educational leader to incorporate ethical frames such as consequential-ist, non-consequentialist, and virtue ethics to reason through the ethical dilemma and its complexity. Here the educational leader reflects, drawing from a virtue ethics frame, on the character of the individuals, as presented, the actions repre-sentative of or that defines the dilemma. He or she also must examine the conse-quential nature of the dilemma in terms of the lives affected, the harm done, the moral codes in question. As a consequentialist, the educational leader cognitively as well as morally examines the nature of the dilemma. As a non-consequentialist, the educational leader is concerned with duty-bound requirements that have or have not been met by individuals identified as integral to the dilemma. The ethical frames enable the educational leader to assess the morally relevant aspects of the dilemma (Freakley & Burgh, 2000; Rachels, 2003; Strike et al., 2005).

The educational leader engages in a critical examination of the essential ver-sus nonessential details of the dilemma, identifying and assessing the values of the individuals involved. The presence of ethical drift is a factor that the edu-cational leader assesses to determine the implications of ethical drift for trig-gering and/or contributing to the dilemma. As well, ethical reasoning enables the educational leader to separate the essential from the nonessential details of a dilemma. As Figure 10.2 depicts, critical self-reflection is a process necessary to the educational leader's engagement in ethical reasoning and analyzing the dilemma, while also preparing to engage in moral imagination, and identifying the options available for making a moral judgment. Ethical reasoning enables the educational leader to give a thoughtful account of an ethical position; it moves beyond intuition or emotions.

Imagining moral options is the *third phase* of the ethical decision-making cycle. What becomes apparent to the educational leader engaged in ethical decision making is that the phases are not discreet, independent steps forward in a pro-cess, but rather dynamic and interactive, often recursive in nature as the ethical dilemma is carefully identified, analyzed, and solutions examined. The interac-tive nature is made apparent through constant critical, self-reflective processing.

Equally apparent to the dynamic nature of the process is the constant interface between the leader's moral character and the moral character of the other individuals who are identified as taking part in or contributing to the dilemma.

Moral imagination enables the educational leader to situate him or herself in the role/position of different individuals involved in the dilemma, while recognizing that different individuals engage in certain actions that often conflict with the values of others and/or are in conflict with varying actions that contributed to the origin of the dilemma. Understanding the nature of actions is essential to identifying alternative actions that might be taken to resolve the dilemma. As well, the educational leader must simultaneously self-recognize his or her dominant mental scripts/schemas and be able to step outside those scripts to see alternative possible solutions. Moral imagination is integral to the educational leader's ability to actualize new alternative possibilities that do not reify existing cultural patterns or decision paths. New solutions that are outside existing patterns are integral to resolving complex ethical dilemmas—to understanding the problématique in the education setting.

The *fourth phase* in the ethical decision-making cycle is making a moral judgment, taking action, and rendering an ethical decision. The interface between phase two and phase four is dependent on critical self-reflection and moral reasoning. Again, the dynamic nature of the ethical decision-making process draws into specific relief the interdependent nature of the educational leader's moral character as a primary factor in ethical sensitivity, ethical reasoning, and moral imagination in coming to a moral judgment that resolves the ethical dilemma (see Figure 10.2).

Perhaps the most important aspect of moral judgment, for the educational leader engaged in ethical decision making, is that the actions which result from the decision-making process faithfully and accurately reflect an individual's moral ideals in concert with a level of conscious deliberation (Hsieh, 1997). Once the educational leader has reasoned through the details of the dilemma and examined the moral solutions to the ethical dilemma, identifying alternative possibilities, he or she then enacts the judgment as an ethical decision/action on behalf of all individuals involved.

As moral agent in the educational setting, the educational leader following a path of moral literacy understands that the goal of ethical judgment "is not to achieve absolute certainty about what is right, but rather to achieve reliability and coherence in behavior, choices, character, process, and outcomes" (Rushton & Penticuff, 2007, p. 325). The morally literate educational leader recognizes that it is the nature of a problématique in educational settings like schools that makes absolute certainty difficult, if not impossible. Making a moral judgment is an attempt to resolve a complex ethical dilemma; however, at the same time an educational leader's moral judgment may resolve the ethical dilemma it may also simultaneously create a new dynamic that eventually emerges as a new problem or set of problems.

Final Reflections

As the challenges facing educational leaders have become more acute, attention to the area of ethics and ethical dilemmas is required (Duignan & Collins, 2003). The ability to evaluate the problématique and ethical dilemmas pervading education requires the leader be self-aware of his or her ethical positioning with respect to theoretical and philosophical frames. As well, the leader must be able to see the factors contributing to the nature of a problématique and ethical dilemma, whether it is a socio-cultural conflict in values on an institutional or personal level. Tensions related to common values, or conflict between values come into play as cultural patterns shift, and the leader is not only responsible for recognizing the emerging education problem but is equally responsible for evaluating the problem from multiple perspectives, theoretical and philosophical as well as cultural and political. And, the leader is responsible, in terms of himself or herself as well as other persons, with respect to discerning when conflicting values, beliefs, and cultural patterns contribute to education problems.

Note

1. For purposes of this chapter, the term *problématique* is used to denote the complex nature of ethical dilemmas and the requisite decision-making model required. Drawing on Warfield's (2009) work, problématique may take on two different forms: (1) some members of a set of problems that arises in an ethical dilemma situation aggravate or antagonize other members of the same set of problems (i.e., in the nature of conflicting values); (2) some problem categories found within a set of problems that arise within an ethical dilemma aggravate or amplify other problem categories found within the same set of problems, primarily due to the dynamic nature of interactions among the problems that are integral to the ethical dilemma (i.e., in the nature of conflicting values, the contributing political and professional factors, the interaction between multiple problems).

References

Aristotle. (2000). *Nicomachean ethics.* (Trans. R. Crisp). Cambridge, UK: Cambridge University Press.

Beachum, F. D., & McCray, C. R. (2010). Cracking the code: Illuminating the promises and pitfalls of social justice in educational leadership. *International Journal of Urban Educational Leadership, 4*(1), 206–221.

Begley, P. T. (1996). Cognitive perspectives on values in administration: A quest for coherence and relevance. *Educational Administration Quarterly, 32*(3), 403–426.

Begley, P. T. (1999). *Values and educational leadership.* Albany, NY: SUNY Press.

Begley, P. T. (2005, April 13). *The dilemmas of leadership: Perspectives on the moral literacy of principals from Ontario and Pennsylvania.* Paper presented at the 2005 Annual Meeting of the American Educational Research Association, Montreal.

Begley, P. T. (2006). Self-knowledge, capacity and sensitivity: Prerequisites to authentic leadership by school principals. *Journal of Educational Administration, 44*(6), 570–589.

Begley, P. T., & Johansson, O. (Eds.). (1990). *The ethical dimensions of school leadership.* Dordrecht, The Netherlands: Kluwer Academic Publishers.

Begley, P. T., & Johansson, O. (Eds.). (2003). *The ethical dimensions of school leadership.* Dordrecht, The Netherlands: Kluwer Academic Publishers.

Burke, C. (1997). *Leading schools through the ethics thicket in the new era of educational reform.* Hawthorne, Victoria: Australian Council for Educational Administration.

Campbell, E. (2003). Let right be done: Trying to put ethical standards into practice. In P. T. Begley and O. Johansson (Eds.), *The ethical dimensions of school leadership* (pp. 107–125). Dordrecht, The Netherlands: Kluwer Academic Publishers.

Cooper, T. L. (1998). *The responsible administrator: An approach to ethics for the administrative role.* San Francisco, CA: Jossey Bass.

Cranston, N. (2002). School-based management, leaders and leadership: Change and challenges for principals. *International Studies in Educational Administration, 30,* 2–12.

Cranston, N., Ehrich, L., & Kimber, M. (2003). The 'right' decision? Towards an understanding of ethical dilemmas for school leaders. *Westminster Studies in Education, 26*(2), 135–147.

Cranston, N., Ehrich. L., & Kimber, M. (2006). Ethical dilemmas: The bread and butter of educational leaders' lives. *Journal of Educational Administration, 44*(2), 106–121.

Dempster, N., & Berry, V. (2003). Blindfolded in a minefield: Principals' ethical decision-making. *Cambridge Journal of Education, 33*(3), 457–477.

Duignan, P. (2006). *Educational leadership: Key challenges and ethical tensions.* Cambridge, UK: Cambridge University Press.

Duignan, P., & Collins, V. (2003). Leadership challenges and ethical dilemmas in front-line organizations. In N. Bennett, M. Crawford, & M. Cartwright (Eds.), *Effective educational leadership* (pp. 281–294). London, UK: Sage.

Enomoto, E. K, & Kramer, B. H. (2007). *Leading through the quagmire: Ethical foundations, critical methods, and practical applications for school leadership.* Lanham, MD: Rowman & Littlefield Education Press.

Freakley, M., & Burgh, G. (2000). *Engaging with ethics: Ethical inquiry for teachers.* Katoomba, New South Wales, Australia: Social Science Press.

Furman, G. C. (2004). The ethic of community. *Journal of Educational Administration, 42*(2), 215–235.

Goldring, E., & Greenfield, W. (2002). Understanding the evolving concept of leadership in education: Roles, expectations, and dilemmas. In J. Murphy (Ed.), *The educational leadership challenge: Redefining leadership for the 21st century. 101st yearbook of the National Society for the Study of Education* (pp. 1–19). Chicago, IL: National Society for the Study of Education.

Hart, D. K. (1994). Administration and the ethics of virtue. In T. C. Cooper (Ed.), *The handbook of administrative ethics* (pp. 391–412). New York, NY: Marcel Dakker.

Haynes, F. (1998). *The ethical school.* London, UK: Routledge.

Herman, B. (1998). Moral literacy. In G. B. Peterson (Ed.), *The Tanner Lectures on Human Values* (vol. 19, pp. 311–373). Salt Lake City: University of Utah Press.

Herman, B. (2007). *Moral literacy.* Cambridge, MA: Harvard University Press.

Hodgkinson, C. (1991). *Educational leadership: The moral art.* Albany, NY: SUNY Press.

Hsieh, D. M. (1997). *Between instinct and habit: Moral judgment and dispositions.* Washington University, St. Louis, Honors Thesis (Magna cum laude). Retrieved from http://enlightenment.supersaturated.com/essays/text/dianamertzhsieh/thesis/01.html

Jarvis, P. (1997). *Ethics and education for adults in a late modern society.* Leicester, UK: National Institute of Adult Continuing Education.

Jenlink, P. M., & Jenlink, K. E. (2012, April 13–17). *Ethical leadership and moral literacy: Incorporating ethical dilemmas in a case-based pedagogy.* Paper presented to Division A, Section 5, at the annual meeting of the American Educational Research Association, Vancouver, British Columbia, Canada.

Johnson, C. E. (2012). *Meeting the ethical challenges of leadership: Casting light or shadow* (4th ed.). Los Angeles, CA: Sage.

Johnson, M. (1993). *Moral imagination.* Chicago, IL: University of Chicago Press.

Kant, I. (1993). Grounding for the metaphysics of morals. In J. W. Ellington (Ed.), *On a supposed right to lie because of philanthropic concerns* (3rd ed.) (pp. 30–32). Indianapolis, IN: Hackett Publishing Company.

Kidder, R. M. (1995). *How good people make tough choices: Resolving the dilemmas of ethical living.* New York, NY: William Morrow.

Kleinman, C. S. (2006). Ethical drift: When good people do bad things. *JONA's Healthcare Law, Ethics, and Regulation, 8*(3), 72–76.

Langlois, L. (2004). Responding ethically: Complex decision-making by school district superintendents. *International Studies in Educational Administration, 32*(2), 78–93.

MacIntyre, A. (1981). *After virtue.* Notre Dame, IN: University of Notre Dame.

Moore, C., & Gino, F. (2013). Ethically adrift: How others pull our moral compass from true north, and how we can fix it. *Research in Organizational Behavior, 33,* 53–77.

Nash, R. J. (1996). *Real world ethics: Frameworks for educators and human service professionals.* New York, NY: Teachers College Press.

Rachels, J. (2003). *The elements of moral philosophy* (4th ed.). New York, NY: McGraw-Hill.

Rest, J. R. (1986). *Moral development: Advances in research and theory.* New York, NY: Praeger.

Robbins, S., & Trabichet, L. (2009). Ethical decision-making by educational leaders: Its foundations, culture and more recent perspectives. *Management in Education, 23*(2), 51–56.

Rushton, C. H., & Penticuff, J. H. (2007). A framework for analysis of ethical dilemmas in critical care nursing. *AACN Advanced Critical Care, 18*(3), 323–328.

Shapiro, J. P., & Stefkovich, J. A. (2005). *Ethical leadership and decision making in education: Applying theoretical perspectives to complex dilemmas.* Mahwah, NJ: Lawrence Erlbaum Associates.

Sims, R., & Keon, T. (1999). Determinants of ethical decision making: The relationship of the perceived organizational environment. *Journal of Business Ethics, 19*(4), 393–401.

Solomon, R. C. (1988). *Ethics and excellence.* New York, NY: Oxford University Press.

Starratt, R. J. (1991). Building an ethical school: A theory for practice in educational leadership. *Educational Administration Quarterly, 27*(2), 185–202.

Starratt, R. J. (1994). *Building an ethical school.* London, UK: Falmer Press.

Starratt, R. J. (2003). *Centering educational administration: Cultivating meaning, community, responsibility.* Mahwah, NJ: Lawrence Erlbaum Associates.

Starratt, R. J. (2004). *Ethical Leadership.* San Francisco, CA: Jossey-Bass.

Stefkovich, J., & Begley, P. T. (2007). Ethical school leadership: Defining the best interests of students. *Educational Management Administration & Leadership, 35*(2), 205–224.

Sternberg, R. J. (2012a). Ethical drift. *Liberal Education, 98*(3), 58–60.

Sternberg, R. J. (2012b). A model of ethical reasoning. *Review of General Psychology, 16*(4), 319–326.

Strike, K. A., Haller, E. J., & Soltis, J. F. (2005). *The ethics of school administration* (3rd ed.). New York, NY: Teachers College Press.

Tuana, N. (2003). *Moral literacy.* Research/Penn State, *24*(2). Retrieved from www.rps.psu.edu/0305/literacy.html

Tuana, N. (2006, October 27). *Moral literacy and ethical leadership.* Paper presented to the 2nd Annual Moral Literacy Colloquium, University Park, PA.

Tuana, N. (2007). Conceptualizing moral literacy. *Journal of Educational Administration, 45*(4), 364–378.

van de Poel, I., & Royakkers, L. (2006). The ethical cycle. *Journal of Business Ethics, 71,* 1–13.

Walker, A. (2003). Developing cross-cultural perspectives on education and community. In P. T. Begley & O. Johansson (Eds.), *The ethical dimensions of school leadership* (pp. 145–160). Dordrecht, The Netherlands: Kluwer Academic Press.

Walker, A., Haiyan, Q., & Shuangye, C. (2007). Leadership and moral literacy in intercultural schools. *Journal of Educational Administration, 45*(4), 379–397.

Warfield, J. N. (2009). *A variety of problématiques.* The John N. Warfield Digital Collection. Fairfax, VA: George Mason University. Retrieved from http://digilib.gmu.edu/jspui/bitstream/1920/3391/1/Variety%20of%20Problematiques.pdf

Warfield, J. N., & Perino, G. H. (1999). The problématique: Evolution of an idea. *Systems Research and Behavioral Science, 16,* 221–226.

Werhane, P. H. (1998). Moral imagination and management decision-making. *Business Ethics Quarterly, Ruffin Series: Special Issue, 1,* 75–98.

Werhane, P. H. (1999). *Moral imagination and management decision-making.* New York, NY: Oxford University Press.

11

JUSTICE AND EQUITY IN EDUCATIONAL PROVISION: THE CASE OF ONTARIO

Marvin A. Zuker

> *The principal is like the caretaker at a cemetery—*
> *there are a lot of people under you, but none are responding.*

Introduction

Canada is a federal system of government. Political and law-making power is shared by two levels of government: the provincial and the federal government. The division of powers is set out in the Constitution between the provinces and federal government. Section 93 of the Constitution Act, 1867 gives the provincial governments the exclusive jurisdiction to make laws governing education. There is no federal department of education in Canada. Education has evolved province specific.

Provincial governments are directly responsible for funding, legislating, regulating, and coordinating education. Some of the sources of provincial education law are education statutes (i.e., Education Act [1990], Teaching Profession Act [1990], Ontario College of Teachers Act [1996]), education regulations, ministry guidelines; policies, procedures, protocols, and by-laws; the common law; and case law.

At both the federal and provincial level, there are other areas of law that intersect with education. For example, federal: Youth Criminal Justice Act (2002); Criminal Code (1985); Divorce Act (1985); and provincial: Human Rights Code (1990); Occupational Health and Safety Act (1990); Labour Relations Act (1995); Child and Family Services Act (1990); and Children's Law Reform Act (1990). These are additional sources of law in education.

The Constitution Act (1982), originally enacted as the British North America Act, 1867 gives the provinces exclusive jurisdiction to enact laws governing public education in Canada. All other provincial and federal laws must be consistent with the Constitution or they may be struck down as "unconstitutional." All education laws passed by the province must be consistent with the Constitution.

Section 93 of the Constitution Act of 1867 gives the provinces exclusive jurisdiction to enact laws governing "education as long as the province does not make laws that affect the rights or privileges of denominational schools recognized by law and in existence at the time of Confederation." Similarly, the Canadian Charter of Rights and Freedoms (1982) (Section 29), recognizes specific rights of denominational (religious), separate, or dissentient schools.

In Ontario, the only denominational schools that existed at the time of Confederation were Roman Catholic French-speaking and Roman Catholic English-speaking. These are the only denominational rights protected under the Constitution in Ontario. Ontario has created a network of French-language school boards both public and Roman Catholic to address this right.

The Canadian Charter of Rights and Freedoms (1982) protects the right to minority language education (Section 23). This section provides that parents who speak the minority official language in their province (i.e., French or English) have specific but limited rights to public schooling for the children in their minority language.

Who Is a Child?

The tangle of legal regulations defining, delineating, or impacting "the child" sets no one standard by which this "junior" status is defined. "Age of majority" and "accountability" legislation regards the graduation date from youth to the standard of 18. Liquor laws commonly demand that no sales be made to individuals under the age of 19. Some legal regimes (such as Ontario's Child and Family Services Act [1990]) accord rights to individuals as young as 7 years old (e.g., for the purposes of consenting to adoption). Still other sources of law consider the issue on the basis of capacity.

There is no one legal definition of "the child." Rather, there are a multitude of standards and definitions of "the child" for the purposes of our laws, which makes understanding the many areas of the law that impinge upon the lives of young persons more challenging.

Simply put, the definition of "the child" for the purposes of the law (and by inference the ascension to adulthood or license for the purposes of various legal standards) varies and must be viewed and applied in the context (and frequently within the statutory or regulatory authority) in which it arises.

Under 21

While rare, the upper limit of childhood does not entirely end at age 19 either, with a handful of public enactments conferring some aspect of "child" recognition (for limited purposes mainly in connection with benefits to dependent "children") to individuals bumping the final threshold of being under the age of 21.

In any situation, "who is the child" is context specific, with definitions and applications of the term being variable and changing even in attempts to apply one statute and its regulations. Anyone who deals with children should be very conscious and attuned to the context (both as a matter of practical application and law) in which this contact occurs.

How many of us would like to be defined, forever, by what we did at 14? Despite almost universal recognition that adolescents are different from adults, many still think they are not. A landmark U.S. Supreme Court decision from 2005 prohibiting capital punishment for crimes committed by children under the age of 18 determined and acknowledged that juveniles are fundamentally different from adults in p. 569 of *Roper v. Simmons* (2005). The court gives three reasons to support its conclusion. First, "a lack of maturity and an underdeveloped sense of responsibility are found in youth more often than in adults and are more understandable among the young." Second, "juveniles are more vulnerable or susceptible to negative influences and outside pressures, including peer pressure." And finally, "the character of a juvenile is not as well-formed as that of an adult. The personality traits of juveniles are more transitory, less fixed," as discussed at pp. 567–570 in *Roper v. Simmons* (2005). They are the general lens through which punishment of children should be viewed.

In an increasingly competitive society, failing to complete high school has detrimental effects on a young person's potential. The first Canadian legislation separating adults from child and adolescent persons was introduced in 1857, placing young persons in training schools and reformatories rather than penitentiaries. Community-based alternatives to imprisonment for young persons were initiated at that time. The first probation officers working specifically with and for juveniles were hired.

The Youth Criminal Justice Act of Canada (2002) (YCJA) came into force on April 1, 2003. The fundamental underlying principles of this legislation are found in s. 3:

3. (1) The following principles apply in the YCJA:

  (b) the criminal justice system for young persons must be separate from that of adults and *emphasize the following:*

    (i) *rehabilitation and reintegration,*
    (ii) *fair and proportionate accountability that is consistent with the greater dependency of young persons and their reduced level of maturity,*
    (iii) enhanced procedural protection to ensure that young persons are treated fairly and that their rights, *including their right to privacy,* are protected,

Section 3(2), moreover, stipulates that the YCJA "shall be liberally construed so as to ensure that young persons are dealt with in accordance with the principles set out in subsection (1)." Section 2(1) defines a "young person" as someone "who is or, in the absence of evidence to the contrary, appears to be 12 years old or older, but less than 18 years old and, if the context requires, includes any person who is charged under this Act with having committed an offense while he or she was a young person or who is found guilty of an offence under this Act."

Moreover, the preamble recognizes society's "responsibility to address the developmental challenges and the needs of young persons and to guide them into adulthood"; encourages "guidance and support"; and seeks "effective rehabilitation and reintegration."

It is also a legal principle that finds expression in Canada's international commitments. The United Nations Convention on the Rights of the Child (1989) (the "Convention"), explicitly mentioned in the preamble to the YCJA, was ratified by Canada in 1992 (Can. T.S. 1992 No. 3). Paragraph 1 of Article 40 of the Convention states:

> States Parties recognize the right of every child alleged as, accused of, or recognized as having infringed the penal law to be treated in a manner consistent with the promotion of the child's sense of dignity and worth, which reinforces the child's respect for the human rights and fundamental freedoms of others and *which takes into account the child's age and the desirability of promoting the child's reintegration and the child's assuming a constructive role in society.*

If the behavior is serious or if the police have other protection concerns, such as apparent parental abuse or neglect, a referral should be made to child welfare authorities. When a child welfare agency receives reports of offending behavior by a child under age 12, which may come from police or other sources, the agency will investigate whether there are parental abuse or neglect concerns that would in themselves merit intervention, with the offending behavior being considered primarily as a symptom of the child's response to an unsatisfactory home situation.

In every Canadian jurisdiction there is, in theory, the possibility of a child welfare or mental health response in the case of serious offending behavior by a child under age 12. However, there are real legal and practical limitations to these responses. In every province, the primary legal basis for a response to offending by children less than 12 years old is child welfare law. When parents are considered unwilling or unable to care properly for their children, in most provinces up to age 16, child welfare legislation authorizes involuntary intervention by a state-sponsored child welfare agency. The agency can become involved in a broad range of circumstances, including physical, emotional, or sexual abuse, physical or emotional neglect, parental death, parental desire to have a child placed for adoption, and other situations where parents are unwilling or unable to care for their children, such as when an adolescent is "out of control."

Student Discipline

There is a need for all children to thrive, which need is more critical now than ever. A shift toward a globally connected economy, a changing workforce, and the increasing diversity of the students we serve in schools require a commitment to two inextricably linked goals: educational equity and excellence. There should be a clear link between safe and supportive learning communities and student achievement. Exclusionary disciplinary strategies should not exclude students from school. They should be used as a last resort to preserve the safety of students and staff. Schools must focus on building professional learning environments. At the heart of this shared vision are meaningful relationships among parents, community members, school leadership, teachers, mental health professionals, and school counselors. These partnerships must be complemented by a culture of caring for the safety and well-being of students who are being suspended— and shared by all in the school and learning community, where ownership of a school vision is built on support for students and believing that all students have the potential to succeed. Students with disabilities too often have their education interrupted by out-of-school suspensions.

A safe and civil environment in schools is necessary for students to achieve high academic standards. Threats, intimidation, harassment, and other bullying behavior are unwarranted and preventable acts of misconduct that interfere with students' ability to learn, disrupt educators' efforts to teach students in a safe and civil environment, and thereby waste essential educational opportunities and resources. Protecting the safety of children and assuring the unimpeded and effective utilization of educational resources are of paramount importance in all schools. Children learn best by example. School administrators, faculty, staff, and student leaders must demonstrate civil and respectful behavior toward all persons and refuse to tolerate threats, intimidation, harassment, or other acts of bullying in their schools.

Schools have the right to adopt reasonable rules and regulations to control student conduct. Such rules are necessary to ensure order and safety and to set the parameters of appropriate behavior. The rights of school officials to adopt and enforce reasonable rules of student conduct are not unlimited as students enjoy certain constitutional, statutory, and regulatory protections from arbitrary and unreasonable discipline. The traditional doctrine of *in loco parentis* is the basis of the school's authority over the students. The forms of discipline imposed vary and depend upon the nature of the infraction, the disciplinary record of the student, and other circumstances. Potential discipline measures span the continuum from a simple verbal reprimand to permanent expulsion.

Disciplining students for off-campus conduct has been recognized as reasonable when the student's action has a direct and immediate effect on school discipline or the safety and welfare of students and staff, causing a material or substantial disruption to the operations of the school. School policy must inform students that they are subject to discipline for such action even though it occurs away from school grounds, and the discipline imposed should relate to school purposes.

The question of what standard should be applied to searches of student persons and property in a school was considered by the Supreme Court of Canada in *R. v. M. (M.R.)* (1998). The summary of that decision, as contained in the head-notes, is that search of student's person or property at a school, by school authorities, is not subject to the same standards that apply to the police.

The Supreme Court found that to require the same kind of prior authorization as is required of the police before a search can be reasonable would be impractical and unworkable in the school environment and, second, that a student's expectation of privacy is lessened to some extent while they attend school or school functions. The headnote indicates:

> A search by school officials of a student under their authority need not be based upon reasonable and probable grounds. Rather, in these circumstances, a search may be undertaken if there are reasonable grounds to believe that a school rule has been or is being violated, and that evidence of the violation will be found in the location or on the person of the student searched.

Another principle, that has come both from *R. v. M.(M.R.)* (1998) and from the cases that have considered it, is that there are different considerations to be applied to a search of the person as opposed to a search of the locker or desk, if you will, or things like that of a student.

A student attending school may have a lessened expectation of privacy in their locker. They may not have a lessened expectation of privacy in their person, and the cases have established that in order to conduct a search of the person, a higher standard must be met.

Privacy

The Municipal Freedom of Information and Protection of Privacy Act (1990) (MIPAD) and/or the Freedom of Information and Protection of Privacy Act (1990) (FIPPA) permit disclosure to aid an investigation of a law enforcement proceeding or from which a law enforcement proceeding is likely to result.

With certain exceptions, s. 21 of the Education Act (1990) imposes a legal obligation to attend school on every school day. In Part XIII of the Education Act (1990), each student is subject to a regime authorizing a school principal to investigate and suspend a student and even commence expulsion proceedings. Essentially, the principal and vice principals are conferred with a disciplinary authority over all their students.

The MFIPPA, with limited exceptions, prohibits the voluntary release of records, containing personal information, which are in the possession, custody, or control of an institution, including a school board. Section 14(3)(J) provides that disclosure of recorded personal information relating, for example, to educational history, constitutes an unjustified invasion of personal privacy. Section 53(1) provides that the provisions of the MFIPPA prevail over confidentiality provisions in other provincial statutes unless the MFIPPA or other statute "specifically provides otherwise." The MFIPPA scheme, to the extent of any overlap or inconsistency, prevails over the Education Act (1990) regime. Sections 14(l) (d) and 51 of the MFIPPA recognize that personal information may be subpoenaed to a criminal trial.

Role of the Principal

When interviewing students, principals often intend to pass on their findings to an investigating officer. The issue then becomes whether that makes the principal a "person in authority" within the meaning of s. 146 of the *YCJA*.

If the principal or vice principal is a "person in authority," s. 146 (2) of the *YCJA* may well govern admissibility. If he or she is a "person in authority," and there is not compliance with the requirements of s. 146 (2), the noncompliance is more than a mere technical irregularity. If the vice principal is not a "person in authority," there is s. 146 (7) and the issue of duress.

The Education Act (1990) sets out the duties of the principal. Those duties include discipline, which is set out in s. 265 (1) (a): to maintain proper order and discipline in the school, and, in s. 265 (1) (d): to maintain pupil records. Pursuant to s. 266 (10), those pupil records are privileged and are to be kept secret subject to the duties of the principal, or with the consent of the pupil or parent.

Teachers and principals must be able to act quickly to protect their students and to provide the orderly atmosphere required for learning. A school official should not be held to the same stringent standard as police when conducting searches of students. The principal has a statutory duty under s. 265 of Ontario's Education Act (1990) to ensure a safe school environment, which implies an authority to conduct reasonable searches and seizures within his school without prior judicial authorization to fulfil that duty.

265. (1) It is the duty of a principal of a school, in addition to the principal's duties as a teacher,

. . . discipline

(a)   to maintain proper order and discipline in the school;

. . . care of pupils and property

(j)   to give assiduous attention to the health and comfort of the pupils, to the care of all teaching materials and other school property . . .;

. . . access to school or class

(m) subject to an appeal to the board, to refuse to admit to the school or classroom
a person whose presence in the school or classroom would in the principal's
judgment be detrimental to the physical or mental wellbeing of the pupils . . .

Teachers and those in charge of our schools are entrusted with the care and
education of our children. It is difficult to imagine a more important trust or duty.
To ensure the safety of the students and to provide them with the orderly environment so necessary to encourage learning, reasonable rules of conduct must be in
place and enforced at schools.

The nature of any inquiry must be viewed in the light of Cory J.'s judgment
in *R. v. M. (M.R.)* (1998), *supra,* at page 401:

> On one hand, it is essential that school authorities be able to react swiftly
> and effectively when faced with a situation that could unreasonably disrupt
> the school environment or jeopardize the safety of the students. Schools
> today are faced with extremely difficult problems which were unimaginable
> a generation ago. Dangerous weapons are appearing in schools with increas-
> ing frequency. There is as well the all too frequent presence at schools of
> illicit drugs. These weapons and drugs create problems that are grave and
> urgent. Yet schools also have a duty to foster the respect of their students
> for the constitutional rights of all members of society. Learning respect for
> those rights is essential to our democratic society and should be part of the
> education of all students. These values are best taught by example and may
> be undermined by those in authority.

Teachers and principals are placed in a position of trust that carries with it
onerous responsibilities. When children attend school or school functions, it is
they who must care for the children's safety and well-being. It is they who must
carry out the fundamentally important task of teaching children so that they can
function in our society and fulfil their potential. In order to teach, school officials
must provide an atmosphere that encourages learning. During the school day they
must protect and teach our children. In no small way, teachers and principals are
responsible for the future of the country.

> It is essential that our children be taught and that they learn. Yet, with-
> out an orderly environment learning will be difficult if not impossible.
> In recent years, problems which threaten the safety of students and the
> fundamentally important task of teaching have increased in their num-
> bers and gravity. The possession of illicit drugs and dangerous weapons
> in the schools has increased to the extent that they challenge the ability

of school officials to fulfill their responsibility to maintain a safe and orderly environment. Current conditions make it necessary to provide teachers and school administrators with the flexibility required to deal with discipline problems in schools. They must be able to act quickly and effectively to ensure the safety of students and to prevent serious violations of school rules.

Courts "assume," without deciding, that the Canadian Charter of Rights and Freedoms applies to schools and boards, particularly in regard to the decision to expel a student.

Clearly, educators want to know more. Fortunately, some educators, such as principals, have had some legal training and, in turn, demonstrate a higher level of legal knowledge. Thus, in building legal literacy within the school, principals play a critical role.

Suicide Prevention

Suicide is a major cause of death among youth. Research and practice demonstrate that suicide is preventable. Accordingly, if we commit to proven suicide reduction programs, the number of unnecessary suicide attempts and deaths can be reduced. One of the more common approaches to youth suicide prevention is to utilize what are called "gatekeeper" programs where adults are trained to be a safety net for vulnerable youth and for students seeking help for their friends. Research shows these gatekeeper programs, which are aimed at identifying and referring suicidal individuals, may not be enough (Wyman, Brown, Inman, Cross, Schmeelk-Cone, Guo, & Pena, 2008). Research also has shown that suicidal youth are usually reticent to seek adult help and that adolescents typically seek help through their peer friendships (Wyman et al., 2008).

This chapter briefly identifies the main policy approaches used by states. It then offers examples of some of the more rigorous state approaches, programs developed by nonprofits, and approaches as successful through research or practice. Wisconsin and Maryland in the United States are illustrative of states that have gone farther than most others in their commitment to school-based suicide prevention. Wisconsin state law establishes that schools must address suicide prevention with students, not just teachers and other adults. Prevention efforts must focus on causation, signs, and services available in local communities (Wis. Stat. S118.295) [2012]. Maryland also has committed to reaching out to all students in a proactive manner. This approach of working directly with students is more aggressive than only training adults or responding to suicidal issues and signs as they arise. The Maryland program establishes a shared responsibility between educational programs at the state and local levels, and community suicide prevention and crisis center agencies (Md. Code Ann. Educ. S7–503).

By decreasing isolation of youth, risk factors such as the opportunity to dwell on suicide or plan for it are lowered. Study results have shown that trained peer leaders in larger schools were four times as likely as were untrained peer leaders to refer a suicidal friend to an adult. The training and intervention increased perceptions among students of adult support for suicidal youths and the suicidal ideation—the process of thinking about ending one's life. Research indicates significant reductions in suicide attempts and ideation as a result of implementation of this program (Wyman, Brown, LoMurray, Schmeelk-Cone, & Petrova, 2010).

"Signs of Suicide" is a suicide prevention program offered through the nonprofit Screening for Mental Health organization (Screening for Mental Health: Signs of Suicide Prevention Program, n.d.; Aseltine, James, Schilling, & Glanovsky, 2007)

Bullying

The general legislative trend is to increase mandates on school districts by requiring, among other things, prevention programs, policies, procedures, reporting, and training, and by addressing in more detail bullying behavior that occurs electronically.

Anti-Bullying Legislation

Anti-bullying statutes should generally define bullying to mean

(1)   Any intentional act by a student, attempted or completed, to harm the person or property of another student, which under the totality of the circumstances a reasonable person would perceive as part of a pattern of conduct intended to threaten, intimidate, or harass; or

(2)   Any intentional threat or display of force by a student including but not limited to threatening statements or gestures, brandishing a weapon, displaying an intimidating presence, or other similar intentional acts that would give another student reasonable cause to fear harm to person or property, and which under the totality if the circumstances a reasonable person would perceive as part of a pattern of conduct intended to threaten, intimidate, or harass; or

(3)   Any other intentional and malicious pattern of conduct by a student that under the totality of the circumstances a reasonable person would perceive as being clearly intended to threaten, intimidate, or harass another student and that causes:

   (A)   Significant physical, psychological, or emotional harm
   (B)   Significant property damage
   (C)   Significant interference with educational opportunities or achievement
   (D)   A threatening or intimidating educational environment
   (E)   Material disruption, substantial disorder, or an invasion of the rights or privacy of others

Parents of both those who bully and the victim should be involved in prevention programs and informed of bullying incidents. Legal issues almost always involve parents who were not informed until several incidents had occurred, serious discipline was imposed, or injury had occurred.

The reality is that students who are "different" are those most at risk. The most frequent victims of bullying and harassment tend to be students who do not conform to the norms as perceived by their peer group, often based on gender stereotypes or disability-based behaviors. School officials must create a culture of acceptance. Schools and parents must take extra, even extreme, precautions when a student presents any risk of suicide. Schools, parents, and communities all desire a school environment free of bullying and harassment. It should be the shared responsibility of all to achieve that goal. Prevention, of course, reduces bullying incidents. Its most important effect is helping to create a nurturing educational environment.

Cyberbullying

Advances in technology have been liberally embraced by the educational community. From Smart-Boards to Netbooks; Wikis to Blogs educators have found novel and useful ways to use current technology to enhance and improve education. But teachers and administrators are not the only ones who have found today's ever-present technology useful. Students have found available technologies and the Internet the perfect method to extend their ability to bully others from just during school hours, to 24 hours a day, seven days a week. The most common forums for cyberbullying are chat rooms, social networking sites, email, and instant messaging systems. The most often seen forms of cyberbullying include stealing an individual's name and password to gain access to a social networking site, altering photos to humiliate, online polls about an individual, posting conversations or video taken without the knowledge of the victim, or posting embarrassing information about an individual.

The most disturbing use of technology which has emerged is "sexting," which is the sending of sexually explicit photos or message via the Internet using cell phones or computers. Students, seemingly without a second thought that these images will remain forever in cyberspace, send this information to their boyfriends or girlfriends. The recipients often will send the images on to other individuals, without realizing that by doing so, if the photos are of minors, they can be found guilty under our child pornography laws.

Traditionally bullying has been handled disciplinarily as a "speech" issue, or perhaps even under "hate speech" policies and procedures. Consequently, the courts have required a clear nexus between the student behavior and the school; the behavior had to have happened during school hours or at school events.

With the advent of the Internet and in the wake of school shootings at Columbine, Santee, and Newtown in the United States in particular, school administrators face the daunting task of evaluating potential threats of violence and keeping their students safe without impinging on their rights. It is a feat like tightrope balancing, where an error in judgment can lead to a tragic result. The challenge for administrators is made all the more difficult because, outside of the official school environment, students are instant messaging, texting, emailing, twittering, tumblring, and otherwise communicating electronically, sometimes about subjects that threaten the safety of the school environment. At the same time, school officials must take care not to overreact and to take into account the creative juices and often startling writings of students.

MySpace is a social networking website that allows its members to set up online "profiles" and communicate via email, instant messages, and blogs (*Layshock v. Hermitage Sch. Dist.*, 2011). Instant messages enable "users to engage in real-time dialogue 'by typing messages to one another that appear almost immediately on the others' computer screens'" (*United States v. Meek,* 2004, quoting *Reno v. ACLU,* 1997).

The U.S. Supreme Court's school speech jurisprudence echoes a common theme: Although public school students do not "shed their constitutional rights to freedom of speech or expression at the schoolhouse gate," (*Tinker v. Des Moines Indep. Cmty. Sch. Dist.*, 1969), "the Constitutional rights of students in public school are not automatically coextensive with the rights of adults in other settings" (*Bethel Sch. Dist. No. 403 v. Fraser,* 1986). The Court has decided four lead student speech cases: *Tinker; Fraser; Hazelwood Sch. Dist. v. Kuhlmeier* (1988), and *Morse v. Frederick* (2007). Each governs a different area of student speech: (1) "vulgar, lewd, obscene, and plainly offensive speech" is governed by *Fraser;* (2) "school-sponsored speech" is governed by *Hazelwood,* and (3) "speech that falls into neither of these categories" is governed by *Tinker.* The Court discussed these areas of student speech in *Chandler v. McMinnville Sch. Dist. (1992).* In *Morse,* at 403, the Court dealt with a fourth, and somewhat unique, category—speech promoting illegal drug use. All four cases involved speech that took place at school or at a school-sanctioned event. Beyond those contexts, in *Morse* at 401, the Court has noted only that "[t]here is some uncertainty at the outer boundaries as to when courts should apply school speech precedents."

The Supreme Court of Canada released a judgment on September 27, 2012, that upheld a minor's right to anonymity in a case involving cyberbullying consistent with provincial education initiatives to codify awareness of bullying (Bill 13 also known as the Accepting Schools Act, 2012).

In *A.B. v. Bragg Communications Inc.* (2012), the Supreme Court considered whether A.B., a 15-year-old girl who had been the victim of cyberbullying, was entitled to anonymously apply for her Internet provider to disclose the names of persons who created a fraudulent Facebook account in her likeness for the purpose of bringing a defamation action against those persons. The Court unanimously reversed the decisions of the Supreme Court of Nova Scotia and the Nova Scotia Court of Appeal that denied A.B.'s right to privacy and anonymity.

The Court held that, in an application for anonymity in a case of cyberbullying, there is no need for a child to demonstrate that he or she is subjectively "vulnerable," because vulnerability is assumed. The law attributes this heightened vulnerability based on "chronology, not temperament." This is a departure from the previous requirement of subjective harm, although the Court stated that subjective evidence of a direct, harmful consequent to an individual applicant may still be relevant in any given determination of vulnerability.

In determining that cyberbullying meets the threshold of "objectively discernable harm," the Court took into account the 2012 Report of the Nova Scotia Task Force on Bullying and Cyberbullying. (See also http://stopbullyingnow.hrsa.gov; www.glsen.org; http://pewinternet.org; www.olweus.org; www.cde.gov)

The above report discussed, in part, the particularly harmful nature of the dissemination of cyberbullying, in that "the content can be spread widely, quickly—and anonymously." The report defines bullying at pp. 42–43 as

> behaviour that is intended to cause, or should be known to cause, fear, intimidation, humiliation, distress or other forms of harm to another person's body, feelings, self-esteem, reputation or property. Bullying can be direct or indirect, and can take place by written, verbal, physical or electronic means, or any other form of expression.

In *Bragg*, the Supreme Court of Canada expressly recognized the widening scope of the traditional notion of bullying, taking it from the schoolyard to the vast and arguably more permeating world of cyberspace. The Court recognized the prevalence of social media in our society and the harm that can result from its misuse, specifically in the context of bullying. This decision supports bullying as a distinct category of harm apart from its link to any human rights or accommodation issues, such as, if the bullying is triggered by victim's race, disability, or another enumerated ground under Human Rights Code of Ontario (1990). Bill 168, Occupational Health and Safety Amendment Act (Violence and Harassment in the Workplace) (2009) amended the Occupational Health and Safety Act (1990) and is another crucial piece of the puzzle.

Teachers, principals, and school boards have both a statutory and common law duty of care to protect their students from bullying. They must proactively implement measures, including but not limited to the creation of anti-bullying policies, in order to prevent and effectively address all instances of bullying and to stay current with what may be required or expected of them under the law. The Province of Nova Scotia took the lead in Canada with the passage of Bill 61, the Cyber-safety Act (2013), which came into force in August 2013. It can be found at www.canlii.ca.

The Health and Safety of Students

Issues of health and safety are important when providing any aspect of an educational program to a student.

- Curriculum hazards in science and technology classes, cooperative placements, physical education, and excursions
- School buildings, portables, and other physical premises occupied by students while attending school
- Natural and human disasters requiring emergency preparedness and response
- Diseases and illness, such as communicable diseases, pandemics, immunization, and emergency plans
- Food and water safety, including allergens
- Transportation to and from school
- Students with special medical and behavioral needs

The courts in Canada have held that the standard of care owed is that of a careful or prudent parent. See *Myers v. Peel County Board of Education* (1981). More specifically, the standard of care may depend on the following:

- The number of students being supervised at any given time
- The age of the students
- The nature of the exercise or activity
- The degree of skill and training that the students may have received in connection with the activity
- The nature and condition of any equipment in use at the time
- The competency and capacity of the students involved

Related to the Education Act (1990) and regulation are the Immunization of School Pupils Act (1990), which addresses the immunization of students, and Sabrina's Law (2005), which requires that school boards implement certain measures for the protection of students, and is also indirectly provided pursuant to the Ontario Human Rights Code (1990) as a result of the duty to accommodate.

Insurance

School boards maintain liability insurance, including accident insurance for students participating in training programs, as well as public liability insurance to protect the board and students should there be loss or damage to the person or property of others while a student is participating in such a program.

The Ministry of Education provides the Workplace Safety Insurance Board (WSIB) coverage to students in cooperative education programs, Ontario Youth

Apprenticeship Programs (OYAP), Supervised Alternative Learning for Excused Pupils (SALEP), job shadowing, and job twinning programs.

Occupiers' Liability

Specifically the duty, pursuant to Section 3(1) of the Occupiers' Liability Act (1990) requires school boards:

> . . . to take such care as in all the circumstances of the case is reasonable to see that persons entering on the premises, and the property brought on the premises by those persons are reasonably safe while on the premises.

Accessibility

When considering the health and safety of school premises, students' accessibility to and from school facilities must be considered, particularly with respect to students with special needs.

The Ontario Human Rights Commission, working under its enabling statute, the Ontario Human Rights Code (1990) provides that, where barriers already exist—such as schools without wheelchair accessible ramps or doors—the duty to accommodate requires that education providers make changes to school premises, up to the point of undue hardship, to provide equal access for students with disabilities.

The obligations to improve accessibility has been further defined by the Accessibility for Ontarians with Disabilities Act (2005) (AODA) as well as Ontario Regulation 429/07 that mandates the creation of accessibility standards to eliminate barriers in key areas of everyday life, including attending school.

Volunteer Drivers

School boards should not permit students to drive other students to or from school activities is supported by Canadian statistics that drivers under 21 years old are up to four times more likely than older drivers to be involved in an accident.

The long-standing advice of the Elementary Teachers' Federation of Ontario (ETFO) to its members is also that members "not volunteer their own vehicles, or drive students around either during or after School hours." (Elementary Teachers' Federation of Ontario, 2006).

Emergency Medication

The Regulated Health Professions Act (1991) creates exceptions for lay persons administering a substance by injection or inhalation where the purpose is either "rendering first aid or temporary assistance in an emergency" or "assisting a person with his or her routine activities of living."

Form

Informed Consent/Permission Form for Education Trips
(Students Under 18 Years)

The _____ is arranging
    (name of school)

_____

    (description of activity and dates)

THIS FORM MUST BE READ AND SIGNED BY EVERY STUDENT WHO WISHES TO PARTICIPATE AND BY A PARENT OR GUARDIAN OF A PARTICIPATING STUDENT.

ELEMENTS OF RISK:

Educational activity programs, such as _____
involve certain elements of risk. Injuries may occur while participating in these activities. The following list includes, but is not limited to, examples of the types of injury which may result from participating in

_____

    (describe activity)

1. _____
2. _____
3. _____

The risk of sustaining these types of injuries result from the nature of the activity and can occur without any fault of either the student, or the school board, its' employees/agents or the facility where the activity is taking place. By choosing to take part in this activity, you are accepting the risk that you/your child may be injured.

The chance of an injury occurring can be reduced by carefully following instructions at all times while engaged in the activity.

If you choose to participate in _____ on
_____, you must understand that you bear the responsibility for any injury that might occur.

The _____ does not provide accidental death,
    (name of school board)
dismemberment or medical expense insurance on behalf of the students participating in this activity.

ACKNOWLEDGEMENT

WE HAVE READ THE ABOVE. WE UNDERSTAND THAT IN PARTICIPAT-
ING IN THE ACTIVITY DESCRIBED ABOVE, WE ARE ASSUMING THE
RISKS ASSOCIATED WITH DOING SO.

Signature of Student: _____ Date: _____

Signature of Parent/Guardian: _____ Date: _____

PERMISSION

I give _____ permission to participate in the _____
   (name of student)   *(description of activity)*

to be held on or about _____
      (date)

Signature of Parent/Guardian: _____ Date: _____

Both the Municipal Freedom of Information and Protection of Privacy Act
(1990), which applies to schools operated by school boards, and the Freedom of
Information and Protection of Privacy Act (1990), which applies to "provincial
and demonstration schools," prohibit institutions from releasing personal information in their custody or under their control to anyone other than the person to
whom the information relates, except in certain circumstances. These circumstances are defined in the legislation, and it is up to the head of an institution to
decide whether or not to grant access to personal information in such circumstances. School boards should therefore consult with their freedom of information
coordinators to determine whether they should develop policies on access to their
students' Ontario school records (OSRs). Any such policies must be developed in
accordance with the legislation.

Every student has the right to have access to their OSRs. The parents of a student
have the right to have access to the student's OSR, until the student becomes an adult
(age 18) or when a student arguably withdraws from parental care. Under both the
Children's Law Reform Act (1990) and the Divorce Act (1985), the legal right of
a noncustodial parent to have access to a child includes the right to make inquiries
and to be given information concerning the child's health, education, and welfare.

Subsection 266(2) of the Education Act (1990) states that the OSR will not
be produced in the course of any legal proceedings. There may be occasions,
however, when access to the OSRs of current students or former students will be
sought. In such cases, boards should obtain legal advice from their lawyers in order
to deal with such issues as the following:

- Whether the Education Act (1990) in fact prevents the production of the OSR
- Whether the OSR in question is relevant to the proceedings
- If the OSR is relevant to the proceedings, whether a copy, rather than the original, may be submitted to the court

Both the municipal and provincial freedom of information acts permit disclosure of personal information for the purposes of law enforcement. The conditions for disclosure and the definition of "law enforcement" are contained in the legislation. School boards should consult with their freedom of information coordinators and their legal counsel to determine whether they should develop policies on the disclosure of personal information in an OSR to courts and law enforcement agencies.

In court proceedings, subject to an appeal, the judge's order must be followed. If a principal receives a court order requiring the release of an OSR, the principal should contact the board's legal counsel. Although court orders must be followed, the principal should obtain legal advice about the issues listed above.

A principal may be served with a subpoena requiring that he or she appear in court on a particular date and bring part or all of an OSR. If a principal receives a subpoena, he or she must comply with it, but should obtain legal advice from the board's legal counsel about the issues involved.

As a general rule, the principal should go to court with both the original OSR and a complete and exact photocopy of it, and should propose to the judge that the photocopy be submitted instead of the original. The principal should also inform the judge that the subpoena is inconsistent with Subsection 266(2) of the Education Act (1990). The principal must, however, relinquish the documents if ordered to do so by the judge.

The Criminal Code (1985) is federal legislation; where there is a conflict between it and provincial legislation, it takes precedence. Therefore, if a principal is served with a search warrant under the Criminal Code (1985) requiring the surrender of an OSR to the police, or is served with a subpoena requiring his or her appearance at court with the OSR, he or she is obliged to comply with the search warrant or the subpoena. The principal should also inform the relevant authority (i.e., the police or the judge) that the use of any part(s) of the OSR as evidence in court proceedings is inconsistent with Subsection 266(2) of the Education Act (1990). The principal should present the police or the judge with both the original OSR and a complete and exact photocopy of it, and should propose that the photocopy be submitted instead of the original.

Under the Child and Family Services Act (1990), a court may order a principal of a school to produce a student's OSR for inspection and copying. A court may make such an order if it is satisfied that (a) a record contains information that may be relevant to a consideration of whether a child is suffering abuse or likely to suffer abuse, and (b) the person in control of the record has refused to permit a Children's Aid Society director to inspect it. If a principal receives a court order under the Child and Family Services Act (1990), he or she should seek legal advice about how to comply with it.

What about the practice or position of a board in permitting any party who has subpoenaed student records to inspect the records in advance of their production to the court itself? Such access was accorded the defense at the accused's preliminary inquiry. In the absence of the written permission of the parent or guardian of an underage student, there is no authority to implement the procedure of informally permitting access to the party who has obtained the subpoena. Indeed, such a practice fundamentally misconceives the nature of a subpoena.

A school principal is statutorily obliged to maintain proper order and discipline in the school (Education Act [1990], s. 265[a]). With the guidance of the Act and Ministry and board policy, the principal is responsible for the increasingly challenging task of securing pedagogical effectiveness in a civilized setting where all participants, including teachers and students, are motivated and respectful of individual dignity and privacy.

The greatest power a principal has is the power of discretion in any given circumstances of minor "offenses" whether to deal with the matter herself or himself, whether to consult the child's parents, and whether to call in the law enforcement authorities. In instances of complaint of serious criminality, the school should report the matter to the police. There is an obvious and significant public interest in the effective investigation of crime within a school.

Conclusion

Charles Dickens began *David Copperfield* asking, ". . . [W]hether I shall turn out to be the hero of my own life, or whether that station will be held by anybody else. . ." (Dickens, 1850). You can choose not to wait for someone else to act but instead to be the hero of your own life—for the good of others. By making that choice, you not only help but inspire, and so keep lit around the world the lights of valor in the cause of justice.

There is no formula or category for moral courage; it can appear in many forms and in any place even—maybe especially—in places it is not supposed to exist. Dr. Larch, the founder of St. Cloud's orphanage in John Irving's "Cider House Rules," lamented, "There are no heroes in the world of lost and abandoned children" (Irving, 1985). But the good doctor was wrong. Ku Klux Klansmen believe African Americans are inferior, but their own superior lawyers, Anthony Griffin and David Baugh, show by their legal representation, both valorous and excellent, just how big is that lie.

"Heroism feels and never reasons, and therefore is always right," wrote Ralph Waldo Emerson. Like all marches, our world march for international human rights must both be shepherded and shared. Cesar Estrada Chavez said, "Compartimos el mismo futuro. No valemos nada solo. Pero juntos, valemos mucho. Si se puede," which, loosely translated, means "We share the same future: We may each be able to do only a little alone, but together we are powerful and can succeed."

Values and motivation are at the core of educational achievement. Kids do well in school when their internal value system encourages achievement, when their parents demand it, and when their peers reinforce it. Education is very different from health care and other professional-client relationships. The most important event is not what the teacher does in the classroom. It is what the student does outside the classroom. To expect that the hundreds of our classroom teachers can lead and motivate to the extent that they overcome the social forces outside the schools is naive at the least.

I see a teenager's report card at school while in detention, and I am amazed by the leaps many make. They often show a year's progress in reading or math, achieved in just a few months. I used to wonder why, but now I understand. The first thing we give a boy or a girl is the gift of feeling safe. No bullets ripping by their door, no need for drop-down drills. A child in terror cannot learn; terror freezes the brain. A child released from terror is liberated to learn, to play, to be a child. Children who live in terror rarely play. A teenager without the necessary protections of childhood, feeling safe, the nurturing of love, ever-present role models, creates his own: the posse, fists, guns, boom-box music, the deep-away swagger that shouts "Don't mess with me."

When an individual has experienced trauma, they lose their sense of control, connection, and meaning. In order to live a healthy, full life, the individual must be able to regain control, connection, and meaning in their life. Trauma erodes one's sense of self, self-esteem, and confidence. There are feelings of blame, guilt, and responsibility for the traumatic event. The pressure to learn can augment feelings of guilt, shame, and low self-esteem. A further effect is the inability to concentrate, which may be manifested by difficulty listening, distraction, or preoccupation.

Our childhoods make us what we are; our hurts and our happiness; our loves and our hates; our successes and our failures. All of our childhood experiences are woven into the fabric of our adult characters. If hate gets out of hand for kids at home, it often is fueled later by hate groups; or sometimes fanned by their anti-hate counterparts. No matter when the hatred gets out of control, it generally is traceable to childhood. Kids learn bigotry from their parents. Bigotry and hate. Love and tolerance. If parents can teach their kids the importance of the difference, they can make a bigger difference than all of our laws.

Studies show the main family situations that put pupils at risk for failing tests, repeating grades, or dropping out of school. The factors—a struggling single parent, parents who did not complete high school, welfare dependency, or a family that speaks a language other than English—all need closer attention from policy-makers and parents who tend to blame schools for the failure. These difficulties cannot be attributed solely to so-called bad schools, because these children are already behind when they reach the classroom door. In fact, waiting until kindergarten may be too late to intervene in the educational trajectory for many children.

The inequalities imposed on children by their home, neighborhood, and peer environment are carried along to become the inequalities with which they confront adult life after school ends. The success of our Russian, Italian, and Irish immigrants a century ago, and many Asian and Hispanic immigrants today, makes it plain that the issue has less to do with poverty as such than with culture, with conscious values as well as unconscious behavior. Kenneth Clark first popularized the phrase "the pathology of the ghetto," in *Dark Ghetto,* published in 1965. Clark wrote about how "the stigma of racial inferiority" leads to self-destructive behavior, including violence, alcohol, and drug abuse, family breakdown, and every social pathology save suicide. But Clark understood this damage as emotional and psychological, not cognitive.

We must be in the business of trying to break cycles. Take the teen mother. She probably dropped out of school. Her child may have had a low-birth weight. No nutrition, prenatal care, and little education. Who takes care of her baby, and makes sure that any developmental lags are diagnosed and treated? Will these mothers go back to high school?

Many of the children I see need an enveloping environment that is secure and nourishing, as the streets and often the home may not be. And school is not enveloping enough. You can't take children away from their mothers, but you can place them in an alternative environment for much of the day (which the end of welfare, in any case, has now made indispensable). There's a strong persuasive argument for universally available after-school activities including the high crime rates between 3:00 and 7:00 P.M.

The message I hear from so many teachers is that kids today come with more emotional baggage than ever before, and we do not have the preparation, training, or time to deal with such issues. Teaching and shaping the minds of young people has always been a demanding and exhausting job. It can be exhilarating but when children with more complex needs are put into larger schools with larger classes, teachers feel overworked, overstressed, and burned out.

It really is all about four words: The Future of Hope. For too many children childhood is not a period of stability, safety, and normal development. Instead, these children are the victims of maltreatment at the hands of family members and caretakers. Although some children seem to have an innate resilience that mediates the damage of early maltreatment, others suffer lasting and wide-ranging negative consequences. Problematic school performance is among the more common problems associated with child abuse and neglect, with neglected children most adversely affected. Similarly, such children often experience difficulties with social relationships, problem solving, and the ability to cope with new or stressful situations. Some abused or neglected children develop aggressive behavior patterns, whereas others become withdrawn. Maltreated children are at risk for delinquency, violence, and other self-destructive behaviors, as well as for posttraumatic stress disorder, major depression, and other psychiatric conditions.

An old cliché says that an ounce of prevention is worth a pound of cure. This argument is even more compelling when young lives are concerned—some early preventative measures can save a lifetime of grief and trouble. It is past time to shine the light on children in the darkness. In many cases, people simply don't know how they can make a difference in the lives of children. Together, individuals in the public and private sectors are working hard to make headway. We must continue to look for ways to inspire community involvement in child abuse prevention. As citizens, legislators, or researchers, we must look for ways to promote community involvement in the prevention of child abuse. The best interests of children should be paramount in all our decisions.

Educators must deliver educational services as required by law. More importantly, they are responsible for knowing and respecting the rights of their students and teachers. There are a wide range of legal issues that influence the lives of teachers, students, parents, and administrators. Despite the intimidating size of this body of law, school officials sometimes ignore the law at their peril and may be held personally liable in damages for violating students' clearly established rights. By knowing what educators know about school law and identifying gaps in how they obtain, maintain, and disseminate legal information, changes to policy and practice can be made to help them confidently assume the role of child law instructor in schools. Subsequently, they will be better able to help staff become legally literate by helping them understand the laws that affect them, how the legal system works, and their responsibilities thus improving their ability to protect their students, their staff, and themselves.

References

Statutes and Bills

Accepting Schools Act, S.O., C. 5 (2012), amended the Education Act (1990), Royal Assent June 19, 2012.

Accessibility for Ontarians with Disabilities Act, 2005, SO, c. 11 (2005).

Bill 13, the Accepting Schools Act, S.O., C. 5 (2012), amending the Education Act (1990), with Royal Assent June 19, 2012.

Bill 61, the Cyber-safety Act, SNS 2013, c.2

Bill 168, Occupational Health and Safety Amendment Act (Violence and Harassment in the Workplace), 2009, amended the Occupational Health and Safety Act, R.S.O. 1990, c. O.1

Canadian Charter of Rights and Freedoms (1982).

Child and Family Services Act, RSO, c. C. 10 (1990).

Children's Reform Act, RSO, c. C. 12 (1990).

Constitution Act, The Schedule B to the Canada Act 1982 (UK) (1982).

Criminal Code, RSC, c. C. 46 (1985).

Divorce Act, RSC, C. 3 (2nd Supp.) (1985).

Education Act, RSO, c E. 2 (1990).

Freedom of Information and Protection of Privacy Act, RSO, c. F. 31 (1990).

Health and Safety Amendment Act (Violence and Harassment in the Workplace), 2009.

Human Rights Code, RSO, c. H. 19 (1990).

Immunization of School Pupils Act, RSO, C. I. 1 (1990).

Labour Relations Act, 1995, SO, C. 1, Sch. A (1995).

Md. Code Ann. Educ. S7–503. Maryland State Department of Education: Youth Suicide Prevention Program. Retrieved from www.msde.maryland.gov/MSDE/divisions/student schoolsvcs/student_services_alt/suicide/

Municipal Freedom of Information and Protection of Privacy Act, RSO, c. M. 56 (1990).

Occupational Health and Safety Act, RSO, c. O. 1 (1990).

Occupiers' Liability Act, RSO, c. O. 2 (1990).
Ontario College Teachers Act, 1996, SO, C. 12 (1996).
Regulated Health Professions Act, 1991, SO, c. 18 (1991).
Sabrina's Law, 2005, SO, c. 7 (2005).
Teaching Profession Act, RSO, c. T. 2 (1990).
United Nations' Convention on the Rights of the Child (1989) ratified by Canada, Can. T.S. 1992 No. 3, Arts. 3, 9, 12.
Youth Criminal Justice Act, SC, C. 1 (2002).

Case Law

A.B. v. Bragg Communications Inc., [2012] 2 S.C.R. 567.
Bethel Sch. Dist. No. 403 v. Fraser, 478 U.S. 675, 682 (1986).
Chandler v. McMinnville Sch. Dist., 978 F.2d 524, 529 (9th Cir. 1992).
Hazelwood Sch. Dist. v. Kuhlmeier, 484 U.S. 260 (1988).
Layshock v. Hermitage Sch. Dist., 650 F.3d 205, 208 & n.2 (3d Cir. 2011) (en banc).
Morse v. Frederick, 551 U.S. 393 (2007).
Myers v. Peel County Board of Education (1981), 123 D.L.R. (3d) 1, [1981] 2 S.C.R. 21.
R. v. M. (M.R.), 3 Sch. 393 (1998).
Roper v. Simmons, 543 U.S. 551, 569 (2005).
Tinker v. Des Moines Indep. Cmty. Sch. Dist., 393 U.S. 503, 506 (1969).
United States v. Meek, 366 F.3d 705, 709 n.1 (9th Cir. 2004) (quoting Reno v. ACLU, 521 U.S. 844, 851–52 [1997]).

Books, Journals, and Reports

Aseltine, R., James, A., Schilling, E., & Glanovsky, J. (2007). Evaluating the SOS suicide prevention program: A replication and extension. *BMC Public Health, 7,* 161. doi:10.1186/1471-2458-7-161
Clark, K. (1965). *Dark Ghetto: Dilemmas of Social Power.* Retrieved from http://books.google.com
Dickens, C. (1850). *David Copperfield.* Retrieved from http://books.google.com
Elementary Teachers' Federation of Ontario. (2006). Use member's own vehicle to drive students to board-sponsored events. Toronto. Canada: Author. Retrieved from www.etfo.ca/AdviceForMembers/PRSMattersBulletins/Pages/default.aspx
Emerson, R. W. (1841). *Essays and English Traits.* Retrieved from http://books.google.com
Irving, J. (1985). *Cider House Rules.* New York, NY: Morrow. Retrieved from http://books.google.com
Screening for Mental Health: Signs of Suicide Prevention Program. (n.d.). Retrieved March 28, 2012, www.mentalhealthscreening.org/programs/youth-prevention-programs/sos/
Wis. STAT. S118.295. (2012). Wisconsin Department of Public Instruction: Youth suicide prevention strategies. Retrieved from www.dpi.wi.gov/sspw/suicideprevstrategies.html
Wyman, P. A., Brown, C. H., Inman, J., Cross, W., Schmeelk-Cone, K., Guo, J., & Pena, J. B. (2008). Randomized trial of a gatekeeper for suicide prevention. *Journal of Consulting and Clinical Psychology, 6*(1), 104–115.
Wyman, P., Brown, C. H., LoMurray, M., Schmeelk-Cone, K., & Petrova, M. (2010, September). An outcome evaluation of the sources of strength suicide prevention program delivered by adolescent peer leaders high schools. *American Journal of Public Health, 100*(9), 1653–1661. doi: 10.2105/AJPH.2009.190025

12

EDUCATIONAL LEADERSHIP AND DECISION MAKING: MAKING THE POLITICS AND POLICY VISIBLE

Howard Stevenson

Introduction

Education systems around the world increasingly reflect a global orthodoxy that has emerged and formed in recent years and which asserts that economic success in a globalized and knowledge-based economy depends on the capabilities of its labor force and, by inference, their educational achievements. From virtually all sides of mainstream political opinion, and across nations with the most diverse histories and backgrounds, there exists an almost unchallengeable truth that, in a hypercompetitive globalized economy, individual nation states will only survive and thrive through the endeavors of human labor, and human labor requires investment. Almost everywhere, education policy has been transformed into economic policy, with wider educational aspirations acknowledged, but largely subordinated to economic imperatives (Rizvi & Lingard, 2010).

As the discourse of global competition dominates all else, then so, too, does the drive for "change" and "improvement" in education systems intensify. Nowhere is this better exemplified than in the titling of the Obama administration's key education strategy, *Race to the Top* (Department of Education, 2009). The message is clear, there is a competition, and there is no time to delay. The implication is equally clear, those who delay, will lose. This is education as competition.

Within this environment, school leaders experience policy as a relentless pressure to change, perform, improve. There is always an urgency, and a restlessness, that requires action. Those who question, let alone challenge, this discourse are characterized as being rooted in the past and resistant to change. According to Michael Gove, secretary of state for education in the U.K. government, they rejoice in failure and are "enemies of promise" (BBC, 2012).

Such is the power of this discourse that it assumes the status of the common sense. It becomes the accepted way that the world is, with the assumptions and values that underpin it being taken for granted and unquestioned. What happens every day in schools is framed by education policies that are rooted in this new common sense, with schools expected to implement and comply. School leaders make important decisions countless times every day, but they do so within a wider policy context that itself reflects a particular view of the world. The realities and pressures of life as school leaders mean that the policies that frame their world are often seen as inevitable and determined. Policy is recognized as being "political," but, paradoxically, it is also seen as something beyond influence. The danger is that school leaders become uncritical implementers of policy as they see themselves as powerless in a politicized environment.

In this chapter, I seek to argue that school leaders' actions, and the decisions they make, need to recognize the political nature of every aspect of their practice, including the values and assumptions that underpin the taken for grantedness of what they do. Rather than invoke a mythical claim to being apolitical, school leaders need to name the politics and policy visible in their decision making. Only then does it become possible for school leaders to identify the spaces within which they can assert agency, and shape their own policy environment, rather than be shaped by it. School leaders must therefore recognize the fundamentally political nature of their work.

> [Q]uestions of pedagogy, the fundamental questions of teaching and learning, and wider questions of institutional organisation and structure are always and everywhere questions of politics. Any learning context is one framed by a political context, and any action of educators must be either reinforcing or challenging of that political context. It follows that there can be no understanding of the work of educators, leaders and teachers, without an understanding of education policy. Therefore, the work of educational leaders and educators must start from an understanding of the political context within which they function.
>
> (Bell & Stevenson, 2013, p. xxviii)

The chapter begins with a discussion of the global shift in political orthodoxy as capitalist crisis in the 1970s presaged a shift from welfarism to postwelfarism (Gewirtz, 2001; Tomlinson, 2006) in the industrialized nations of the West. Understanding how this orthodoxy has emerged is critical to understanding current trajectories in education policy, and thereby identifying future possibilities. Educators cannot hope to shape the future unless they can understand the past and critique the present. The key features of the paradigm shift in education policy are identified and, following this, there is a discussion of the implications for education as post-welfarist and market-driven structures increasingly drive school-level policy environments.

The chapter concludes by identifying the dispositions school leaders need to adopt if they are to reclaim education as a service committed to social justice and the achievement of all.

From Welfarism to Post-Welfarism: Crisis and the New Orthodoxy

Current global orthodoxy in relation to both economic and education policy emerged in the wake of the capitalist crisis of the 1970s. In the postwar period, the advanced capitalist nations of the West had developed substantial welfare states (Gough, 1983). Although the precise form of these differed significantly between individual nation states, their common elements were a commitment to public sector provision of welfare services, including education, combined with an aspiration to reconcile needs-based provision with principles of universalism. These welfare states represented a political settlement between capital and organized labor and were underpinned by the economic principles of Keynesian demand management. Not only did Keynesianism appear to confirm that the state could manage the market, but the ability to ensure full employment (through policies of demand management) appeared to make a comprehensive welfare state "affordable."

What is now clear is that this compromise between capital and labor was not sustainable. By the mid-1970s, critics from both Right (Bacon & Eltis, 1976) and Left (O'Connor, 1973) argued that the increasing size of the state placed unsustainable demands on capital accumulation and that fundamental change was required. Keynesianism appeared to no longer offer a solution. Stagflation suggested the inflation-unemployment trade-off no longer applied, whilst Keynesianism's nation-state-based approach seemed unable to contain a resurgent neoliberalism that was straining to exploit international markets.

This was the point at which a new global orthodoxy emerged; or perhaps more accurately, a new global hegemonic settlement in which the priorities of international capital and global markets were seen as primary. It was from this point that capital began to push back against the welfarist settlement in the Western economies whilst also seeking to transcend national borders in the search for new markets, most notably in the global south. Stuart Hall's (1979) analysis of the emergence of Thatcherism in the United kingdom argued that the crisis experienced across the advanced industrial economies of the West was political and social as much as economic. Furthermore, when applied to this period, the term crisis should not be seen as meaning near to collapse, but rather as a period of rapid, substantial, and conjunctural change from which new possibilities emerge. This was the point at which political discourses began to shift and new policy trajectories became visible. These were not a matter of detail, but represented a fundamental realignment of politics and were accompanied by equally profound changes in relation to state formation and concepts of governance (Gamble, 1988).

These changes are central to understanding contemporary welfare policy in very many parts of the world, north, south, east, and west. They have had a particular impact on education policy at a global and national level. Although they emerged from an organic crisis in the west, the global reach of these developments extends around the globe. In this chapter, I highlight three key features of the global hegemonic settlement, at both a global and national level, that now have a significant influence on how policy is experienced by leaders, teachers, and students in schools. All of these features are interdependent of each other, both horizontally and vertically.

First is the development of a strident globalization in which economic, political, and cultural borders have diminished in significance (Held & McGrew, 2007). The most obvious manifestation of globalization is the increased movement of goods, service, and people around the world, on a scale, and at a pace, unimaginable not so many years ago. However, what is also significant is the emergence of global forms of governance, including supranational bodies such as the World Bank and the Organisation for Economic Co-operation and Development, and the growing importance of regional trading blocs such as the European Union. Such developments have led many to argue that the sovereignty of individual nation states is now substantially diminished. Although this is clearly a key development, it is also possible to exaggerate this trend and to ignore the very significant influence that individual nation states continue to have. There is clearly a need to balance the relative influence of global and local pressures (Ball, 1998). However, what is apparent is that, in relation to education policy for example, the influence of supranational bodies is now substantial.

One obvious consequence of these developments has been the international migration of education policy initiatives on an unprecedented scale. The term *policy borrowing* is widely used in this context although, as Dale (1999) asserts, rather inappropriately. It is not that policies are "borrowed" in the traditional sense but, rather, they are reproduced in much the same way that globalized product markets spawn imitators. There is a desperate search for "what works" and, therefore, an apparent desire to reproduce those polices that appear to be adopted by the most successful countries. Indeed the dominance of global league tables, and the power of the organization that promote them, can be considered one of the defining features of globalization's impact on education (Sellar & Lingard, 2013). While this is clearly a phenomenon, evidenced by the many journeys of policy-makers, practitioners, and academics to Finland, Shanghai, and South Korea, it does not explain why policy options at a national level sometimes continue to develop in quite distinct ways. Rather, it is necessary to look for more complex explanations of policy reproduction that take account of the globalized movement of educational capital and policy entrepreneurs (Ball, 2007, 2012).

A second feature of the new global hegemonic settlement at a national level is a shift in the form and nature of the state itself. At the time of the crisis in the 1970s, the New Right argued vigorously that the state was too large. The problem was one of "big government" that drained private resources, restricted personal liberty and encouraged dependency. Margaret Thatcher famously set herself the objective of "rolling back the frontiers of the state" (Gamble, 1988). Accompanying this analysis was the argument that the private sector, subject to the discipline of market forces, would always provide a more efficient solution than a public sector option (Friedman & Friedman, 1980). Although this is a view that reflected a particular New Right ideology at the time, it is a narrative that has since become mainstream with governments of both right and center-left engaging in actions to reduce the scale and scope of the state.

Perhaps the most striking feature of this development has been a "hollowing out" of the state in many contexts, whereby direct public provision of services, such as education, has increasingly been subcontracted to private sector providers. In this "competition state" (Jessop, 2002) the role of government is to specify the detail of work to be performed, and to then award the work to the private sector through a competitive bidding process. Performance is ensured through rigorous processes of target setting and performance monitoring, with no removal or termination of contracts providing the incentive for providers to perform. In many instances, performance rewards and penalties are reinforced through the use of quasi-markets whereby providers are also subject to the demand preferences of "consumers." Under such circumstances, public participation in democratic decision making is subordinated to an accountability fused from a mixture of managerial target setting with market forces (Stevenson & Wood, 2013).

A third and final development that flows from the new global hegemonic settlement is a drive to link the nature of educational output more closely to the needs of the economy (Bell & Stevenson, 2006). The logic of this approach is informed by the increasing influence of Human Capital Theory (HCT), in which economic success is linked directly to the productive capacity of a nation's labor force which, in turn, is linked to educational achievement. These arguments were most clearly articulated by Becker (1964), and have gained in currency since. According to HCT, knowledge has emerged as the new factor of production and is central to competitiveness in a "knowledge economy." Investment in human capital, therefore, becomes pivotal to being competitive in a globalized market economy. This is an analysis particularly attractive to the established economies of advanced industrialized nations, for whom there is little realistic possibility of competing with emerging economies on low labor costs in the short or medium term. Rather, HCT offers the possibility of securing competitiveness through high levels of labor productivity and value-addedness. Education and training is clearly central to this strategy. Such is the purchase of this global orthodoxy within governing elites that policy statements supporting this approach are commonly found in almost every country of the world. One such example is provided by Tony Blair, speaking when he was prime minister of the United Kingdom:

> [E]ducation is our best economic policy . . . This country will succeed or fail on the basis of how it changes itself and gears up to this new economy, based on knowledge. Education therefore is now the centre of economic policy making for the future. What I am saying is, we know what works

within our education system, we can learn the lessons of it. The key is now to apply those lessons, push them right throughout the education system, until the young children . . . wherever they are, they get the chance to make the most of their God given potential. It is the only vision, in my view, that will work in the 21st century.

(Tony Blair, quoted in Ball, 2008, p. 12).

Quite what this looks like in the context of individual countries is not clear, and much remains uncertain. What is apparent is that the relative importance of economic and labor market issues within school curricula, and the extent to which these are balanced against other objectives of education policy, will vary between countries. Such variations will partly reflect the specificities of particular labor market requirements, but wider questions are also at play. For example, what is the balance between a knowledge- and skills-based curriculum, or what might be the relative priority of academic and vocational issues? Such issues will play out differently in different contexts, but a common theme is the dominance of economic considerations over wider educational aspirations.

The consequences of these developments for education policy are substantial. Globalized neoliberalism advances ever faster as the deregulation of financial markets combines with developments in technology to increase the speed and mobility of capital, thereby intensifying the competitive pressures experienced by producers (Robertson, 2000). Given the claimed importance of education for economic success, it follows that increasing intensity in economic markets is, in turn, experienced by increased pressure on education systems to "perform." As economic markets move at an increasing pace, and with a relentless drive for capital accumulation, it should come as no surprise when education policy mimics this rapid turbulence.

Fast Capitalism and Quick Fixes

Given the rapidity of change in the economic sphere, and the ways in which globalization has compressed both time and space, it is inevitable that education is impacted similarly. Levin (1998) has described the pace and scale of education policy development in recent years as akin to an "epidemic," whilst Hess (1999) has referred to "policy churn" to describe the relentless change experienced by educators. However, for all this change and the search for "solutions," there is little evidence of policy change delivering recognizable improvements. In a later article, Levin (2010) reflected on some of the reasons why such substantial policy development has often failed to achieve any corresponding progress in educational systems. His arguments focus on two issues—inappropriate policies and insufficient attention to implementation.

Levin's argument is that education policy tends to focus on the wrong issues, and seeks to change the factors that have minimal impact on the quality of teaching

and learning. He singles out the focus on structural changes in the form of schooling, exemplified by the drive to create quasi-markets in education. This represents
a major plank of the post-welfarist reform agenda but, as Levin argues, "To sum
up many studies in a few words, it is hard to find much evidence of sustained
improvements in outcomes resulting from these efforts. Structural changes have
almost always had disappointing results" (Levin, 2010, p. 740). Levin highlights,
in particular, the issue of choice and competition in schools, where there is little
evidence that this has impact on educational quality.

Levin argues that developments in accountability reforms demonstrate more
impact on educational outcomes, but he also argues that this still depends on
leaders and teachers understanding how to bring about change and improvement,
as much as knowing that improvement is possible and required. In short, it is
important for structural changes related to accountability measures to be linked to
corresponding changes in professional practice. This aspect of Levin's analysis links
to his second broad explanation of policy failure as a failure of implementation.
Levin's critique of poor implementation is divided into two subarguments. First,
he argues that policies need to be adapted to their context and that crude forms
of policy reproduction are unlikely to succeed. Rather, policies need to be formed
for the specific context into which they are being introduced and then appropriately supported with resources and professional development. This often requires
long-term planning, but the imperatives of political systems encourage what is
short term and high profile over what may be less headline grabbing, but far more
enduring. Electoral cycles, as much as economic ones, drive the search for quick
fixes, rather than focusing on longer term change that may deliver tangible results.

Levin's second argument in relation to implementation is what he identifies as
a failure to engage with, and mobilize, those charged with policy implementation.

> Far too many education reforms, based on conventional ideas about organi-
> zation, have seen teachers as the equivalent of assembly line workers whose
> job is simply to follow instructions or, in some cases, as an opposition to be
> controlled through policy. This cannot work. Governments that belittled
> teachers may have reaped short-term political benefits but failed to create
> the conditions that could produce better outcomes for students.
>
> (Levin, 2010, p. 742)

Levin's analysis highlights many of the key tensions in current education policy,
visible in different forms in many parts of the world. Education policies in many
countries are subject to change on a scale and at a pace that is unprecedented.
The volume of change is vast—as are the resources required for implementation. These problems are compounded when policies are implemented and then
reversed, often before any meaningful implementation has been undertaken.

Understanding why this is the case requires an understanding of the global
neoliberal project that is linking education ever more closely to the needs of the

global market, seeking to transform the nature of public education systems. This is something Levin himself recognizes when he asserts, "No amount of research will displace or replace politics" (Levin, 2010, p.744). It is important, therefore, to understand the politics of neoliberalism because the underlying assumptions of neoliberalism begin to explain why education reform begins to assume a specific form. At the base of this analysis is a view about the role of public and private sector interests in education, and of the specific interests of those who work in these sectors.

Ideas that inform the new orthodoxy in relation to governance and public policy are deeply antithetical to public provision. This is based on traditional choice theory which asserts that only markets are the guarantors of quality, and that public provision is inherently inferior. It is claimed that public provision lacks the incentives to ensure quality and efficiency and, therefore, public provision should be replaced, where possible, with private provision and quasi-markets. Within the analysis, it becomes logical to argue that producer interests are in conflict with "consumer" interests and that, in the absence of sufficient safeguards, producers will act in self-interest, rather than the interests of service users. This is what is meant by "producer capture" (Adam Smith Institute, 1984) whereby market advocates argue that public service monopolies are vulnerable to being "taken over" by producer interests, with public policy determined in favor of providers of services, rather than users.

Such an analysis often asserts that professional interests working within public services are inherently resistant to change. From this analysis it is but a short step to argue that producer interests must be confronted and defeated, and change imposed. Consensus is rejected as an unacceptable compromise and a price too high to pay.

> The structural change is we've got to *bust open* [my emphasis] the state monopoly on education and allow new schools to be established. It's what's happened in Sweden, in parts of America it's hugely successful in terms of making sure there's excellence, there's competition, there's innovation and new excellent schools come along. It's a big chance. It will mean some big battles with forces of resistance. Some LEAs might not like it, some of the education establishment won't like it . . . There are forces in the education establishment that have to be taken on and defeated on this.
>
> (*The Telegraph*, 2009)

These are the words of David Cameron who, within 12 months, was to become the prime minister of the United Kingdom. They provide a consummate example of the market-driven neoliberal analysis. The problem is state monopoly, and the solution is private enterprise. The enemy is the "education establishment" (generally taken to refer to teacher unions, local authorities [school districts], and university based education departments). These are the "enemies of promise," and they must be defeated. It is a model of change and improvement that eschews partnership and consensus, and which sees confrontation as a creative force for progress.

Given the direction of travel outlined above, it is possible to identify a shifting environment in which school leaders increasingly do their work. First is a drive for "efficiency" within school systems, expressed as a need to maximize "output" whilst containing costs. I have already argued that international league tables of system performance have become increasingly influential in driving the education policies of individual nation states. This will create a pressure to increase "output" in the form of student performance in standardized tests. However, the need for "efficiency" will generate a corresponding pressure to ensure that costs are controlled. In such a context school systems are likely to come under increased pressure to increase performance, whilst functioning with tightly controlled—possibly diminishing—budgets. This creates substantial tensions within the system. The imperative is to deliver more with less.

Within individual countries the emphasis on maximizing output is often reflected in a drive to quantify the value produced by individual schools. This is most commonly represented as student performance in standardized tests and, as the focus on school performance intensifies, so too does the pressure to increase student performance in standardized tests. More and more aspects of school life will be reduced to what is measurable. From this point, it is a short step to quantify the value generated by individual teachers, and to link pay to performance. Such a process requires a much greater emphasis on the quantification of value within the school system than has hitherto been the case. The danger is that school leadership is reduced to a crude managerialism (Clarke, Gewirtz, & McLaughlin, 2000) in which teacher performance is scrutinized forensically, with rewards and punishments being dispensed accordingly. Such developments are already well established in those nation states, most notably the United States and England, that fly the flag for the neoliberal restructuring of public services.

Facing the Future: Three Dispositions of Leadership

There is a global orthodoxy that is shaping education policy around the world. This can assume different forms in different countries and the pace and form of change is likely to be extremely uneven, but there is enough evidence of common trajectories to suggest that the features of education policy I have identified are likely to have a decisive influence on the future development of education systems worldwide. There are extremely powerful forces driving these changes forward, not least the power of global capital, and it is a serious error to underestimate the drive of the "global education reform movement" (Sahlberg, 2010). However, it is a mistake of equal magnitude to fall victim to a fatalism that asserts that the future is predetermined, and that alternative possibilities do not exist. Rather I want to argue that the future is always uncertain and that there is much to play for. In such circumstances, leadership is pivotal and the role of leaders is crucial.

The challenge for school leaders is to avoid becoming functionaries in systems in which schools become business units, and complex educational processes are reduced to a focus on a narrow range of functional skills. This is what Hargreaves and Fullan (2012) describe as the "business capital" model of schooling, and it is already deeply embedded in the education systems of many parts of the world. If school leaders are to resist such developments, and if the trajectory of policy reform is to be interrupted, then I want to argue that school leaders must adopt three distinct dispositions.

Understand and Critique

Much education reform relies on school leaders being so overwhelmed by the pace and scale of the changes imposed on them that they have insufficient opportunity to think deeply about the demands being made on them, and the consequences for children. Moreover, not only is there a constant urgency to implement, but there are often fearsome consequences for a failure to implement. In increasingly high stakes environments, in which potential dismissal is never far away, the imperative is to look down and focus on the immediate. In such environments, it can be difficult to stand back and to not only seek to understand, but also to develop powerful and serious critiques. However this is what school leaders must do, constantly, if they are to begin to identify the spaces in which alternative visions of education can be nurtured.

In particular, school leaders need to develop a powerful understanding of the role of the market in school systems, and how market forces shape professional values and judgments. In a market-based environment managerial decisions become driven by market considerations, and the moral purpose of education is defined not by public service values, but by what the market values. Whatever is claimed about markets—they produce winners and losers and, in a market, winners are valued more than losers.

Decision making by school leaders therefore is not value free, whatever the evidence base that might be invoked to support it. Management by numbers needs to critiqued in a way that recognizes that numbers are not just values in a numeric sense, but that numbers embody values. In a market context, higher numbers represent higher value. Those who score more highly are valued more highly. Such an approach is difficult to reconcile with a commitment to the values of equity. Understanding how these phenomena shape education practice and developing a powerful critique are the departure point for developing an alternative.

Reframe and Articulate

If school leaders are to resist these developments, the challenge is to go beyond critique and to articulate a much more optimistic vision of education. The starting point for such a project must be for school leaders to return to basic questions about the moral purpose of education. In short, to return to the question posed by Hargreaves and Fullan in 1998 in *What's Worth Fighting for in Education?*, school leaders therefore need to reassert the moral purpose of education and ground their decision-making processes within that context. There is an imperative to reject management by numbers, and to reframe and articulate a much richer vision of the educational process. This would be very much evidence based, but it would recognize the complexity of the educational process and make a virtue out of a plurality of ideas. Rather than search for simplicity, school leaders must learn to be comfortable with uncertainty and to celebrate complexity.

This is an immensely difficult task. Part of the attraction of the market-based approach is that simple league tables communicate clear messages about who is good, and who is poor. It does not matter that such measures are crude, take no account of social context, are often unreliable and present only a small part of what is important. The intention is to provide an easily digestible means of ranking schools, thereby encouraging a hierarchy that can sift and sort.

The challenge for leadership is to present a much more hopeful and optimistic vision of education, about what that might look like and its possibilities. This must be based on a recognition that the thin democracy of the market is a poor substitute for a much richer and participatory form of education and that education for democracy must itself be democratic (Apple & Beane, 1999). Rejecting management by numbers must never mean a "leave it to the experts" view of teacher professionalism in which students, parents, and communities are passive recipients of a service that "professionals" have decided is "good for them." Such an approach merely represents an alternative form of thin democracy. Rather, the goal must be to reframe and articulate a much more inclusive vision of thick democracy in which learning is a genuine partnership between the school, its students, and the community (Gandin & Apple, 2002).

Organize and Challenge

The third disposition school leaders must adopt in the new policy environment is perhaps the most challenging but, without it, there can be little prospect of progress. The task for school leaders is to not only *think* politically, in the sense of engaging with the policy environment within which they work, but to *act* politically too. Market visions of schooling intentionally isolate because this inevitably weakens. Driving forward unpopular change becomes easier when schools experience a toxic mix of potential failure, system fragmentation, and politically driven fear (Stevenson & Wood, 2013). In an environment where deviation from the orthodoxy becomes an act of resistance, then, such actions are much less likely if the state determines "failure," and failure brings with it profound consequences. It should not be a surprise if what results is standardization, conformity, and compliance, however much the rhetoric of policy may speak of freedom, innovation, and diversity.

The only effective means to challenge this is for school leaders to organize and act collectively, and to take on the role of "the activist profession" (Sachs, 2003). Agency needs to be conceived of collectively as, without organization, there can be little scope for influence. However, collective organization requires school leaders to act in ways that consciously overcome the divisiveness of the market. School leaders must learn, and relearn, how to organize for change. This requires school leaders to not only find new ways to work together as school leaders, but also to find new ways to work together with their colleagues in schools and their wider communities. School leaders need to rediscover the power of alliances.

Conclusion

It is becoming increasingly apparent that stark choices are opening up about the future trajectory of education policy. Under such circumstances, school leaders face the considerable challenge of how to navigate an extraordinarily complex policy environment, in which policy change is both substantial in scale and rapid in pace. However, what is equally clear is that the policy directions that are becoming more apparent have significant implications for students in schools. Policies need to be seen as the authoritative allocation of values, and it is the values shift in public education that needs to be understood and critiqued.

School leaders must recognize the political environment within which they function. It might be argued that this has always been an essential feature of school leadership and, indeed, it has. However, it is not only the scale and pace of current change, but the values that underpin change that create a new urgency for school leaders to think and act politically, and to do so collectively. Such actions offer the possibility of not only interrupting the direction of current policy trajectories, but forging a much more hopeful and optimistic alternative in which social justice values triumph over what the market values.

References

Adam Smith Institute. (1984). *The Omega Report: Education policy.* London, UK: Adam Smith Institute.

Apple, M. W., & Beane, J. A. (Eds.). (1999). *Democratic schools: Lessons from the chalk face.* Buckingham, UK: Open University Press.

Bacon, R., & Eltis, W. (1976). *Too few producers.* London, UK: MacMillan.

Ball, S. J. (1998). Big policies/small world: An introduction to international perspectives in education policy. *Comparative Education, 34,* 119–130.

Ball, S. J. (2007). *Education PLC.* London, UK: Routledge.

Ball, S. J. (2008) *The education debate: Policy and politics in the 21st century.* Bristol, UK: Policy Press.

Ball, S. J. (2012). *Global Education Inc.* London, UK: Routledge.

BBC. (2012). Michael Gove: Academy school critics "happy with failure." Retrieved October 10, 2013, from www.bbc.co.uk/news/education-16409940

Becker, G. (1964). *Human capital.* New York, NY: Columbia University Press.

Bell, L., & Stevenson, H. (2006). *Education policy: Process, themes and impact.* London, UK: Routledge.

Bell, L., & Stevenson. H. (2013). Editors' introduction: Organizing public education. In L. Bell & H. Stevenson (Eds.). *Organizing public education*. London, UK: Sage.

Clarke, J., Gewirtz, S., & McLaughlin, E. (Eds.). (2000). *New managerialism, new welfare?* London, UK: Sage.

Dale, R. (1999). Specifying globalization effects on national policy: A focus on the mechanisms. *Journal of Education Policy, 14,* 1–17.

Department of Education. (2009). *Race to the top.* Retrieved October 10, 2013, from www2.ed.gov/programs/racetothetop/executive-summary.pdf

Friedman, M., & Friedman, R. (1980). *Free to choose.* New York, NY: Avon Books.

Gamble, A. (1988). *The free economy and the strong state: The politics of Thatcherism.* London, UK: Macmillan.

Gandin, L. A., & Apple, M. W. (2002). Thin versus thick democracy in education: Porto alegre and the creation of alternatives to neo-liberalism. *International Studies in Sociology of Education, 12,* 99–116.

Gewirtz, S. (2001). *The managerial school: Post-welfarism and social justice in education.* London, UK: Routledge.

Gough, I. (1983). Thatcherism and the welfare state. In S. Hall & M. Jacques (Eds.), *The politics of Thatcherism.* London, UK: Lawrence and Wishart.

Hall, S. (1979, January). The great moving right show. *Marxism Today,* pp. 14–20.

Hargreaves, A., & Fullan, M. (1998). *What's worth fighting for in education?* Buckingham, UK: Open University Press.

Hargreaves, A., & Fullan, M. (2012) *Professional capital: Transforming teaching in every school.* London, UK: Routledge.

Held, D., & McGrew, A. (2007). *Globalization/anti-globalization: Beyond the great divide* (2nd ed.). London, UK: Polity.

Hess, F. (1999). *Spinning wheels: The politics of urban school reform.* Washington, DC: Brookings Institution.

Jessop, B. (2002). *The future of the capitalist state.* Cambridge, UK: Polity.

Levin, B. (1998). An epidemic of education policy: (What) can we learn from each other? *Comparative Education, 34,* 131–141.

Levin, B. (2010), Governments and education reform: Some lessons from the last 50 years. *Journal of Education Policy, 25,* 739–747.

O'Connor, J. (1973). *The fiscal crisis of the state.* New York, NY: St. Martin's Press.

Rizvi, F., & Lingard, B. (2010). *Globalizing education policy.* London, UK: Routledge.

Robertson, S. (2000). *A class act: Changing teachers work, the state, and globalisation.* London, UK: Routledge.

Sachs, J. (2003). *The activist teaching profession.* Buckingham, UK: Open University Press.

Sahlberg, P. (2010). *Finnish lessons: What can the world learn from educational change in Finland?* New York, NY: Teachers' College Press.

Sellar, S., & Lingard, B. (2013). The OECD and global governance in education. *Journal of Education Policy, 28,* 710–725.

Stevenson, H., & Wood, P. (2013). Markets, managerialism and teachers' work: The invisible hand of high stakes testing in England. *International Education Journal: Comparative Perspectives, 12*(2), 42–61.

The Telegraph. (2009). *David Cameron: Tory leader talks to the Daily Telegraph about education.* Retrieved October 10, 2013, from www.telegraph.co.uk/news/politics/conservative/4537403/David-Cameron-Tory-leader-talks-to-the-Daily-Telegraph-about-education.html

Tomlinson, S. (2006). *Education in a post-welfarist society.* Buckingham, UK: Open University Press.

ABOUT THE CONTRIBUTORS

Henry Braun is the Boisi Professor of Education and Public Policy and Director of the Center for the Study of Testing, Evaluation and Education Policy at Boston College. He holds a Ph.D. in mathematical statistics from Stanford University. After serving as an assistant professor of statistics at Princeton University, he joined the Educational Testing Service in 1979, where he served as vice president for research management from 1990 to 1999 and held the title of distinguished presidential appointee from 1999 to 2006. A fellow of the American Statistical Association and of AERA, he is a corecipient of the 1986 Palmer O. Johnson Award of the AERA and a corecipient of the NCME's 1999 Award for Outstanding Technical Contribution to the Field of Educational Measurement. His interests include school and teacher accountability, the role of testing in education policy, and the analysis of large-scale survey data.

Stephanie Chitpin is an associate professor of Leadership, Evaluation and Curriculum at the Faculty of Education, University of Ottawa, Canada. Her research in leadership, curriculum, and professional development focuses on how practitioners construct the requisite professional knowledge and skills to do their work competently. Her studies funded by The Social Sciences Humanities Research Council of Canada (SSHRC) and The Ontario Ministry of Education, Canada are international in scope. Her research initiative on The Knowledge Network for Applied Education Research (KNAER) funded by the Ontario Ministry of Education/ University of Toronto/Western University is the first of its kind to explore how principals across Canada and on different sides of the globe (Australia) cope with and respond to high-stakes demands, demands that affect diverse stakeholders and require wise and astute decision making. She has also served on many committees in the capacity of editorial board member, reviewer, chair, presenter, and discussant.

Rozanne Donald is a research student at The University of Auckland. She has a teaching background and is currently the Director of Professional Learning at St Cuthbert's College. Auckland, New Zealand. Her research interests are in organizational change and teacher professional learning.

Colin W. Evers is Professor of Educational Leadership in the School of Education at the University of New South Wales. He has a disciplinary background in mathematics and philosophy and research and teaching interests in the areas of educational administration and leadership, philosophy of education, and research methodology. He is coauthor and coeditor of seven books and nearly 100 scholarly papers. He is currently doing research with coauthors for a book on teacher leadership (to be published by Routledge) and a book on realist research in social science (to be published by SAGE).

Dean Fink is an international consultant and "best-selling" author. He is a former superintendent and principal with the Halton Board of Education in Ontario Canada. In the past 19 years, Dean has made presentations or conducted workshop in 31 different countries. He has published numerous book chapters and articles on topics related to organizational effectiveness, leadership, and change. Dean is the author or coauthor of *Changing Our Schools* (McGraw-Hill, 1996) with Louise Stoll of the University of London in England, *Good Schools/Real Schools; Why school reform doesn't last* (Teachers College Press, 2000), and *It's About Learning and It's About Time* (Taylor Francis, 2003) with Louise Stoll and Lorna Earl of the University of Toronto, *Sustainable Leadership* with Andy Hargreaves of Boston College for Jossey Bass (2006), and *Leadership for Mortals: Developing and sustaining leaders of learning* for Corwin (2006). His most recent book is *The Succession Challenge: Building and sustaining leadership capacity through Succession Management* (Corwin, 2010).

Peter P. Grimmett is Professor and Head of the Department of Curriculum and Pedagogy in the Faculty of Education at the University of British Columbia (UBC). A former Associate Dean at Simon Fraser University (SFU), he also served as Director of the Institute for Studies in Teacher Education at SFU, was appointed by the BC Cabinet as the BC Deans of Education appointment to the Council of the BC College of Teachers (the professional body that governs teaching and teacher education in the province) between 2007 and 2010. His most recent (2012) book (written with Jon Young), *Teacher Certification and the Professional Status of Teaching in North America: The New Battleground for Public Education* (Information Age Publishing) locates recent developments in teacher certification in North America within a broader, international policy context characterized as hegemonic neoliberalism wherein economic rationalism has begun to trump professional judgment.

Alex M. Gurn is a Ph.D. candidate in the Lynch School of Education at Boston College. He is coauthor/editor of the recent book, *The Myth of the Normal Curve*.

His thesis, titled "Troubling Public-Private Partnerships in Education," critically examines the role of corporate philanthropy in urban public schools. His multidisciplinary research interests reflect a commitment to rupturing deficit models of youth and learning.

Andy Hargreaves is the Thomas More Brennan Chair in the Lynch School of Education at Boston College. He was the founding editor-in-chief of the *Journal of Educational Change* and leading editor of the first and second International Handbooks of Educational Change. His books have achieved outstanding writing awards from the American Educational Research Association, the American Libraries Association, the National Staff Development Council, and the American Association of Colleges for Teacher Education, and are translated into many languages. His most recent books are *The Global Fourth Way* (with Dennis Shirley—Corwin, 2012), and *Professional Capital* (with Michael Fullan—Teachers College Press, 2012). His current research is on whole school and system reform strategies that especially benefit students with special educational needs.

Patrick M. Jenlink is a professor in the Department of Secondary Education and Educational Leadership and Director of the Educational Research Center at Stephen F. Austin State University. Dr. Jenlink has served as a classroom teacher at the junior high and high school level as well a K–12 counselor. He has also served as building administrator and school district superintendent in Oklahoma. In addition to his current appointment, Dr. Jenlink's university teaching experience includes Northwestern Oklahoma State University, Western Michigan University, and assignments in Europe with University of Oklahoma and NATO. Dr. Jenlink's teaching emphasis in doctoral studies at Stephen F. Austin State University includes courses in ethics and philosophy of leadership, research methods and design, and leadership theory and practice. Currently Dr. Jenlink serves as editor of *Teacher Education & Practice* and coeditor of *Scholar-Practitioner Quarterly*.

Gabriele Lakomski is best known for her critical work on leadership and organizational learning in both public and private sector organizations. Her research is based on the most recent scientific understanding of human knowledge acquisition and the processing of information, developed by connectionist cognitive science. In her work she examines how such empirical knowledge affects current theories of organizational learning, leadership, organizational culture, and change, as well as the training of managers and administrators. Her research program includes the analysis of Knowledge Management (KM) as a new tool for managing organizational development and change. Located in the Centre for the Study of Higher Education at the University of Melbourne where she is a professorial fellow, Professor Lakomski was founding director of the Centre for Organizational Learning and Leadership, a research center of the University of Melbourne established to focus on organizational expertise and knowledge with aspects of leadership. She is a member of the Academy of Management (USA),

Beth Morton is a doctoral candidate in the Educational Research, Measurement, and Evaluation program at Boston College and research analyst at the Center for Education Policy Research at Harvard University. Her current research interests include educators' use of data to improve teaching and learning. Prior to starting her doctoral program, Beth was an analyst at the American Institutes for Research where she supported the work of the National Center for Education Statistics and the Schools and Staffing Survey. Beth holds a B.A. in sociology from Castleton State College and an M.A. in sociology from the University of New Hampshire.

Viviane Robinson is a distinguished professor in the Faculty of Education at The University of Auckland and Academic Director of its Centre for Educational Leadership. She specializes in school improvement, leadership, and the relationship between research and the improvement of practice. She is the author of five books and numerous chapters and journal articles. Her latest book titled *Student-Centred Leadership* was published by Jossey Bass in August 2011. Viviane has consulted on leadership development and research to government agencies and organizations in England, Singapore, Chile, Canada, Australia, and New Zealand. She has received awards from national and international professional organizations including the Australian Council for Educational Leaders, the New Zealand Secondary Principals Association, and the U.S.-based University Council on Educational Administration. In 2011 she was made a fellow of the American Educational Research Association for sustained excellence in educational research.

Karen Starr is the Foundation Chair, School Leadership and Development in the Faculty of Arts and Education at Deakin University, Australia. Prior to this she was a school principal for 15 years, she was the Chief Writer of South Australia's Curriculum, Standards and Accountability Framework and in 2004 won the Australian Telstra Business Women's Award for the not-for-profit sector. She is a Fellow of the Australian Institute of Company Directors, the Australian Council for Educational Leaders and the Australian College of Educators. Her research interests lie in educational leadership, change, professional learning, governance, educational policy, gender, and equity.

Howard Stevenson is Professor of Educational Leadership and Policy Studies, and Director of Research, in the School of Education, University of Nottingham. He has written widely in the areas of school leadership, education policy, and teachers' work/school sector labor relations. He is currently co-convenor of the BELMAS-UCEA sponsored International School Leadership Development Network, an international research collaborative involving 40 scholars undertaking work in over 20 countries.

Jingping Sun is an assistant professor at the University of Alabama (starting in August 2012). Prior to that, she worked in the Ontario Ministry of Education as a policy analyst and senior research and evaluation analyst. She obtained her Ph.D. in Educational Administration at the Ontario Institute for Studies in Education, University of Toronto in 2010. Her research interests are educational leadership, leadership preparation, school improvement and educational change, policy evaluation and improvement, and research synthesis methods (e.g., meta-analysis), ethics and leadership, and comparative studies of leadership. She has communicated her work in referred journals such as *Educational Administration Quarterly,* book chapters, and at both international and national conferences. She won awards for her research or research manuscripts. She promotes dialogues between scholars in the West and East in the field of educational leadership (e.g., comparison of transformational leadership developed in North America and Confucian idea of transformation developed in Asia).

Marvin A. Zuker is a justice of the Ontario Court of Justice. He holds the rank of Associate Professor at OISE/UT where he has taught Education Law since 1982. Justice Zuker is the author and coauthor of several books, including *Canadian Women and the Law* and *The Law Is Not for Women,* with June Callwood; *Ontario Small Claims Court Practice* (30th anniversary edition 2011); *Education Law,* with Anthony Brown (4th edition 2007); Consulting Editor, *Sexual Misconduct in Education: Prevention, Reporting and Discipline* with Grant Bowers and Rena Knox (2nd edition 2006); and *Children's Law Handbook,* with Rod Flynn and Randy Hammond (2nd edition 2009). He is coauthor with Nick Scarfo of *Inspiring the Future: A New Teacher's Guide to the Law,* Thomson Carswell 2011. He serves on the Editorial Boards of the *Education and Law Journal,* the *International Journal of Law and Education* (ANZELA), and *Risk Management in Canadian Education.*

INDEX

Page numbers in *italic* refer to figures.